Agency Operations and Sales Management

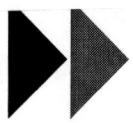

**Agency Management Tools and Processes
Segment C**

Agency Operations and Sales Management

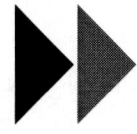

Agency Management Tools and Processes
Segment C

Cheryl L. Koch, MBA, CPCU, CIC, ARM, AAI, AAM, AIM, AIS, API, ARP, ASCR
Principal
Agency Management Resource Group

Mary Ann Cook, CPCU, AU, AAI
Director of Curriculum
American Institute for CPCU/Insurance Institute of America.

Third Edition · Seventh Printing

American Institute for Chartered Property Casualty
Underwriters/Insurance Institute of America
720 Providence Road, Suite 100
Malvern, Pennsylvania 19355-3433

Third Edition • Seventh Printing • March 2009

Library of Congress Control Number: 2006931531

ISBN 978-0-89463-300-3

Foreword

The American Institute for Chartered Property Casualty Underwriters and the Insurance Institute of America (the Institutes) are not-for-profit organizations committed to meeting the evolving educational needs of the risk management and insurance community. The Institutes strive to provide current, relevant educational programs in formats that meet the needs of risk management and insurance professionals and the organizations that employ them.

The American Institute for CPCU (AICPCU) was founded in 1942 through a collaborative effort between industry professionals and academics, led by faculty members at The Wharton School of the University of Pennsylvania. In 1953, AICPCU coordinated operations with the Insurance Institute of America (IIA), which was founded in 1909 and remains the oldest continuously functioning national organization offering educational programs for the property-casualty insurance sector.

The Insurance Research Council (IRC), founded in 1977, is a division of AICPCU supported by industry members. This not-for-profit research organization examines public policy issues of interest to property-casualty insurers, insurance customers, and the general public. IRC research reports are distributed widely to insurance-related organizations, public policy authorities, and the media.

The Institutes' new customer- and solution-focused business model allows us to better serve the risk management and insurance communities. Customer-centricity defines our business philosophy and shapes our priorities. The Institutes' innovation arises from our commitment to finding solutions that meet customer needs and deliver results. Our business process is shaped by our commitment to efficiency, strategy, and responsible asset management.

The Institutes believe that professionalism is grounded in education, experience, and ethical behavior. The Chartered Property Casualty Underwriter (CPCU) professional designation offered by the Institutes is designed to provide a broad understanding of the property-casualty insurance industry. Depending on professional needs, CPCU students may select either a commercial or a personal risk management and insurance focus. The CPCU designation is conferred annually by the AICPCU Board of Trustees.

In addition, the Institutes offer designations and certificate programs in a variety of disciplines, including the following:

- Claims
- Commercial underwriting
- Fidelity and surety bonding
- General insurance
- Insurance accounting and finance
- Insurance information technology
- Insurance production and agency management
- Insurance regulation and compliance
- Management
- Marine insurance
- Personal insurance
- Premium auditing
- Quality insurance services
- Reinsurance
- Risk management
- Surplus lines

You can complete a program leading to a designation, take a single course to fill a knowledge gap, or take multiple courses and programs throughout your career. The practical and technical knowledge gained from Institute courses enhances your qualifications and contributes to your professional growth. Most Institute courses carry college credit recommendations from the American Council on Education. A variety of courses qualify for credits toward certain associate, bachelor's, and master's degrees at several prestigious colleges and universities.

Our Knowledge Resources Department, in conjunction with industry experts and members of the academic community, develops our trusted course and program content, including Institute study materials. These materials provide practical career and performance-enhancing knowledge and skills.

We welcome comments from our students and course leaders. Your feedback helps us continue to improve the quality of our study materials.

Peter L. Miller, CPCU
President and CEO
American Institute for CPCU
Insurance Institute of America

Preface

The Accredited Adviser in Insurance (AAI) program is designed to meet the educational needs of insurance producers, customer service representatives, and other insurance agency and brokerage personnel. In that regard, the courses in the AAI program focus on three primary areas: (1) the technical aspects of the insurance business, including coverage and pricing; (2) the marketing of insurance products, including producer relationships with both customers and insurer representatives; and (3) the operation and management of agencies and brokerages, including both financial and sales management.

AAI 83, *Agency Operations and Sales Management*, is one of three courses that must be passed to complete the Accredited Adviser in Insurance designation. Each AAI course contains three segments that group topics of similar subject matter. This text, *Agency Management Tools and Processes* (Segment C), is the third of the three segments that comprise AAI 83. Although the Institutes do not require that students take AAI courses in sequence, they may prefer to do so. However, the Institutes strongly recommend that students complete each course's segments in sequence.

In its first assignment, *Agency Management Tools and Processes* describes and proposes solutions to the various issues agency principals and managers face managing agency IT. The second assignment discusses agency management of customer services. Issues including revenue and expense control are covered in the third assignment on agency financial management. The fourth assignment examines producers' legal and ethical responsibilities.

This text is based on former *Agency Operations and Sales Management* texts. Many people contributed to those texts as authors. The Institutes recognize their efforts, especially those of Peter R. Kensicki, DBA, CPCU, CLU, FLMI, and Carol A. Hammes, CPCU. Additionally, the Institutes recognize the previous contributions of Daniel P. Hussey, Jr., CPCU, AAI, ARM, to the AAI program.

We extend our thanks to the reviewers from both inside and outside the Institutes who contributed to this text edition by providing guidance during its planning and development stages. These individuals include the following members of the AAI Advisory Committee:

Thomas B. Ahart, CPCU, AAI

Christopher J. Amrhein, AAI

Noreen Brawley, AAI, ARM

Cheryl L. Koch, CPCU, ARM, AAI, AAM, AIM, AIS, API, ARP, ACSR

Lynne S. Lovell, CPCU, RHU, CLU, ChFC, CRM, ARM, CIC, ASLI

Christine McLeod, CPCU, AAI, AIM, AIS, ARM, API

David Surles, CPCU, AAI

For more information about the Institutes' programs, please call our Customer Service Department at (800) 644-2101, e-mail us at customerservice@cpcuiia.org, or visit our Web site at www.aicpcu.org.

Cheryl L. Koch

Mary Ann Cook

Contents

Direct Your Learning

Managing Agency Information Technology

Educational Objectives

After learning the content of this assignment, you should be able to:

1. Describe the purposes of agency information technology.

2. Describe agency IT business practices.

3. Explain how agencies conduct their IT planning.

4. Explain how IT management influences the ability of agencies to increase their efficiencies and cost-effectiveness with respect to the following:

   a. Productivity issues

   b. Internet issues

   c. Security issues

5. Describe the goals of agency/company interface.

6. Describe the two types of agency/company interface and the organizations that support the interface process.

7. Explain how an agency's information needs may be categorized based on how the information is being used, with respect to the following:

   a. Strategic planning

   b. Management information

   c. Operational information

8. Describe the three types of agency management systems.

9. Explain how agency management systems are used in various agency operational areas.

10. Describe the ways an agency workplace of tomorrow would implement its IT solutions in the course of its daily insurance transactions.

11. Define or describe each of the Key Words and Phrases for this assignment.

ASSIGNMENT

Develop Your Perspective

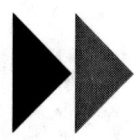

What are the main topics covered in the chapter?

Agencies rely on business practices formulated around information technology, and IT planning must play a significant role in the agency business plan in order to maximize efficiencies and cost-effectiveness. An agency's information needs can be categorized based on how the information is used and can be delivered by the selected agency management system. Agencies that focus on supporting new IT technology will be prepared to meet the challenges of the workplace of tomorrow.

Identify what an agency's IT plan should accomplish.

▶ How does the IT plan guide the agency through integrating with current technological changes and allowing for the rapid pace of future changes?

▶ How does the IT plan align with the agency's business plan?

Why is it important to learn about these topics?

When an agency develops and adopts an IT plan, its producers and CSRs can use its IT systems to conduct business more efficiently and more cost-effectively.

Consider the benefits of using IT to conduct business.

▶ How can agency managers use IT to accelerate work processes and communication and to facilitate decision making?

▶ How can agencies use IT to improve the timeliness of customer service?

How can you use what you will learn?

Evaluate the IT plan used in your workplace.

▶ What questions should you ask when reviewing the plan?

▶ Is the IT plan aligned with your organization's business plan?

▶ How well-positioned is the plan to address future IT challenges?

Managing Agency Information Technology

ASSIGNMENT 1

Outline

▶ **Purposes of Agency Information Technology**
A. Improving Customer Service
B. Maximizing Productivity and Efficiency
C. Maximizing Profitability
D. Reducing Errors and Omissions Loss Exposures

▶ **Agency IT Business Practices**

▶ **IT Planning**

▶ **IT Management**
A. Productivity Issues
1. Training
2. Ergonomics
3. Telecommuting
B. Internet Issues
1. Obtaining Information
2. Marketing Products and Services
3. Improving Customer Service
C. Security Issues

▶ **Agency/Company Interface**
A. Goals of Agency/Company Interface
B. Types of Agency/Company Interface
1. Interactive Interface
2. Single-Entry Multiple-Company Interface
C. Organizations That Support Agency-Company Interface
1. ACORD
2. ACT

▶ **Insurance Agency Information Needs**
A. Strategic Planning Information
1. Internal Information About Agency Performance
2. External Information About Competitors, Industry Information, and Economic Information
B. Management Information
1. Sales Management Information
2. Budgeting and Financial Information
3. Employee Performance Information
C. Operational Information
1. Prospect Information
2. Customer and Policy Information
3. Rating Information
4. Claim Information
5. Standardized Information
6. Premium Accounting Information

▶ **Agency Management Systems**
A. Types of Agency Management Systems
B. Use of Agency Management Systems
1. Sales Management
2. Customer Database Management
3. Claim Management
4. Transactional Filing
5. Electronic Filing
6. Rotational Servicing

▶ **The Agency Workplace of Tomorrow: A Case Study**

▶ **Summary**

▶ **Appendix**

Managing Agency Information Technology

Nothing in recent history has had a greater effect on how an insurance agency conducts its daily business than advances in information technology. In this assignment, the term **"information technology" (IT)** refers to a system that helps produce, manipulate, store, communicate, and distribute information. Rapid changes in such IT components as hardware and software have presented both opportunities and challenges to agency owners and managers and have transformed how insurance transactions are processed.

IT advances have helped agencies improve performance in such areas as customer service, agency-insurer relationships, and agency management. If an agency is to successfully achieve its goals, producers and agency managers must understand the role of IT and its importance. In fact, many large agencies and brokerage firms have created a new management position, chief information officer (CIO), or chief technology officer (CTO), who is responsible for administering all IT activities. As the cost of personal computers and software continues to decline, IT has become affordable to even the smallest agencies. The pervasiveness of the Internet has also given agencies access to IT tools once considered beyond the reach of smaller organizations.

Even more crucial to an agency's success is how, using technology, information is gathered, input, manipulated, transmitted, accessed, and delivered to both the agency's external customers and its employees. Rather than managing technology alone (such as hardware, software, and related equipment), an agency should be managing information technology and using it to its best strategic advantage.

This assignment focuses on agencies that represent more than one insurer, for two reasons. First, the IT concepts described for use in a multiple-insurer environment can easily be adapted by an agency that represents only one insurer. However, the reverse is not true. Second, achieving smooth interaction between insurers and agencies that represent many insurers has proved to be one of the greatest IT challenges.

This assignment also discusses why and how agencies can plan for, manage, and use their IT, because a key IT challenge for agencies is how they interface (electronically communicate) with the insurers they represent, this assignment discusses the goals of agency/company interface.

Information technology (IT)
A system that helps produce, manipulate, store, communicate, and distribute information.

PURPOSES OF AGENCY INFORMATION TECHNOLOGY

IT serves many purposes throughout an agency, including the following:

- Improving customer service
- Maximizing productivity and efficiency
- Maximizing profitability
- Reducing errors and omissions (E&O) loss exposures

Improving Customer Service

IT has a major effect on an agency's ability to provide service to its customers. An IT system with a detailed customer information database can provide customer service representatives (CSRs) with immediate access to customer records. When a telephone call is received, the CSR can access the customer's electronic file without having to put the caller on hold or call back after a paper file has been located. CSRs can enter information into the system and any necessary changes can be made while the customer is on the phone, making this information immediately available to others in the agency.

IT can also allow for quicker service to the customer. CSRs can fax or e-mail correspondence to the customer or the insurer and change requests and other documents via computer without leaving their workstations.

Maximizing Productivity and Efficiency

A sound practice of agency management is to continually look for ways to maximize productivity and efficiency using IT. One of the overall goals of agency management is to maximize agency productivity and efficiency by enabling CSRs to enter data (such as a customer's address) in a system only once, and then using the data for multiple purposes, such as in an insurance claim form or for a newsletter mailing. This process is called single entry, multiple use. **Single entry, multiple use** eliminates redundancies by updating customer files throughout the system without the need to re-enter information. This technology gives agency employees immediate access to accurate, up-to-date customer information.

IT also maximizes the speed and efficiency of communications between the agency and the insurer if the agency is interfaced with the insurer. Employees are more productive, and the agency can often handle new business without adding staff because fewer activities are needed to process the same volume of work.

Single entry, multiple use
A process that eliminates redundancies by updating customer files throughout the system without the need to re-enter information.

Maximizing Profitability

Through the use of IT, agencies have come to maximize their profit potential. Agencies that apply IT in their operations typically have higher profit margins than agencies using manual systems because of their improved operating efficiencies and reduced transaction costs. Additionally, effective IT use can maximize agency profitability by lowering overall labor costs and raising per-employee revenue. Properly used, IT increases new-business sales and improves account development—additional ways to maximize profitability. Further, IT maximizes profitability by refining the agency's marketing processes, allowing producers to segment both customers and prospects based on specific criteria contained in the database. Along with more effective selling and service, the IT tools available to monitor the agency's financial performance can enhance profitability through better analysis, budgeting, and development, leading to a more desirable and stable book of business.

Reducing Errors and Omissions Loss Exposures

IT helps agencies reduce errors and omissions loss exposures by standardizing office procedures, including those relating to policy processing, claim handling, and customer documentation. However, IT alone cannot eliminate all of an agency's E&O loss exposures. In fact, some agency personnel document information in their IT system that could harm the agency from an E&O standpoint. For example, a CSR might document that a request to remove a vehicle from a customer's auto policy came from a car dealer and endorse the policy accordingly. However, the car dealer, not being a named insured under the personal auto policy (PAP), is not authorized to request any changes to the policy. The CSR should always follow up such change requests by confirming them with the insured before endorsing a policy. Proper use of well-designed agency procedures by all personnel does reduce the likelihood of an error or omission that might lead to an E&O claim. IT functionality enables an agency to quickly perform audits to ensure adherence to those procedures.

E&O Alert!

Unlike paper records, computer-generated correspondence has the date and time the document was produced embedded in the system. This information cannot easily be altered. Courts have made this information and other computer records admissible as evidence in errors and omissions cases if witnesses can attest to facts related to the record.

AGENCY IT BUSINESS PRACTICES

Even though a majority of agencies report they use some type of IT, the extent of use among those agencies varies. Simply having IT does not mean that agency owners and staff fully and efficiently use it. Features the agency did not need may have been included in the agency's IT system when it was purchased. Alternatively, agencies may have yet to address IT issues—for example, employee training—that could lead to better business practices.

According to the *Best Practices* study of the Independent Insurance Agents and Brokers of America (IIABA), the top-performing agencies in the United States have not only recognized the importance of IT to their success, but also have found ways to use IT more fully and efficiently. Exhibit 1-1 lists some of the key business practices cited by these agencies with respect to IT.[1]

EXHIBIT 1-1

Key Business Practices Related to IT

- Hire a full-time IT manager or assign responsibility to one employee.
- Provide employees with ongoing in-house IT training.
- Make certain that owners and senior managers are committed to supporting, understanding, and using IT.
- Encourage IT managers to network with other users and attend users' group meetings.
- Load all policy details to fully tap IT potential.
- Understand IT's capabilities and limitations.
- Establish an IT committee made up of representatives of all user departments and charge this committee with finding ways to use IT capabilities more effectively.
- Standardize the use of IT.
- Periodically test employees to ensure accurate and consistent use of IT.
- Set IT usage goals at least annually.
- Require all employees, including producers, to use IT.
- Be aware of new IT developments, but resist the urge to be the first to try them.
- Use transactional filing in personal lines and elsewhere whenever possible.
- Maintain good communications with IT vendors.
- Provide a PC for each employee.
- Invest in only as much IT as the agency is committed to using.
- Strongly encourage employees to depend on IT.
- Be willing to invest in IT when required.
- Use outside experts to help provide training and to assist in achieving broader IT use.

IT PLANNING

Virtually all agencies require IT because most insurers require their agents to communicate and initiate insurance transactions using the Internet. Because IT is such a key aspect of agency operations and because of the rapid pace of changes in IT, agency owners and managers must realize that IT planning is a dynamic and ongoing process. Answers to the following questions can help agencies conduct their IT planning:

- *What agency operations require IT and how will new and existing IT be integrated?* Until recently, IT applications software was not available for some areas of agency operations, for example, surety bonds and employee benefits. Consequently, many agencies must continually monitor which operations need IT and how new IT can be integrated with existing IT. If agencies do not plan for these developments, new IT may not be used most efficiently and may even be counterproductive to existing IT.

- *Which processes will use IT?* Agencies must determine which processes within or across their operations need IT. An agency should examine each of the processes it uses for customer transactions, then streamline those processes and apply appropriate IT to them. Customer transaction processes that may benefit from IT include new business, endorsements/ policy changes, policy renewals, claims, certificates and other evidence of insurance, audits, bonds, and policy cancellations and nonrenewals. Applying IT to these customer transaction processes improves customer service, maximizes the productivity of agency staff, maximizes profitability, and reduces E&O loss exposures.

- *What are the IT requirements?* Typically, decisions regarding changes to software guide hardware decisions. Before decisions are made to upgrade existing software or to purchase new system software, hardware needs also must be evaluated. Servers are the primary hardware devices used to store and access an agency's data. Therefore, the decision to make a software change, such as switching to a new data management program, can also entail a hardware upgrade. With the cost of such hardware declining, upgrading those devices is becoming easier, but it can still result in significant additional costs to the agency.

- *When should IT be upgraded?* Determining when IT should be upgraded is a challenge. Sometimes, it may seem easiest to agency managers to continue using existing systems. But even systems that are still operational will eventually become outdated. To encourage customers to upgrade, most vendors (companies that sell IT systems) discontinue their support of older IT systems. An agency that wants to continue using an older system may find that it must provide its own IT support to the older system and solve software or hardware problems. However, when determining whether to upgrade its IT, an agency should avoid being the first to adopt a new version of the vendor's software without considering the inevitable bugs that will require correction. Consequently, an agency must consider the costs and technical resources involved in supporting an old system, the costs of the new system, and the timing of converting systems.

- *How can agencies keep current about new IT?* Agency owners and managers must continually evaluate new IT that may be able to help the agency achieve its goals. One way agencies typically stay current with IT is for their principals or IT managers to become active participants in user groups of other agencies that have the same or similar IT. Often, members of these user groups represent the cutting edge of agency IT and can be helpful in avoiding mistakes when purchasing IT.

IT planning must be aligned with the agency's business plan. Software is available to assist agencies, particularly small ones, in developing a business plan. Business plans can reveal whether IT is adequate to accomplish the agency's goals.

IT MANAGEMENT

Although agencies and insurers may disagree to some extent about IT system selection, all agree that they must continually strive to use IT systems to conduct business more efficiently and more cost-effectively. The following are three issues addressed by IT management that affect the ability of agencies and insurers to increase their efficiency and cost-effectiveness:

1. Productivity issues
2. Internet issues
3. Security issues

Productivity Issues

Employee productivity is a primary concern of management. Among the ways IT can help employees improve productivity are to speed up work processes and communication and to facilitate decision making through easy access to information. Management must support IT and its use by training employees and by considering any ergonomic concerns and telecommuting opportunities.

Training

One of the most important issues facing industry today is the evolution of the workforce of clerical processors into one of knowledge-based employees. The skills once required to perform jobs in an insurance agency are very different from those required today. IT advances and the ability of employees to access millions of pieces of information without leaving their desks have profoundly affected how customer service, sales, and management personnel perform their jobs. Although management must provide ongoing training and education for its employees, employees are ultimately responsible for keeping their job skills up to date. Employees must have the opportunity to be trained on the IT resources that relate to their work and that can enhance their job performance. They must also be aware that training is vital to their continued employability.

Ergonomics

Ergonomics, also called human engineering, is the science of designing work space and equipment based on the needs of the people who use the work space and equipment. Ergonomics is important because computers, office furniture, light sources, and other workstation elements affect an employee's productivity and health.

For example, some support functions in insurance involve long hours of computer work. Such computer keyboarding involves constant, repetitive motion that may, in severe cases, lead to neurological damage. If such ergonomic issues are not addressed, productivity gains made possible through IT could be reduced and worker job satisfaction could decline.

Ergonomics
The science of designing work space and equipment based on the needs of the people who use the work space and equipment.

Telecommuting

With the availability of portable computers, fax machines, and cellular phones, many organizations have found that some employees do not need to spend all of their work hours in the office. This is particularly true for salespeople and others whose daily activities involve being out in the field. Even support staff such as CSRs can be connected electronically from their homes, allowing them to work without coming to the office. Telecommuting offers many advantages to insurance agencies. For example, many employees find greater job satisfaction and a better work-life balance, which can benefit agencies in the form of increased productivity. Additionally, agencies can attract, hire, and retain the most qualified employees to perform sales and service functions, regardless of where they are located geographically.

Internet Issues

The Internet has significantly affected insurance agency operations. Internet usage facilitates communication between agencies and their insurer partners and has become a common method of communicating with customers. The growth of the Internet has reduced transaction costs throughout the insurance supply chain. Agencies can use the Internet for obtaining information, marketing products and services, and improving customer service.

Obtaining Information

Agencies can use the Internet to retrieve public information for sales, marketing, and operational purposes. Financial statements of publicly owned businesses, technical information, government information, and even information about competitors are readily available. Most insurers and agencies have Web sites that provide general information about the industry, specific product information, access to information at the policy level, and links to individuals in insurance company and agency offices. Various professional insurance associations, such as ACORD, the CPCU Society, the Risk and Insurance Management Society (RIMS), and the Professional Liability Underwriting Society (PLUS) maintain Web sites to provide information to their members and the public. Industry trade associations, state insurance departments, and other organizations also use the Internet to disseminate information, perform routine transactions, and enable access to individual accounts and members-only areas. A brief list of Internet resources for agencies appears in the appendix to this assignment.

Marketing Tip

When a producer encounters business that is difficult to place, the Internet can help solve the problem. An Internet search based on the type of business, linked to the word "insurance," will probably reveal insurers willing to quote that type of business. In fact, Internet search engines may produce an overwhelming number of resources that can be used to gather information about the class of business as well as potential markets.

Marketing Products and Services

Some producers have placed advertisements and information on the Internet intended to market their products and services. Customers are demanding more information delivered more quickly than ever before, and, unlike an office-based insurance agency, the Internet is available twenty-four hours a day, seven days a week. Many agencies and insurers solicit business via the Internet, providing real-time quotes and the opportunity to complete routine transactions. Such efficiencies increase the productivity of an agency by helping it sell its products quickly and economically.

E&O Alert!

Agencies are advised to beware of the E&O loss exposures that Web sites could create. Do prospects expect coverage to be bound? What type of content is provided on the Web site, and whose responsibility is it to update the content? Who is responsible for Web site security? These and similar concerns should lead Web site owners to carefully consider how they design their Web sites and what information and promises those Web sites offer.

Improving Customer Service

Most producers acknowledge that agencies that provide what customers want, when they want it, and at the price they are willing to pay will be successful. The Internet has become a tool to help meet the expectations of insurance customers. For example, agencies can use e-mail to improve the timeliness of customer service, allowing customers to request information at any time. Likewise, producers can respond to customers at any time.

Also, millions of customers are making stock transactions, purchasing airline tickets, and buying consumer products online. Although some customers still prefer to purchase insurance through an insurance agent, the growing consumer interest in purchasing personal insurance online is likely to continue. Agencies should be ready to meet the changing purchasing preferences of their customers.

Security Issues

The information stored in the agency's IT management system is one of its most vital assets and must be protected. Loss exposures in both the external and internal agency environments pose threats to agency information.

The physical destruction of the agency's IT, with consequent information loss, can result from external causes of loss, such as lightning or windstorm, or from internal equipment problems. "Crashes" are IT equipment or software failures that result in damage to or destruction of the information contained on the system storage devices or application and system software. However, only about one in ten cases of information loss is attributable to environmental causes.

Most incidents of information loss result from the actions of individuals. From data entry errors to outright crime, people can cause a variety of computer information losses. Some of these incidents are caused by individuals inside the organization who have access to the agency management system. Employees (past and present), consultants, service providers, and vendors all present a threat to the integrity of the information stored in the agency management system. Outsiders such as hackers and other criminals also pose threats. The introduction of viruses, worms, and Trojan horses into computer systems for purposes of data destruction is increasing. Additionally, the unauthorized use of illegally obtained information and the theft of funds by electronic means are only a few of the security problems associated with IT.

Exhibit 1-2 shows statistics developed by the Computer Security Institute (CSI) and the Federal Bureau of Investigation (FBI) concerning the types of cybersecurity attacks or misuse experienced by survey participants in a twelve-month period.

Many of the security problems an agency faces can be lessened by using loss control techniques. Frequent change of passwords, limited system access, a good virus protection program that is continually updated, and regular backups of the system can eliminate many of these potential security problems. Additionally, redundant systems, such as those using an application service provider, and the increased use of the Internet to access agency and insurer servers provide a layer of defense against threats from both the environment and people. A comprehensive disaster plan is a must for all agencies, to deal with not only IT issues, but also all aspects of maintaining agency operations in the event of a disaster.

Safeguarding the agency's IT and controlling IT security loss exposures will improve agency efficiency and cost-effectiveness.

EXHIBIT 1-2

Types of Attacks or Misuse Detected in the Last Twelve Months (by percent)

Virus	74%
Insider abuse of net access	48%
Laptop/mobile theft	48%
Unauthorized access to information	32%
Denial of service	32%
Abuse of wireless networks	16%
System penetration	15%
Web site defacement	10%
Telcom fraud	10%
Financial fraud	8%
Theft of proprietary information	8%
Misuse of public Web site applications	6%
Sabotage	4%

2005 CSI/FBI Computer Crime and Security Survey. Used with permission of CSI/FBI copyright 2005.

AGENCY/COMPANY INTERFACE

Agency/company interface
The electronic exchange and communication of data between agencies and companies.

Perhaps the most challenging aspect of agency operations has been the attempt to electronically link agencies to their insurer partners. This connection is called agency/company interface. **Agency/company interface** is the electronic exchange and communication of data between agencies and companies. This electronic communication occurs between the agency management systems and multiple insurer systems, either directly or through some type of IT network. Ideally, the information communicated from system to system is fully usable and ready for processing upon receipt.

Because insurer IT needs were once more complex than those of agencies and because insurers began using IT before their agencies, insurer IT was rarely compatible with newer agency IT. Consequently, for many years, agency management systems were unable to interface with insurer systems. Solving the interface problems required locating single-company, insurer-dedicated terminals in the agency. Although such terminals allowed the agency and the insurer to interface, they actually impaired the agency's work flow because the same information had to be entered in both the agency's management system and the insurer's system. This requirement prohibited single entry and multiple use of the same information.

Goals of Agency/Company Interface

The goals of agency/company interface are as follows:

- Reduce information input errors when completing policy and customer information
- Eliminate the duplication of work processes by agency and insurance company personnel
- Reduce costs for both the agency and the company
- Improve the relationship and communication between the agency and the company
- Improve the competitive position of agencies and their insurance company partners
- Improve customer service

The most important goal of agency/company interface is improved customer service. Although interfacing also enables the agency to lower its internal costs and improve its internal work flows, it is the external result—improved customer service—that ultimately provides the greatest benefit to the agency. Improved customer service increases customer retention and, by enhancing the agency's reputation, promotes sales.

Types of Agency/Company Interface

Insurance agencies typically choose between the two most common types of agency/company interfaces—interactive interface and single-entry multiple-company interface. Each of these types of agency/company interfaces has advantages and disadvantages.

Interactive Interface

Interactive interface is a process by which the agency's IT and insurer's IT are connected, engaging in two-way communication. This type of interface is used for inquiries about policy status, accounting, and claim information and to perform transactions such as new business and policy changes. An interactive system may also be used for rating purposes when rating information is not already stored in the agency's IT management system.

The most important advantage of interactive interface is the agency's ability to provide faster customer service by immediately accessing the insurer's database. An additional advantage of this feature is that it may reduce errors by immediately detecting incorrectly entered information, which the user can correct before proceeding with a transaction. Another powerful advantage of interactive interface is the ability of agency and insurer personnel to view the same information at the same time. This enables issues to be resolved more easily and quickly between the underwriter and the agency representative.

Interactive interface
A process by which the agency's and the insurer's IT are connected, engaging in two-way communication.

A final advantage is that the agency, with proper interface training provided by the insurer, has the ability to control all information entered into its IT management system.

Interactive interface has disadvantages as well. Not all insurer systems are alike, and agency personnel who work with multiple insurers may require extensive training in order to use the interface. Without standardization, interactive interface may not provide an agency with a cost-effective, competitive IT communications tool. Another disadvantage is that information may have to be entered twice—once in the agency's IT management system and once in the insurer's IT system—resulting in inefficiencies.

E&O Alert!

Interactive interface presents two serious issues that can create E&O loss exposures. First, agency personnel must be trained on multiple systems. Second, double entry of information presents more chances to enter incorrect information. Both of these issues can cost the agency more in E&O expenses than the interactive interface saves on processing expenses. Agencies may want to designate specific interface personnel to handle the task and emphasize training and attention to detail.

Single-Entry Multiple-Company Interface

Single-entry multiple-company interface (SEMCI) A method of using one IT system, typically an agency management system, to enter data only once so that it can be transmitted to multiple insurers or used for other designated purposes, such as quoting or policy issuance.

The second and preferred type of agency/company interface is the **single-entry multiple-company interface (SEMCI)**. SEMCI is a method of using one IT system, typically an agency management system, to enter data only once so that it can be transmitted to multiple insurers or used for other designated purposes, such as quoting or policy issuance. This type of interface allows the agency to enter information a single time, yet have it available to obtain quotations from several insurers with which it interfaces or use for entry onto a claim form.

The information the agency enters is sent to the insurers for processing. Quotations from the insurers are then returned electronically to the agency. The agency's database is automatically updated when the information is received from each insurer. The agency can then prepare proposals without re-entering the information.

Capturing an agency's information electronically, using that information to produce output for the insurer, and receiving the returned output at the agency in a usable form has been a challenge for agencies and insurers. Much of the challenge has been caused by differences between the agency's and insurer's IT. Insurers typically use mainframe computers, while agencies typically use servers or personal computers. Additionally, the insurer and agency often use different operating systems. Other software used during the information exchange is often incompatible as well. A lack of standards for information input and transmission has also created interface problems.

> **Marketing Tip**
>
> SEMCI is more efficient for the agency than interactive interface and also gives the producer access to proposals from several insurers. Producers can provide their customers with more options tailored to customers' needs and can therefore increase their chances of closing sales.

SEMCI offers agencies several advantages, including lower costs compared to interactive interface costs, and improved customer service. Additionally, communication costs are usually lower than with interactive interface because upload and download usually occur at off-peak hours when telecommunications rates are lower. Because the data entry format is standardized, training costs for agency personnel are reduced. Finally, agency personnel need to learn only the agency's system, because the information is transmitted to the insurer directly from the agency's database.

However, SEMCI is not without disadvantages. Among them is the fact that only agencies using an agency management system can take full advantage of it. Additionally, agencies that do have agency management systems must be using current systems to fully use SEMCI. An ACORD User Groups Information Exchange survey indicated that many agencies do not have the current version of their agency data management systems for maximum interface effectiveness.[2] When compared to interactive interface, SEMCI may also produce more errors that require further input because errors are not detected until each insurer's system receives and reviews the information. Software costs may also be higher because vendors must work closely with both insurers and agencies to develop a standard method of transmission.

SEMCI is most appropriate for transactions involving information required by both the agency and insurer databases. Applications, endorsements, cancellations, and other service requests are examples of these types of transactions.

Organizations That Support Agency-Company Interface

Two industry organizations have emerged as the primary supporters of agency/company interface over the past several decades. These organizations, ACORD and ACT, and others like them, support agencies and insurers who seek to standardize and simplify their agency/company interface.

ACORD

The Association for Cooperative Operations Research and Development (ACORD) is a global, not-for-profit insurance industry organization that has played a key role in the evolution of interface processes in the property-casualty and life insurance industries. ACORD was organized in 1970 to standardize the paper forms that were used for routine insurance transactions. Before forms standardization, all insurers used their own applications, claim forms, and other insurance forms. The standards established by ACORD for paper forms provided the basis for the standards of electronic transaction used today.

ACORD's efforts to establish standards for the insurance industry have been successful. Electronic transaction formats have been standardized so that each piece of information, such as a vehicle type or the personal automobile liability coverage limit, is expressed in the same way. The development of these consistent standards has facilitated more-integrated interface software development.

Additionally, ACORD provides a great deal of support for agents with respect to IT issues. ACORD works closely with agency IT vendors and insurers to enhance electronic communications and collaboration. The ACORD Advantage[3] program was designed especially to provide agents with access to a variety of IT-related resources, such as the following:

- Printable ACORD forms—printable forms that include instructions for completion

- Fillable ACORD forms—forms that can be completed online by agents who may not have access to current forms in their agency management systems

- Benchmark Calculator Evaluation Tool—a tool providing an external benchmark against which to measure agency performance

- HR Snapshot from LawRoom.com—access to a Web site that provides agency human resources staff the information to help manage employees, administer employee benefits, and comply with employment laws

- Resource Center—an online service that provides access to a variety of tools dealing specifically with IT issues

- Advantage e-Newsletter—an online publication that provides information about current IT issues

- Online education—continuing education via the Internet

- Audio Insurance Outlook—a monthly audio service featuring interviews with top agency principals

- ACORDMailNOW—which helps create direct mail marketing campaigns

ACORD also sponsors its own user group, AUGIE (ACORD User Groups Information Exchange), a forum for agents, brokers, insurers, vendor user groups, and trade associations to share ideas and work together to shape the future of insurance IT. AUGIE's goal is to improve agency productivity and efficiency.

ACT

The Agency Council for Technology (ACT) is associated with the IIABA for the purpose of providing an open, action-oriented approach to critical IT issues. ACT has helped coordinate agents', vendors', and insurers' interface efforts. Organizations such as ACT provide tools and resources that help organizations make the transition from paper to electronic processes.

REVIEW

Key Words and Phrases

Define or describe each of the words and phrases found in this assignment.

Information technology (p. 1.5)

Single-entry, multiple-use (p. 1.6)

Ergonomics (p. 1.11)

Agency-company interface (p. 1.14)

Interactive interface (p. 1.15)

Single-entry multiple-company interface (SEMCI) (p. 1.16)

Review Questions

1. How do agencies use IT to improve agency performance? (p. 1.5)

2. What are the purposes of agency information technology? (p. 1.6)

3. What are the ways in which the application of IT in agency operations increases agency profitability? (p. 1.7)

4. IT planning requires ongoing agency assessment. What questions can help agency managers ask to help structure their IT planning? (pp. 1.9–1.10)

5. What are three aspects of IT management that influence the ability of agencies and companies to increase their efficiency and cost-effectiveness? (p. 1.10)

6. How has the increased use of the Internet helped reduce agency transaction costs? (p. 1.11)

7. List the common causes of IT information loss. (p. 1.13)

REVIEW

8. What are the goals of agency/company interface? (p. 1.15)

9. What are two common types of agency/company interface? (p. 1.15)

Application Questions

1. As part of structuring an IT plan, an agency manager must determine what agency processes might benefit from IT.

   a. Identify typical customer transaction processes in the agency that may benefit from IT.

   b. Describe how the use of IT in the agency can streamline these customer transaction processes.

2. Yolanda Fernley, owner of Fernley Insurance Agency (Fernley), has learned that proper IT management enables her to efficiently and cost-effectively operate her business. Yolanda understands that three aspects of IT management influence her agency's ability to increase its efficiency and cost- effectiveness. For each aspect of IT management, describe how it can affect Yolanda's agency and its ability to increase efficiency and cost-effectiveness.

   a. Productivity issues

   b. Internet issues

   c. Security issues

REVIEW

Answers to Assignment 1 Questions

NOTE: These answers are provided to give students a basic understanding of acceptable types of responses. They often are not the only valid answers and are not intended to provide an exhaustive response to the questions.

Review Questions

1. The purposes of agency information technology are as follows:
   - Improve customer service
   - Maximize productivity and efficiency
   - Maximize profitability
   - Reduce errors and omissions loss exposures

2. Application of IT in agency operations increases agency profitability in the following ways:
   - Improves operating efficiencies and reduces transaction costs
   - Lowers overall labor costs and raises per-employee revenue
   - Increases new-business sales
   - Improves account development
   - Refines the agency's marketing processes by allowing producers to segment both customers and prospects based on specific database criteria
   - Provides tools to monitor the agency's financial performance and manage the book of business

3. Agencies use IT to improve agency performance in the areas of customer service, agency-insurer relationships, and agency management.

4. Agency managers can structure their IT planning by answering the following questions:
   - What agency operations require IT and how will new and existing IT be integrated?
   - Which processes will use IT?
   - What are the IT requirements?
   - When should IT be upgraded?
   - How can agencies keep current about new IT?

5. The three aspects of IT management that influence the ability of agencies and insurers to increase their efficiency and cost-effectiveness are as follows:
   (1) Productivity issues
   (2) Internet issues
   (3) Security issues

6. Agencies have been able to reduce their transaction costs by using the Internet for the following purposes:
   - Obtain information
   - Market products and services
   - Improve customer service

7. IT information loss can occur as a result of fire, windstorm, internal equipment problems, and the actions of individuals.

8. The goals of agency/company interface are as follows:

   • Reduce the agency's information input errors

   • Eliminate duplication of agency and company work processes

   • Reduce agency and company costs

   • Improve communication and relationships between the agency and the company

   • Improve the competitive position between agency and interface partners

   • Improve customer service

9. The two most common types of agency/company interface are as follows:

   (1) Interactive interface—The agency's and insurer's IT systems are connected in "real time" that allows for two-way communication.

   (2) Single-entry multiple-company interface—Information is entered and stored in the agency management system until it can be transmitted to insurers.

Application Questions

1. a. Customer transaction processes found in a typical agency that should benefit from IT typically involve new business, endorsements/policy changes, policy renewals, claims, certificates and other evidence of insurance, audits, bonds, and policy cancellations and nonrenewals.

   b. The agency might apply IT or upgrade its existing IT to improve its customer service, productivity, and efficiency; increase its profitability; and reduce errors and omissions loss exposures. For example, in the area of customer service, a CSR can view a customer's electronic file when the customer is on the telephone and make policy changes in real time. In the area of improving productivity and efficiency, IT allows CSRs to enter data into agency management systems only once, from where it can be exported to a number of other agency and insurer applications as needed. IT can increase the agency's profitability by improving operating efficiencies and revenue per employee and reducing transaction and labor costs. Finally, IT can reduce the agency's E&O loss exposures by standardizing office procedures.

2. a. Productivity issues can affect Yolanda's agency in several ways. She understands that increases in productivity can be related to her workers' feelings and attitudes about their jobs. Therefore, she should be attentive to such productivity issues as the following:

   • Training—ensuring that employees have the knowledge and skills required to perform their jobs. An employee may require specialized training for an insurer's new rating program.

   • Ergonomics—ensuring that her employees are in comfortably designed work environments and have the equipment needed to perform their jobs.

   • Telecommuting—considering whether some employees may be more productive working away from the agency, whether on the road, from home, or from another remote location.

REVIEW

b. Internet issues can affect Yolanda's agency in numerous ways. She may use the Internet primarily as a means of communication, but she should also consider its effect as a means of obtaining information, of marketing her agency's products and services, and of improving customer service. For example, if Yolanda acquires a significant portion of her leads and new business via the Internet, she should determine whether her customers will then expect twenty-four-hour service access via the Internet from her agency in return.

c. Yolanda also must consider security issues as an aspect of IT management. The information contained in her agency's management system is one of her agency's most valuable assets and must be protected. Yolanda should ensure that security measures are in place to safeguard her IT against losses generated by both the internal and external environment. No safeguard is entirely foolproof, however, so the more loss control measures Yolanda can implement, maintain, and constantly upgrade, the better.

INSURANCE AGENCY INFORMATION NEEDS

Some functions and tasks are performed in the same way in all agencies; therefore, the information needs of different agencies are often similar. Most agencies can sort their information needs into three categories: strategic planning, management, and operations—each requiring more-detailed information than the last. IT can help an agency organize this information for its individual use.

Exhibit 1-3 illustrates the different levels of information needs and examples of specific information used at those levels.

EXHIBIT 1-3

Levels of Information Needs

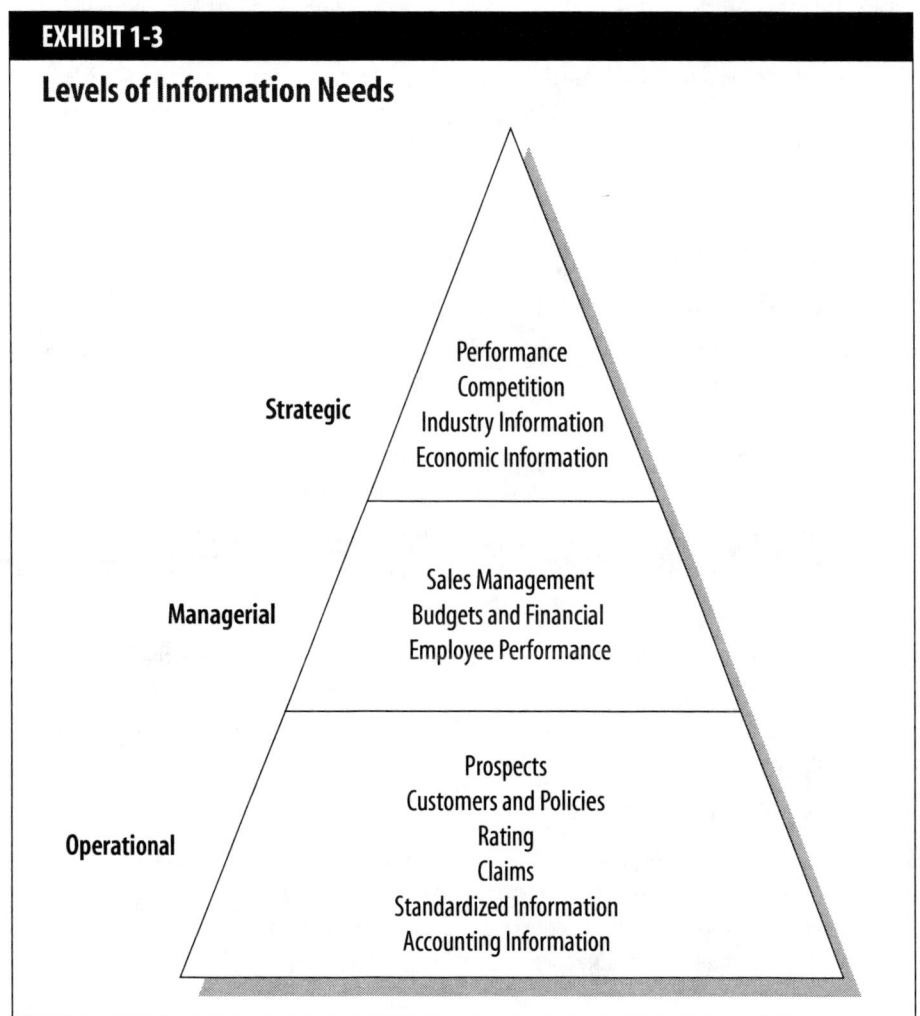

Strategic
- Performance
- Competition
- Industry Information
- Economic Information

Managerial
- Sales Management
- Budgets and Financial
- Employee Performance

Operational
- Prospects
- Customers and Policies
- Rating
- Claims
- Standardized Information
- Accounting Information

Strategic Planning Information

Strategic information is data an agency collects that form the basis for the agency's strategic planning. Strategic information can include (1) internal information about agency performance and (2) external information, including information about competitors, industry information, and economic information.

Strategic information
Data an agency collects that forms the basis for the agency's strategic planning.

Internal Information About Agency Performance

Senior management uses internal reports on prospective and existing business to evaluate how the agency is performing relative to its strategic goals. Internal reports typically relate to financial and productivity measures. Executives compare information about current performance results with established budgets and projections to determine whether the agency is on or off target. Mid-course corrections may be made based on an analysis of this strategic information.

External Information About Competitors, Industry Information, and Economic Information

Agencies gather external information about competitors, the insurance industry, and economic factors. Agencies consider this information in combination with their internal information to generate strategic plans. Sources of such external information can include professional associations, trade associations, industry periodicals, and daily and weekly online subscription services.

Marketing Tip

From a strategic perspective, some of the most important information stored in the agency's database is why a customer moved an account from the agency or why a quotation was not accepted. This vital information, if properly collected, captured by the agency's IT, and interpreted, can change how the agency operates to improve its retention and hit ratios.

Management Tip

Strengths, weaknesses, opportunities, and threats (SWOT) analysis is a thorough analysis of both internal and external factors. SWOT allows management to consider what the agency does best, where it needs improvement, what challenges and opportunities may be on the horizon, and what obstacles could prevent the agency from achieving its strategic goals.

Managing Agency Information Technology   1.29

Management Information

Management information assists managers and supervisors in planning, budgeting, and staffing the agency's functions. The following are types of management information:

- Sales management information
- Budgeting and financial information
- Employee performance information

Management information
Information that assists managers and supervisors in planning, budgeting, and staffing the agency's functions.

Sales Management Information

Even if an agency does not have an employee with the title of sales manager, sales management functions must still be performed to maintain the agency's focus on sales. For example, sales productivity requires detailed information to establish agency and individual sales goals and to measure progress. Information about the number of sales calls, hit ratios, premium and commission volume, and retention rates for each member of the sales staff should be available for producers and managers. Monitoring and measuring success with the agency's insurers in terms of sales goals are also important.

Budgeting and Financial Information

Managers and supervisors are often responsible for preparing budgets. These budgets, which are essential for the agency's sound financial management, can include revenue projections, estimated expenditures, and anticipated profit or loss.

The financial information an insurance agency maintains serves as the basis of financial management. Just as for other businesses, this information includes a general ledger, accounts receivable and payable, income statements, and balance sheets. Unique to the agency, however, is its fiduciary role with both the insurer and the insured. In this role, the agency must maintain funds collected from customers separately from operating accounts until the funds are remitted to the insurer. This additional facet of financial management requires special expertise and must be supported by financial reports available through the use of IT.

Employee Performance Information

Producer performance is usually measured based on information regarding commission levels, hit ratios, attainment of production goals, retention of existing business, and quality of submissions. This information is readily available through an agency's IT. For CSRs and other support personnel, performance is typically measured based on the amount of premium and/or number of commissions handled, number of accounts serviced, number of transactions processed, and retention rates. Additionally, CSRs who are responsible for account development may also be evaluated based on coverages or policies added to existing accounts.

All this information can be entered and maintained in the agency's database, from which reports can be produced in several formats for management to use. However, some financial reports examine quantitative factors that overlook the overall quality of the employee's work and the speed with which business transactions are processed. Managers must adopt a multidimensional approach to evaluating employee performance that considers both the quantity and the quality of an employee's work.

Operational Information

Operational information
Data needed to conduct the agency's daily activities.

Operational information is data needed to conduct the agency's daily activities. It can include the following:

- Prospect information
- Customer and policy information
- Rating information
- Claim information
- Standardized information
- Premium accounting information

Prospect Information

When used effectively, a database containing prospect information, such as names, addresses, telephone numbers, and coverage codes, can dramatically improve a producer's sales performance. Producers can use information reports generated by their IT to analyze their agencies' marketing results and trends. They can then concentrate their marketing efforts where they are most likely to result in sales.

Prospect information can also be especially helpful to new producers and producers new to a market segment, enabling them to learn about the segment's needs. This segmented marketing approach usually results in better hit ratios than providing proposals to a wide variety of prospects.

Stored prospect information provides another benefit to the agency—it can easily be compared to insurer preferences. When submitting applications for quotations or policy issuance, the agency can identify the insurer or insurers that would be most interested in this type of prospective customer. The use of a prospect information database makes the agency's sales efforts more efficient and helps accommodate insurer preferences.

> ### Marketing Tip
> How can prospect information be used in market segmentation? Stored information can be sorted into segments by categorizing prospects by similar characteristics. In commercial insurance, prospects can be grouped by revenue size, type of industry, number of employees, workers' compensation classification, and similar criteria. Personal insurance prospects can be categorized by occupation, income, or needs for specific types of coverage. Producers and others involved can then focus their marketing efforts on prospects with characteristics that meet the agency's insurer preferences or on prospects with which the agency has had the greatest marketing success.

Not all agencies have IT that can support a prospect information database, forcing some agencies to use third-party contact management software. However, such software may not be compatible with the agency's IT and should be used only after careful consideration of its benefits versus the costs of dual entry, that is, entering information into both the agency system and the third-party software.

Customer and Policy Information

Customer information begins in most agencies' IT as prospect information. When a sale is made, the prospect is converted electronically to a customer, with no need to re-enter information. However, additional information, including detailed customer coverages and limits, claim history, and accounting information, should be added to the database at this time in order to provide efficient customer service. The availability of this information in the database eliminates the need to pull a paper file when a CSR or another staff member receives a request for service. Those data, along with detailed information about any transactions and how they were generated and any correspondence pertaining to the account, should also be included in the database. These electronic files should be the primary source of customer information and should be readily available to all agency representatives.

Rating Information

In an agency that fully uses IT, all information required to quote new or renewal business should be in the agency's database. The promptness with which an agency responds to a prospect's or customer's request for a premium quotation can often make the difference between writing and not writing the account.

Ideally, an agency should use IT to produce multiple quotations with various insurers using different limits and coverages, without duplicating the input information. This IT, called comparative raters, is available for personal and small commercial accounts. Large or complex accounts are usually submitted to the insurer for rating and quoting.

Some agencies use proprietary rating IT (developed by or on behalf of an individual insurer for that insurer's use and for the agent's use, with the insurer's permission). Or they may access the insurer's IT via the Internet to provide quotes to customers. Both of these approaches are inefficient because information must be entered in both the agency's and the insurer's IT systems. For optimum productivity and efficiency, proprietary rating IT should be used sparingly.

Claim Information

Some insurers prefer that customers report claims directly to the insurance company if losses occur. Other insurers prefer that customers report claims to their insurance agents. When a claim is reported to an agency, the agency needs to respond quickly and efficiently. Because customer and coverage information is already in the agency's database, the process of communicating the insured's claim information to the insurer becomes seamless. Using IT, loss notices can be produced and sent to the insurer, and the claim can be monitored until it is closed. Claim histories can be produced to assist agency management in determining an individual customer's profitability to the agency and to the insurer, as well as to provide risk management assistance to the customer. Because most claim transactions are performed by the insurer, IT application is ideal for transmitting agency information needed by the insurer.

If an insurer requires claim information to be entered into its proprietary Web site, the agency should inquire about the possibility of downloading that information into its own management system. Otherwise, dual entry of information is required to maintain the agency's claim records.

Standardized Information

Most agency correspondence with prospects, customers, and insurers involves using database-generated form letters. All customers require similar information for policy processing, and these forms avoid the redundancies of recreating letters, memos, and confirmations for every transaction. Once generated, this standardized information is linked to the customer account. For example, producers can view binders, certificates of insurance, and insurance identification cards issued for a particular account, as well as form letter type and the date it was issued. Awareness of such account activity is useful when agency staff is considering account servicing issues. Proposal formats and customer coverage summaries should also be standardized and included in the agency's IT system.

Marketing Tip

In addition to streamlining the quotation process, standardized proposals also help reduce E&O claims because important wording or disclaimers can be automatically included in each proposal. Although standard proposals can be created using information in the agency's database, care should be taken when creating summaries of insurance that use the same underlying data. Summaries are meant to be internal documents, for use by producers and CSRs when reviewing coverage with a customer. If provided to a customer, a summary may appear to be a substitute for the actual policy. Consequently, the agency might be held legally responsible for any misstatements in the summary.

Premium Accounting Information

Premium accounting, one part of transaction processing, is completed by the CSR when a policy, endorsement, or premium audit is received. All agency personnel must be able to access a customer's accounts receivable history to determine whether any premiums are outstanding. IT ensures that all premium accounting transactions per account are viewable. Premium accounting also serves as the basis for the agency's general accounting system, and IT supports this function.

AGENCY MANAGEMENT SYSTEMS

An **agency management system**, sometimes called a management information system (MIS), is a system that integrates customer, policy, and accounting information with service and sales information, insurer communications, and information about other agency operations. Computerized agency management systems are becoming more common. The cost of this new technology must be considered as part of an agency's operating budget.

ACORD's AUGIE survey of independent agents revealed that some agencies do not budget for this technology. Approximately half the survey respondents stated that they pay for technology only as needed. Only four in ten agencies budget for technology annually; those that do are typically at the high end of the revenue scale in the survey.[3] Once an IT investment has been made, an agency should strive to maximize its newly acquired IT capabilities. After agency management systems have been installed, some systems may not be used to their full potential. Training and new office procedures will help employees and agencies use the new system to enhance the efficiency and quality of their business.

Types of Agency Management Systems

Agency management systems range from simple to complex and include the following types:

Agency management system
A system that integrates customer, policy, and accounting information with service and sales information, insurer communications, and information about other agency operations.

- Integrated agency management systems
- Insurer proprietary management systems
- Manual management systems

Most agencies use integrated agency management systems that are either single, full-function agency management systems or agency management systems combined with other IT. The single, full-function agency management system is intended to handle all agency functions. It is often purchased from a single vendor and may include both hardware and software. Over time, an agency may develop needs that are not addressed by these original systems. Widely available business application software enables many agencies to expand their IT to meet these needs. The percentage of agencies that rely solely on single, full function agency management systems continues to decrease as more agencies combine their agency management systems with other standard software products. An important consideration for agency principals purchasing an agency management system, therefore, is how well that system integrates with the other hardware and software the agency is already using, including Internet access. For example, insurance networking and interface leader IVANS, in a study of independent agents, reported that 52 percent of agents prefer to process policyholder information through their agency management systems, while approximately 31 percent of agents prefer to process policyholder information directly through insurers' Web sites.[4]

Insurers are huge repositories for the data necessary to underwrite policies and adjust losses. Their system needs are often different from an agency's system needs. Because of the substantial cost involved in changing or upgrading their systems, insurers have tended to maintain their old systems. Therefore, some agencies use insurer proprietary management systems (developed and maintained by an individual insurer) because the insurers they do business with require their agencies to have a separate computer dedicated to transacting business with that insurer using that insurer's management system. This approach is usually inefficient and requires dual entry of information.

Finally, a few agencies, typically small in premium volume, may not use computers. These agencies generally use direct billing to handle their accounting needs. They have manual management systems and keep paper files rather than electronic ones. Often, an outside service is employed to perform bookkeeping functions. Adhering to standard procedures is crucial to ensure operational efficiency and limit E&O loss exposures.

Use of Agency Management Systems

Agencies use management systems as convenient information repositories that enhance the efficiency of all aspects of insurance transactions. They can also be used to facilitate sales. An agency management system is most useful in the following areas: sales management, customer database management, claim management, transactional filing, electronic filing, and rotational servicing.

Sales Management

In addition to management reports that track new and lost business, the agency management system provides information that can be used to generate new sales. Profiles of current customers indicate what coverages the agency provides. Reports can be generated and used for cross-selling and account development. Newer agency management systems often include prospecting software that enables producers to gather and store detailed information on prospective customers, generate solicitation letters, monitor sales calls and appointments, and monitor the progress of new business. Proposals generated from the agency management system can include complete descriptions of coverages offered as well as summaries of those that may be needed but are not included in the quotation.

Despite the potential sales capabilities offered by agency management systems, some agencies do not use their management systems for important activities such as qualifying prospects, sales promotions, cross-selling, and generating leads. This nonuse may be because of inadequate IT training or lack of management direction. Most agencies, however, report that they use their management systems for sales tracking.

Marketing Tip

Account development can be much more effective using an agency management system. An agency can easily perform a search for all customers with a personal auto policy but no homeowners policy, or those with a watercraft policy but no personal umbrella policy. These customers' information can then be merged with form letters stored in the system to create quotations or solicitation letters.

E&O Alert!

Using the agency management system for account development also reduces an agency's E&O loss exposures and enhances the producer's and the agency's professional image.

If the agency management system does not include sales management software, off-the-shelf software products are available that can accomplish many of the same tasks, although such products may not be able to interface with the agency's database.

Customer Database Management

Most agencies use their agency management systems to create customer profiles and to store and retrieve customer policy information. The ACORD application is the primary tool used to create a policy and coverage database. Without the information from the ACORD application and that stored in the database, many routine tasks, such as issuing certificates of insurance, binders, notices of cancellation, and loss notices, would require additional input by a CSR. Each of these forms requires access to much of the same information. Therefore, any such information not stored for future use results in inefficient use of the agency management system and may cause database errors.

Claim Management

Another area in which the agency management system is useful is claim management. An agency can use accurate, up-to-date claim information three ways. First, loss histories sorted by customer and by type of coverage enable the agency to automatically generate detailed claim information for use in renewing a customer's coverages. Second, the agency can produce internal reports showing the loss ratios of each customer, which can help determine which accounts the agency should continue to service. Third, the agency can produce reports that show loss ratios by insurer and type of business, for use in negotiating with insurers. Previously, agents had to rely on the claim information provided by the insurer, which might not have been accurate or timely.

Transactional Filing

Transactional filing, or "t-filing," can redefine how work processes are completed in an agency. Transactional filing involves creating two types of files. First, a permanent paper file is created for each customer and is stored alphabetically. These files contain signed applications, appraisals, financial statements, photographs, and other information that is not typically stored via IT unless these documents are scanned and the images are stored in the system.

Transactional file
A file that contains one division for each day of the year, so that all documents are filed by the transaction date.

A second file, the actual **transactional file**, is also created. This file contains one division for each day of the year, so that all documents are filed by the transaction date. All documents that support computer entries in policyholder records (such as requests for coverage increases or changes in vehicle schedules) are filed in the transactional file by the transaction date. If and when the paper file needs to be retrieved, the agency management system can determine the date the transaction was processed. That day's transactional file can then be used to locate the paper document needed.

Transactional filing allows an agency to virtually eliminate the time and expense of filing required to store paper documents in individual customer files. It also encourages agency personnel to rely on the electronic file rather than on paper documents.

Electronic Filing

The current generation of storage and retrieval systems is electronic filing, or e-filing. Unlike transactional filing, which still retains paper, agencies that use e-filing scan paper documents to capture digital images and attach those images to the customer's electronic file. The images can be viewed by anyone with access to the system. The paper can be destroyed once it has been saved into the system because the information can be reproduced as needed.

Agencies that rely on electronic scanning and filing benefit from improved workflow and are also able to significantly reduce their storage needs for paper documents such as photographs, correspondence, claim forms, and policy removals and endorsements.

E&O Alert!

Agents should be thoroughly familiar with all state and federal statutes and regulations that relate to the retention of agency records. In some cases, original paper documents must be retained for a minimum period.

Rotational Servicing

Rotational servicing, which is the automatic routing of an incoming customer call to any CSR who is not already assisting a customer, also uses the agency management system. Rotational servicing is based on the assumption that customers are more interested in having their problems solved than in who solves them.

Rotational servicing
Automatic routing of incoming calls to any CSR not already assisting a customer.

The ultimate goal of rotational servicing is to handle service requests quickly and immediately. With immediate access to the customer's electronic file, any available CSR can handle the request for service. This kind of quality service reflects favorably on the agency, but it requires a commitment by senior management, full use of IT and the agency management system, and a great deal of teamwork on the part of support staff.

THE AGENCY WORKPLACE OF TOMORROW: A CASE STUDY

A case study using a hypothetical insurance agency of tomorrow can help illustrate the current trends in agency IT. Because changes in IT occur constantly and rapidly, the case study approach can provide the best glimpse of what is currently being used and what is possible in the future, demonstrating how an agency stays abreast of current IT, trains its staff, and invests in IT resources.

The agency workplace of tomorrow that fully utilizes IT creates an environment that provides extraordinary levels of customer service, maximizes sales opportunities, fosters growth, and optimizes employees' job satisfaction. For example, the agency uses IT to establish timeframes for the completion of transactions: five working days for commercial insurance transactions and three working days for personal insurance transactions. Using a simple work flow and desk management system helps agency staff adhere to service standards. As a result, no transaction in the agency remains unresolved for longer than five days. Agency managers electronically track adherence to the standards and adjust the work flow as necessary to keep service levels high.

The workplace of tomorrow maintains no paper files. Information for each customer is stored electronically. When a transaction is processed, all information is entered in the agency management system. Producers can keep track of all prospect details, quotes, and proposals in the system. When the business is written, the e-file is transferred to a CSR for processing.

When the agency receives a written document, it is retained only until it has been scanned and stored in the agency management system. When scanned, the document receives a barcode for later document retrieval, if necessary. Scanned files are attached to the customer's electronic file and are viewable by anyone with access to the system.

The workplace of tomorrow does not use or maintain database software in-house. Rather, access to the software is maintained and provided by an application service provider (ASP), an offsite server that hosts the software and allows the agency to access it using the Internet. The software is available to any agency employee with access to the Internet. The ASP could maintain backup or redundant systems in various parts of the country in the event of failure of its primary IT equipment. The agency's software is always current because it is maintained by the vendor rather than the agency. The agency's offices, at multiple locations, maintain communication through the agency management system. Additionally, high-speed Internet connections allow quick communication between offices and with insurers and customers.

The agency workplace of tomorrow adheres to standards and practices regarding faxes received from and sent to each employee's desktop. All employees have printers at their workstations for greater efficiency and higher levels of customer service. When possible, e-mail is used for all internal and external communications. Documents are scanned and attached to electronic mail.

To better serve customers' needs, the agency joins with several other agencies to form an "agency cluster" that may operate twenty-four hours a day. Agency management allows several employees who desire more flexibility in their work schedules to work from home using laptop computers, cellular phones, and fax machines provided by the agency. Employees can work a flexible schedule while also serving customers by being available to provide normal business-hours service and response at any time, day or night.

The agency of tomorrow has a Web site where customers can access their policy information. The site is secure to ensure the privacy of the customer's information. Customers can conduct routine transactions, such as changing addresses, adding or deleting insured vehicles, completing simple certificates of insurance, and requesting quotes. The agency also uses the Web site to advertise for available staff positions. The number of prospects who find the agency via the Web site is monitored weekly.

Tomorrow's workplace uses technology to keep its employees connected to the office. All producers have personal digital assistants (PDAs) that allow them to access e-mail, edit documents, make customer presentations, and transfer information to the office from almost anywhere. They use digital cameras to photograph customer locations and transfer the photos to the agency for attachment to the application and the company submission. Each office location also maintains digital cameras in the event they are needed to assist with a claim or to document other customer information. All laptops, PDAs, and cell phones used by agency personnel are enabled with wireless technology.

The agency workplace of tomorrow requires a comprehensive business plan that includes an IT component. Budgeting for IT is crucial because use of the agency management system and ancillary products will enable the agency to sustain its current growth rate, lower transaction costs, and enhance its ability to provide excellent customer service.

Although the workplace of tomorrow is hypothetical, some agencies are currently using many of these IT solutions while also looking for the next new IT improvements. Such agencies recognize the changing needs of their customers and their employees and are committed to providing the highest level of IT resources.

To prosper, insurance agents must be proactive rather than reactive with respect to IT. Like all aspects of agency management, IT must be constantly improved to meet the agency's strategic goals and, most important, to meet or exceed customer expectations.

REVIEW

Key Words and Phrases

Define or describe each of the words and phrases found in this assignment.

Strategic information (p. 1.29)

Management information (p. 1.30)

Operational information (p. 1.31)

Agency management system (p. 1.34)

Transactional file (p. 1.37)

Rotational servicing (p. 1.39)

Review Questions

10. What kind of information may an agency use for strategic planning? (p. 1.29)

11. What kind of information may an agency use in management? (p. 1.30)

12. What kind of information may an agency use in operations? (p. 1.31)

13. What are three types of agency management systems? (p. 1.35)

14. What are two insurance agency operational areas in which agency management systems are most useful? (p. 1.36)

15. Describe the types of files used in transactional filing. (p. 1.37)

16. What could be the service response standard time frames for a typical agency workplace of tomorrow? (p. 1.39)

REVIEW

Application Questions

3. Joe, the operations manager at XYZ Agency, is working with Linda, the IT manager, to ensure that their new agency management system meets all of XYZ's information needs. What information should Joe include in the system software from an operations perspective and why?

4. The Gold Insurance Agency has just installed its new agency management system. The agency's president, Cheryl Gold, has two goals for the new system: (1) to use the agency management system to its fullest and (2) to have the agency become as "paperless" as possible. Cheryl has decided that the agency will immediately switch to a transactional filing system to work toward her goals.

   a. How can a transactional filing system help Cheryl achieve her goals?

   b. Explain how a transactional filing system is designed.

Answers to Assignment 1 Questions

NOTE: These answers are provided to give students a basic understanding of acceptable types of responses. They often are not the only valid answers and are not intended to provide an exhaustive response to the questions.

Review Questions

10. An agency uses the following information for strategic planning:
    • Internal information about agency performance
    • External information, which includes information about competitors, industry information, and economic information

11. An agency uses the following information in management:
    • Sales management information
    • Budgeting and other financial information
    • Employee performance information

12. An agency uses the following information in operations:
    • Prospect information
    • Customer and policy information
    • Rating information
    • Claim information
    • Standardized information
    • Premium accounting

13. Three agency management systems are as follows:
    (1) Integrated agency management systems—Include purchased hardware and software and are intended to handle all agency functions
    (2) Insurer proprietary systems—Stand-alone computers dedicated to transacting business with a particular insurer
    (3) Manual systems—Use manual billing systems, generally employ outside bookkeepers, and keep paper files

14. Insurance agency operational areas in which agency management systems are most useful are as follows (any two):
    (1) Sales management
    (2) Customer database management
    (3) Claim management
    (4) Transactional filing
    (5) Electronic filing
    (6) Rotational servicing

15. Types of files used in transactional filing include the following:
    - Permanent customer file—Documentation for each customer (signed applications, appraisals, financial statements, photographs, and other information not easily stored via IT) is filed alphabetically.
    - Transactional file—Documentation for all policyholders (requests for coverage increases or changes in vehicles) is filed by the transaction date.

16. The service response standard time frames for a typical agency workplace of tomorrow could be as follows:
    - Commercial lines—five working days
    - Personal lines—three working days

Application Questions

3. Joe should ensure that the new system allows XYZ Agency to use and access operational information needed to conduct the agency's daily activities. Such information can include the following:
   - Prospect information—Contains information such as names, addresses, telephone numbers, and coverage codes, which producers can use in their sales efforts. The sales manager can request that reports be generated from the IT system, segmented to specific target markets based on the prospect information profiled in the system.
   - Customer and policy information—All policy detail contained in the declarations page either received or downloaded from the insurer should be stored in the agency management system. Additional information, such as claim information, is useful in the event that the account needs to be remarketed.
   - Rating information—All information needed to provide a quote for the customer should be contained in the agency management system. This is a critical customer service feature and can be most important when the customer requests multiple quotes on his or her account. With the customer's information already stored in the database, a comparative rating system attached to the agency's IT can immediately provide multiple quotes.
   - Claim information—Claims must be reported to the insurer immediately, and with the customer's coverage information already in the agency's database, the claim form can be quickly completed and transmitted to the insurer.
   - Standardized information—Standardized information, including form letters, ID cards, memos, and certificates of insurance, can be quickly completed with information already stored in the agency management system.
   - Premium accounting information—An accounting of premiums received by the agency as well as those received directly by the insurer can be accessed on the agency management system. Agency personnel can access a customer's accounts receivable history to provide prompt customer service.

4. a. If Cheryl's agency uses transactional filing, all customer information is entered in the agency management system. All customer service will then be provided by accessing that information from the computer. This filing system achieves goal #1 (to use the system to its fullest) by using one of the important features provided by the system and by making all of the agency's personnel rely on the computer for information.

   The filing system meets goal #2 (to have the agency become as "paperless" as possible) because the staff will not use paper to provide customer service. After any paper request for action is received (by mail or fax), the staff takes the appropriate action on the computer and files the paper in the transactional file. If the request for action is phoned in, all activity is done directly in the computer file and no paper is used. Although this approach is not totally paperless, it decreases the agency's reliance on paper and increases its use of the computer.

   b. A transactional filing system has three types of files. The first is the computer file. All policy information is stored in the computer and this is the only source for information and client service. The second file is the permanent customer file, in which the agency keeps paper documents such as signed applications, financial statements, and other important documents for each client. This file looks like the traditional paper file, but it is much smaller because it does not include policies or other similar documents. The third file, also a paper file, is used to store paper documents that do not belong in the permanent file. These documents include policies, endorsements, and any paper correspondence. As these paper documents are received, the client's computer file is updated and the paper is filed in the transactional file on the date the action was taken. Although the agency may not need to use this information again, anyone who needs to find information in this file can locate it easily because the date of each transaction is recorded in the client's computer file.

SUMMARY

Advances in information technology (IT) have greatly affected how insurance agencies conduct business. For example, IT advances have helped improve customer service, agency-insurer relationships, and agency management.

The purposes of agency information technology include the following:

- Improving customer service
- Maximizing productivity and efficiency
- Maximizing profitability
- Reducing errors and omissions loss exposures

Simply having IT does not mean agency owners and their staff are fully using it. Agencies can follow established key business practices to help them use IT more fully and efficiently. Proper training and office procedures must support IT implementation.

Agencies structure their IT planning based on the answers to a series of needs-based questions, including the following:

- What agency operations require IT, and how will new and existing IT be integrated?
- Which processes will use IT?
- What are the IT requirements?
- When should IT be upgraded?
- How can agencies keep current about new IT?

IT planning should be aligned with the agency's business plan. The business plan can reveal whether IT is adequate to accomplish the agency's goals.

As agency owners consider IT needs in order to conduct business operations more efficiently and cost-effectively, they address the following three issues:

1. Productivity issues—Because increases in productivity are largely determined by workers' feelings and attitudes about their jobs, management considers issues such as training, ergonomics, and telecommuting.

2. Internet issues—Agency managers use the Internet for such business purposes as obtaining information, marketing products and services, and improving customer service.

3. Security issues—The information an agency stores on its agency management system must be protected from internal and external threats. Security safeguards are vital.

Agencies and insurance companies communicate electronically by agency/company interface. This electronic communication occurs between the agency management systems and multiple insurer systems, either directly or through some type of IT network. The goals of agency/company interface are as follows:

- Reduce information input errors when completing policy and customer information
- Eliminate duplication of work processes by agency and company personnel
- Reduce costs for both the agency and the company
- Improve communication and the relationship between the agency and the insurer
- Improve the competitive position of agencies and their company interface partners
- Improve customer service

The two types of agency/company interface are interactive interface and single-entry multiple-company interface (SEMCI). Interactive interface allows for two-way communication between the agency and the insurer. Single-entry multiple-company interface is a method of using one IT system, typically an agency management system, to enter data only once so that it can be transmitted to multiple insurers or used for other designated purposes, such as quoting or policy issuance. Among organizations that support agency/company interface are ACORD (Association for Cooperative Operations Research and Development) and ACT (Agency Council for Technology).

An agency's information needs may be categorized based on how the information is being used. Strategic information includes an agency's internal performance reports, external reports about the agency's competition, current industry information, and economic factors. Management information, which includes information about sales management, budgets and other finances, and employee performance, assists managers in planning, staffing, and agency functions. Operational information, which helps the agency conduct its daily activities, can include prospect information, customer and policy information, rating information, claim information, standardized information, and premium accounting information.

Agency management systems range from simple to complex and include full-function integrated agency management systems purchased from vendors; insurer proprietary systems, which are stand-alone computer systems dedicated to a single insurer; and manual, non-computerized management systems, typically used in small, low-premium-volume agencies. Agency management systems are used to facilitate various insurance transactions, including the following:

- Sales management
- Customer database management
- Claim management
- Transactional filing
- Electronic filing
- Rotational servicing

Agencies will continue to pursue their operational goals through IT. The agency workplace of tomorrow case study illustrates how one such hypothetical agency might at optimal IT levels.

ASSIGNMENT NOTES

1. Independent Insurance Agents and Brokers of America and Reagan Consulting, *Agency Self-Diagnostic Tool* (Alexandria, Va.: IIABA, 1994), p. B-15.

2. ACORD User Groups Information Exchange (AUGIE), *2002 Independent Agency Principals & CSRs: Technology & Workflow Challenges: An Industry Sponsored Survey of Independent Agents*, p. 5, www.acord.com (accessed Sept. 15, 2004).

3. *2002 Agency Principals & CSRs*, p. 2.

4. IVANS, *"2003 Independent Agency Survey,"* March 15, 2004 (Old Greenwich, Conn.: Ivans, Inc., 2004), p. 4.

Appendix

Technology Resources

TECHNOLOGY RESOURCES

The American Institute for CPCU/Insurance Institute of America, www.aicpcu.org, include on their Web site complete lists of educational programs offered, distance learning information, and program updates.

Association for Cooperative Operations Research and Development (ACORD), www.acord.org, is a worldwide insurance organization that researches and develops insurance industry standards. Information on ACORD Advantage is also available on the site.

The CPCU Society, www.cpcusociety.org, is the professional association for those who have earned the CPCU designation. The site includes information on how to become involved in a local CPCU chapter.

Independent Insurance Agents and Brokers of America (IIABA), www.iiaba.org, a professional trade association, includes on its Web site links to Best Practices information, ACT, and Trusted Choice.

The Insurance Information Institute, www.iii.org, compiles insurance industry facts and statistics in support of its primary mission of improving the public's understanding of insurance. The III site is regularly updated with industry information and statistics.

Insurance Services Office (ISO), www.iso.com, is a leading creator of property-casualty industry policy forms and endorsements, as well as a leading industry supplier of statistical, actuarial, underwriting, and claim data.

The National Association of Insurance Commissioners (NAIC), www.naic.org, is the national organization of state insurance regulators that promotes uniformity in insurance by offering educated opinions and drafting model laws and regulations. The NAIC also provides statistical information to state insurance departments.

The Professional Liability Underwriting Society, www.plusweb.org, is a professional society for industry professionals focused in the professional liability underwriting field.

Direct Your Learning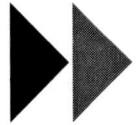

Management of Customer Services

Educational Objectives

After learning the content of this assignment, you should be able to:

1. Describe three tasks agencies should complete to create a customer services organizational structure.

2. Describe the three major support services functions of agencies.

3. Describe the three major technical services functions of agencies.

4. Explain how agencies process new business, renewals, and endorsements and adjustments.

5. Explain what agency managers should evaluate to facilitate work flow and optimize efficiency.

6. Describe the two standard agency accounting reports used for financial transactions.

7. Explain how agencies measure productivity and solve productivity problems.

8. Given an insurance agency case, explain why the agency may exhibit low productivity and poor customer service and recommend solutions to these problems.

9. Define or describe each of the Key Words and Phrases for this assignment.

 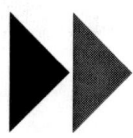

Develop Your Perspective

What are the main topics covered in the assignment?

An agency's customer services organizational structure is determined by an analysis of customer services functions. Over time, as the agency's environment changes, the organizational structure may also require change. In addition to implementing an efficient and effective customer services organizational structure, agencies should use benchmarking to measure productivity and solve productivity problems.

Identify the tasks an agency must complete to perform a customer services organizational structure analysis.

▶ What is the benefit of performing a customer services task analysis?

▶ What questions should be asked when grouping and ranking customer service tasks?

Why is it important to learn about these topics?

To be successful, an agency must satisfy its customers. A carefully developed customer services structure can help it meet this goal. Structures are tailored to the business the agency writes and the functions within the agency.

Contrast a customer services organizational structure based on line of business with a structure based on function.

▶ Why might an agency that predominantly writes large commercial accounts establish a structure based on function?

▶ Why might an agency that predominantly writes personal and commercial accounts for professionals (physicians, attorneys, architects) establish a cross-functional work team?

How can you use what you will learn?

Evaluate your agency's customer services organizational structure.

▶ How does the structure facilitate customer service?

▶ How might a change to the structure improve performance?

▶ How might you benchmark the agency's performance and suggest improvements?

Management of Customer Services

Outline

Management of Customer Services

An agency must efficiently and effectively manage all of its customer services in order to retain current customers and attract new ones. Agencies that can distinguish themselves by offering superior customer services have a competitive advantage. Agencies provide customer service through both support services functions and technical services functions. Support services functions are those relating to processing communications to and from customers as well as managing the customer information that results from these communications. Support services functions also include preparing documentation for products and services proposed or provided to the customer. Technical services functions relate to marketing and sales transactions, claims, and customer billing.

To promote productivity, the organizational structure of an agency's customer services must be sound. It must include the functions of both support services and technical services. In addition, agencies seek to improve their customer services by measuring productivity and solving productivity problems.

In this assignment, the term "manager" is used to describe the individual responsible for the customer services functions discussed, although, in many agencies, this individual handles other duties (such as production). Also, various customer service job titles, such as customer service representative, account manager, and account executive, are used interchangeably within agencies. However, for simplicity, this assignment uses the term "customer service representative" (CSR).

CUSTOMER SERVICES ORGANIZATIONAL STRUCTURE

An agency's customer services organizational structure must promote productivity and facilitate efficient work processing. A carefully constructed, well-managed organizational structure reduces duplication of effort and delegates as many tasks to customer service representatives as they are qualified to handle. Such a structure allows sales personnel to focus on sales.

Different agencies use different customer services organizational structures. Given differences in agency size and business mix, one structure could be highly effective for one agency but highly ineffective for another. An important part of the customer services organizational structure is that the agency principal or manager must recognize the need for change when the existing structure becomes ineffective and no longer supports agency goals.

For an agency to meet its goals, its customer services organizational structure must support its business plan. Agency principals and managers should consider the following guidelines when evaluating how well the customer services organizational structure supports the agency's business plan:

- Determine the customer services goals that are essential to success and build the organizational structure around them
- Build linkages between customer services functions to coordinate delivery of customer services
- Determine the degree of authority necessary to manage each customer services function and to what extent authority is centralized and decentralized
- Determine whether some customer services tasks can best be done by someone outside the agency (outsourced)

With these guidelines in mind, agencies should complete the following three tasks to create a customer services organizational structure that promotes productivity and facilitates efficient work processing:

1. Perform an organizational structure analysis
2. Select a customer services organizational structure
3. Monitor the customer services organizational structure

Perform a Customer Services Organizational Structure Analysis

The analysis of the customer services organizational structure helps the agency determine what tasks must be accomplished to serve the customer and how to accomplish those tasks. The analysis involves four steps.

Four Steps in the Customer Services Organizational Structure Analysis

1. Identify tasks
2. Group and rank tasks
3. Delegate the necessary authority so each task can be effectively performed
4. Coordinate the various job positions that the customer services tasks comprise and communicate the responsibilities for the tasks

---

First, tasks are identified. By generating and analyzing a list of customer services tasks, the agency determines the scope and nature of its customer services. Various employees should be involved in this step because managers may not be aware of the full range of tasks performed.

After identifying the customer services tasks, agency managers group and rank them according to their importance in achieving the agency's overall goals and its specific customer services goals. To do this, managers should ask the following questions: "What customer services tasks are related and can be grouped?" "What groups of customer service tasks must be performed especially well to achieve competitive advantage?" "What customer service tasks, if not performed well, endanger agency success?" and "How are these groups of tasks ranked in order of importance?"

Having ranked the tasks, the manager then delegates authority so that each task can be effectively performed. If authority is not delegated, some agency personnel may be unnecessarily involved in completing customer service tasks, or completion of tasks may be delayed or avoided. Delegating customer service tasks is essential for efficient insurance agency operations because it allows sales personnel to concentrate on sales.

Delegation is the act of empowering an individual or individuals to act on behalf of another. Implicit in delegation is that the person to whom the task is delegated is willing and able to perform it. To delegate effectively, managers must select willing and able personnel and provide them with the training, tools, and resources they need to perform the delegated tasks. Incentives should be provided to encourage employees to seek additional delegated responsibilities.

For a variety of reasons, some managers fail to delegate, even though delegation of tasks can contribute to the agency's overall effectiveness and success. The main reasons managers fail to delegate, and suggested responses, are as follows:

- *Reason*: Managers believe they can perform the job better than anyone to whom they could delegate it.

  Response: Failure to delegate for this reason is not cost-effective for the agency because the managers perform customer services tasks that employees directly responsible for customer services functions should perform.

- *Reason*: Managers lack confidence in the employees and their skills.

  Response: Managers should provide employees with training, new tools, or additional resources needed to perform the tasks.

- *Reason*: Managers lack the ability to direct others.

  Response: Agency principals should assess managers' leadership, management, and supervisory skills and provide training, if necessary.

- *Reason*: Managers have not implemented controls to monitor performance of delegated tasks.

  Response: Performance management systems should be implemented to determine whether remedial action is necessary.

Most of the reasons managers do not delegate customer service tasks result from misconceptions about how and why tasks should be delegated. Such misconceptions indicate the need to train managers in sound delegation techniques.

The final step in customer services organizational structure analysis is to coordinate the various job positions that perform customer service tasks and communicate the responsibilities for the tasks. When employees work at odds with each other or lack the information necessary to perform their customer service tasks, customer service suffers.

Managers can coordinate customer service positions by clearly delineating the customer service tasks related to each position. By evaluating the customer service tasks for each job position, managers can detect gaps in assigned tasks. The manager should also evaluate customer service tasks across all positions to determine whether any overlaps exist and whether each task is assigned to the appropriate job position.

Communicating with employees about who is responsible for each customer service task is an essential part of coordinating job positions. Employees must understand their relationships to co-workers, supervisors, and managers. One way an organization communicates responsibilities is through an organizational chart, which illustrates reporting relationships and organizational structure. A well-designed customer service organizational chart indicates how customer service tasks are grouped and where authority and communication originate.

Written position descriptions listing job duties are also valuable tools for coordinating and communicating reporting relationships, limits of authority, and job responsibilities.

Select a Customer Services Organizational Structure

Depending on the agency's goals, the type and volume of business handled, and staff expertise, customer services work has traditionally been structured in one of two major ways: by line of business or by function. Both structures can be effective, and at various stages in its development an agency may have either structure or a combination of both. In fact, the best customer services organizational structure for a particular agency may be the one that is organized both by line of business and by function.

Line of Business

Structuring customer services by line of business typically creates three divisions: (1) personal insurance, (2) commercial insurance, and (3) life insurance, health insurance, and employee benefits. Some agencies have also added divisions for risk management, loss control, and claim administration, which may be established as separate profit centers. A profit center is a division within an organization that is responsible for generating its own revenue and paying its own expenses with the aim of generating its own profit. These profit centers may each require a different customer services organizational structure.

Management Tip

Many agencies now divide accounts by the expertise required to handle the account rather than dividing them into personal insurance accounts and commercial insurance accounts. Personal insurance and small commercial accounts usually require about the same level of customer service expertise, and, in fact, many of the coverages are similar. Often called "basic accounts," customers in these accounts can generally be handled by the same CSR.

More complex accounts require a higher level of customer service expertise. These accounts are generally large commercial customers with high premiums and complex business insurance needs. CSRs with more experience should service these accounts.

Organizing customer services by line of business is advantageous because it follows traditional divisions of the insurance business. Additionally, training and education is simplified because employees focus on insurer policies, rates, and underwriting guidelines for the specific line of business they handle.

A major disadvantage of the line of business organizational structure is that it often requires duplicate customer service functions. For example, each division must handle the customer service functions of reporting and tracking claims. Although it may be more efficient and productive to move these functions into a separate claim department, making such a change is difficult when the customer services organizational system is rigidly set by line of business. Another disadvantage is that organizing by line of business can impede the flow of information among divisions. For a single customer's account, an agency typically possesses customer services information from a combination of divisions, including personal, commercial, life, and health insurance, as well as employee benefits. If the information flow is slowed, customer service suffers.

Marketing Tip

The birth of a child and the purchase of a new home are major events in a person's life. An agency should have communication procedures in place to notify all divisions when a customer experiences such an event. For example, when a personal lines producer or customer service representative discovers that a customer has purchased a new home, the life insurance division should be informed. If the customer has inadequate levels of life insurance and is a primary wage earner, then the customer's family could suffer financially if he or she dies suddenly. Besides benefiting the customer, this type of cross-selling can result in increased revenue for the producer and the agency.

Another disadvantage of the line of business customer services organizational structure is that it tends to deter management and CSRs from focusing on one customer's total needs. Instead, needs tend to be viewed separately by each division.

Function

An agency's customer services structure can also be organized by function in addition to line of business. An advantage of a functional structure is that CSRs develop specialized expertise in their functions. Also, employee training is simplified because it is focused for each employee. Some of the most common functions include marketing, sales, claims, and accounting.

A major disadvantage of a functional structure is that processing customer transactions involving a life insurance policy can be entirely different from processing those involving a property or liability policy, and employees need different skills to handle these transactions efficiently. As a consequence of this disadvantage, agencies often combine a functional structure with a line of business structure. Large commercial brokerages especially need to split the commercial insurance division into functions, but their personal lines and life/benefits business can often be maintained without such a split. In small agencies, staff must be able to service customers from the commercial insurance division as well as both the personal insurance and life/benefits divisions.

Large agencies with slightly more commercial business than personal insurance or life insurance usually have separate marketing, sales, claim, and accounting functions for personal insurance and life insurance but retain line of business structures for commercial, personal, and life insurance.

Cross-functional work team
A customer services organizational structure in which all customer services functions are contained in a single business unit.

An emerging customer services organizational structure for medium and large agencies is a **cross-functional work team**. In this structure, all customer services functions are contained in a single business unit. Because customer service functions are interdependent in any agency, combining them in this way makes sense. Most cross-functional teams are self-managing, with no one team member having authority over the others, and are results-oriented. Therefore, every team member is responsible to and for every other member. The team as a whole reports to another agency employee who has line authority over them. Often, team members provide input regarding decisions related to hiring, retaining, and rewarding other team members.

No single customer services organizational structure is appropriate for all agencies. Each agency must design its own structure based on its mix of business, its customer needs, and the skill and experience of its employees. An agency may expect to adjust its customer services structure until it identifies the structure that most efficiently produces the highest quality of customer service.

Monitor the Customer Services Organizational Structure

Once a customer services organizational structure has been selected and implemented, a customer services manager must monitor its effectiveness in light of changing work flows, revise procedures and job positions when necessary, and ensure that job positions are properly coordinated. The manager should be involved in human resources management, including hiring, training, and evaluating employees, even if the agency employs a human resources professional.

To accomplish this monitoring most effectively, an agency must have someone with the designated responsibility and authority to manage customer services. The agency's size determines whether this person is part-time or full-time. In small agencies, this person is usually the owner. In large agencies, a full-time customer services manager may be necessary.

As the agency grows, it becomes more difficult for it to function smoothly without a customer services manager. At that point, it may be advisable for an agency principal who functions as a customer services manager to separate and assign the customer services management tasks so that he or she can focus on sales and/or other management tasks.

SUPPORT SERVICES FUNCTIONS

A primary customer services function is support services, which includes processing communications, managing information, and preparing documentation. Support services functions should be handled by entry-level employees or those with clerical and computer skills. Employees who understand the complexities of insurance coverages should be assigned to marketing, sales, and claims, customer services functions for which they are optimally qualified. Often, in agencies representing insurers supporting the exclusive agency system or the direct writer system, producers are assigned customer service representatives. However, in order to keep their focus on sales, even producers in agencies with only a few employees can delegate some functions to customer service staff members.

Processing Communications

An essential element in managing customer services is effectively processing communications with insureds, prospects, insurers, and others—in person; by telephone, mail, or fax; or electronically.

Building and maintaining customer relationships is critical to agency success. The strength of such relationships depends on the quality of customer communication and how it is processed.

Reception

Initial communications create critical first impressions. As the first person in the agency to greet people, the receptionist may, in some respects, have the most important job in the agency, making an important first impression on the customer or prospect.

Handling customer interactions politely and promptly, whether in person or by telephone, is crucial. Prospective customers who telephone may be lost because of long hold times or misdirected calls.

Many agencies mistakenly staff the receptionist position with their newest employee or a temporary employee. The receptionist should instead be one of the agency's most knowledgeable and most personable employees. Because callers often do not know their agency contact person, the receptionist must know what questions to ask and must be familiar enough with the agency to accurately direct callers to the appropriate employees. The receptionist must also be trained on the agency's computer system so that phone messages can be entered in the system rather than recorded on paper if the agency does not use voice mail, and so that the receptionist can perform basic policy inquiries.

When filling the position of receptionist, agency managers should also consider someone who can tactfully handle customers who may be upset. When reporting claims, customers can be under stress. Tactful treatment of both insureds and claimants is an important part of the claim handling process.

Management Tip

Even for an agency that maximizes its use of technology, the positive effect of someone personally answering the phone cannot be overstated. One agency thinks so highly of its receptionist that it has bestowed on her the title "Director of First Impressions."

Voice Mail

Voice mail is a quick and easy way for customers to communicate information. However, some people may be uncomfortable with automated attendants because they seem impersonal. Consequently, voice mail should be structured to meet the agency's needs in a user-friendly way. Voice mail systems should always offer the customer the option to speak to the receptionist and should inform the customer of this option early in the answering message so that the customer need not wait unnecessarily through multiple voice mail options.

E&O Alert!

When using voice mail to answer calls while the office is closed, an agency must take precautions to avoid possible errors and omissions claims. The outgoing message should clearly state the agency's office hours, including when the office will reopen. Callers should be informed that new claim reports and requests for new coverage or modified coverage should not be left on voice mail. If possible, the agency should include an emergency phone number for callers to use if they need immediate assistance. When closed, some agencies activate an announcement-only feature that allows callers to listen to a message but not record one of their own. For individual voice mail boxes, each person's greeting should include the day and date, whether the person is in the office, and a brief disclaimer that coverage may be arranged or confirmed only by speaking directly with an agency staff member. Additionally, agency personnel should not leave detailed voice mail messages about coverages, premiums, and the like, which customers may later question.

Agencies should have guidelines for processing voice mail. The agency may require that employees answer voice mail messages within a specified period, for example, twenty-four hours; access voice mail messages a specified number of times each day; follow a certain protocol when leaving outgoing voice mail messages, for example, to follow up certain types of voice mail requests (such as coverage requests) with written communications; and change outgoing voice mail messages regularly so that the information provided to the caller is current. When used properly, voice mail can help an agency provide efficient customer service.

Regular Mail

Although much agency correspondence is now received by e-mail or fax, the volume of incoming regular mail—typically consisting of such items as policies, endorsements, letters, binders, and invoices—is still significant. Effective processing of incoming mail involves receiving, opening, and reviewing the mail on a daily basis.

To effectively process regular incoming mail, agencies should arrange with the local post office to receive it as early as possible in the work day. However, mail is usually delivered once a day, and the time when mail is delivered to the agency may be subject to the agency's location on the mail route. Many agencies find that daily processing mail is more efficient if they use a post office box rather than await delivery. With a post office box, an employee can pick up the mail at the post office on the way to work, and processing can begin as soon as staff members arrive. In some cases, mail can be picked up several times a day, especially when the agency is expecting payment checks.

Opening and reviewing the mail as quickly as possible after it is received contributes not only to efficient mail processing but also to good customer service. Managers who open and review the mail may gain a better understanding of personnel performance and workload. For example, the first signs of a CSR's backlog occur when second or third processing requests are received from insurers or complaint letters are received from customers. Having managers review the mail before distributing it to employees may also help protect confidential information. However, many agencies see opening and reading mail as a relatively routine task that should be handled exclusively by support staff. Some agencies use a combination of these approaches, with a manager opening and reviewing the mail and support staff distributing the mail to employees.

How an agency decides to process regular mail depends partly on its size. In a small agency, the person who opens the mail knows the recipients. Large agencies, in which the person opening the mail could be far removed from other agency activities, may prefer to have a manager review the mail. The information gained from reviewing incoming mail can help managers better manage agency work flows.

E&O Alert!

Once the mail is opened, place a date and time stamp on the agency copy of the document enclosed. The date is important for defense if an E&O claim is made or if a customer has a question about service. Date stamping also helps staff prioritize their work.

Management Tips

- Sort and distribute all mail from insurers and insureds about policy transactions, based on the agency's organizational structure. For example, premium checks should be immediately routed to the accounting department so they can be deposited.

- Route miscellaneous items such as insurer bulletins, advertisements, and magazines to a designated person—often the administrative manager—for further consideration or distribution.

- Ensure that the mail processor knows the current postal rules and regulations so the agency can provide faster customer service and save money by applying the correct postage.

- Because sorting mail is routine, a customer service representative should handle it. However, despite the fact that it is routine, promptly and efficiently handling outgoing mail is as important as the courteous, friendly handling of incoming phone calls.

- Before using an overnight service, determine whether the documents must reach their destinations by the next business day and whether the cost for overnight service is justified.

E-Mail

E-mail allows agencies to process both customer and insurer communications quickly and can greatly improve customer service. For example, agencies can transmit applications, submissions, and other documents to the insurer electronically. Internally, e-mail allows agencies to document and communicate decisions made by staff members.

Although processing communications through e-mail can improve agency productivity, it is not without its disadvantages. For example, individuals tend to be more casual when using e-mail than when writing traditional letters. The nearly instantaneous response capability of e-mail may contribute to more errors or misunderstandings than the deliberative process typically associated with composing a formal letter. Additionally, e-mail recipients may be more inclined to ignore or delete the correspondence than would traditional letter recipients, creating problems if documentation is needed.

Fax

Responsibility for processing faxes can be placed with the same individual who processes regular mail. Because most agencies have fax machines located throughout the office, CSRs or support staff should be assigned to distribute material received via fax as soon as possible.

Two considerations should affect the decision of whether to fax or mail a document. First, confidential information that is faxed may not remain confidential because many people at the receiving end may have access to the fax machine. Consequently, the intended recipient of a confidential fax should be notified of the fax transmission and asked to confirm receipt. Second, the cost of the fax may not always justify its use. If fax transmission is via telephone line fax modems (rather than through personal computers) during office hours, phone rates may be high depending on the type of telephone service used. Faxing a lengthy document, such as an application that could have been mailed, can be costly. This cost should be justified by the benefits of faxing the document.

E&O Alert

Because of new privacy laws, any information of a sensitive or confidential nature must be handled properly by the agency. When faxing anything that may be considered personal or private, agency personnel should be sure the intended recipient is aware of the transmission and available to receive the information directly. Agency fax cover sheets should contain a disclaimer stating that the fax being sent is intended to be viewed only by the person to whom it is addressed. Agencies should always confirm receipt of a fax using the fax's confirmation function, and, for any faxes the agency characterizes as being of top priority, a confirmation phone call should be placed.

Managing Information

In addition to managing communication, managing information is a major customer services function. Managing (storing and retrieving) account information, for example, can affect all employees' productivity. Agencies must store information after completing a customer transaction, such as a final claim settlement and notice, as well as after completing each step in the process of a transaction, such as loss control inspection report receipts.

Agencies increase efficiency by properly managing information. Agencies can efficiently handle information and records by properly managing their information systems. An efficient filing system for retrieving information, whether paper or electronic, is essential. Information must be logically and consistently stored because time wasted trying to retrieve information that is not easily accessible is money wasted. Anything that affects an employee's ability to promptly handle a customer's request adversely affects customer service.

Information Storage Systems

Agencies use two basic types of storage systems for their information: paper storage systems and electronic storage systems that are maintained by the agency information technology (IT) management staff. Agencies of all sizes use some type of agency IT management system, which reduces dependence on paper files. However, as previously discussed, some agencies maintain both paper and electronic storage systems because they believe that doing so prevents errors and omissions. For example, one system could be used to document the agency's position in an E&O case if the other system fails or is lost or destroyed.

E&O Alert

Agencies that maintain both electronic and paper files should be aware that failing to update both files may increase errors and omissions loss exposures. Because both files are legally required to be provided in an E&O case, the accuracy of the files can be questioned. Consequently, consistency of files should be carefully monitored.

Sometimes agencies are required to keep primary files in a paper system by the insurers they represent or by their E&O carriers. Agencies may also use a paper system as a backup because of legal and regulatory requirements or because electronic systems are not being used to their fullest capacities. Regardless of the storage system used, all agencies have a policyholder information system.

Policyholder Information Systems

Because a variety of policyholder information must be stored, the storage system used varies among agencies. Agencies must keep active policies or binders (those in current use). Employees must also have immediate access to correspondence relating to the policies, applications, motor vehicle records (MVRs), photographs, and summarized claim information. Additionally, employees must have access to records of contacts with insureds, particularly insureds whose requests for coverage are rejected.

Other policyholder information agencies should store includes open and closed claims, pending transactions or suspense records (items such as binder renewal or policy remarketing), policy expiration information, and accounting data. Producers must also keep expired and canceled policies for occasional reference and to satisfy state regulatory requirements.

Most agencies typically keep all this information in electronic form. Applications, correspondence, billing, and accounting information are part of a customer's electronic file. Policies, photographs, appraisals and similar documents are often scanned into the system and attached to the customer's electronic file.

Agencies can efficiently manage their policyholder information by using the following six policyholder information systems:

1. Active filing system
2. Dead filing system
3. Claim filing system
4. Pending filing system
5. Expiration filing system
6. Policyholder accounting filing system

The active filing system contains all policies and related information for active policyholders. Many agencies maintain both an electronic and a paper storage system for policy information, which can result in duplication as well as inconsistent files.

Efficient customer service depends on the immediate availability of up-to-date information in the active file. The electronic file is the most efficient method of providing this information. Detailed policy information should be entered for each customer. When policy changes are made, they are entered in the customer's file in the agency database, allowing all agency personnel immediate access to this information. Using the electronic file, a producer who receives a phone call from a customer does not need to pull the paper file to determine the current status of the account. In fact, using Wide Area Networks (WANs) and the Internet, producers and service personnel can access current customer information from virtually any location. Transactional and electronic filing and agency/company interface, discussed previously, greatly enhance an agency's ability to electronically maintain customer information.

The paper file is a backup to the electronic file in the active filing system. Some documents, such as financial statements, photographs, and applications, remain stored in paper files unless the agency uses document imaging. Although paper files continue to be maintained for some time, agencies should place as much information as possible in the electronic file. Paper files can be kept in a centralized location or can be decentralized by department or workstation. A centralized system saves space by requiring fewer filing cabinets and may require only one person to maintain it.

However, a centralized location may delay retrieving and returning files. Lost paper files are a problem because usually no backup exists. Decentralization allows more rapid access to the file, and, because fewer people handle them, files are easier to track. Decentralization is probably most effective in an electronic system, in which paper files become less necessary. Decentralization allows faster access to files by those individuals in the agency who are most likely to need the information. However, proximity of paper files may contribute to increased dependence on them rather than on the electronic file. Ultimately, the best location is the one that allows the agency to most effectively serve its customers.

Because of legal, regulatory, and insurer requirements, insurance agencies may continue to maintain paper files. For example, many insurers require agents to maintain original signed personal auto policy applications and related forms. If possible, all active information for an account should be contained in one file.

Electronic scanning and electronic transactional filing greatly reduce the amount of paper agencies must maintain in individual customer files because the agency no longer needs to retain certain paper documents on file. For instance, accounting records and correspondence are entered in the transactional files after they have been scanned into the electronic file. Paper files decrease, and customer services staff can view customers' transaction histories by accessing e-files.

The second policyholder information system is the dead filing system, used for storing expired and canceled policies. Highly automated agencies may not need a dead filing system, because all past customer information, including copies of policies, can be scanned and stored electronically in the agency IT management system, usually as some type of history file. Other agencies move policies from the active filing system to the dead filing system once they have expired or been canceled.

These dead file policies may be needed for reference, for possible resolution of errors and omissions claims, and for legal and regulatory reasons. Agents usually keep records for three to five years, depending on the type of policy and state requirements. However, certain policy files, such as for professional liability policies, are kept indefinitely.

The most commonly used dead file system arranges policies in a folder by year and then by alphabet. When information is no longer needed, purging files is simple if they are maintained by year.

Dead file storage should be centralized for the entire agency. If only limited access is necessary, files may be stored off-site. Many storage facilities offer courier or retrieval services for a fee. Alternatively, many agencies use scanning and imaging to store dead files. Scanned files do not have to be updated and can be accessed electronically as often as necessary.

In addition to active and dead filing systems, agencies use a third policyholder information system for claim files. The type of claim filing system used depends on both the agency's customer services organizational structure and its level of computer use. For example, if the organizational structure is organized by function, the agency may have a separate claim department that maintains claim files.

In agencies with separate claim departments, paper files are usually kept alphabetically by policyholder name. In fully automated agencies, claim information is part of the policyholder's electronic file. Because the ability to access the current status of claim information is essential to efficient handling of a policyholder's account, updated information should be entered as soon as it is received. Follow-up procedures should be established for determining the status of open claims. Once a claim is closed, final claim information is entered in the claim filing system as part of the policyholder's electronic file.

The fourth policyholder information system is the pending filing system. When a request for a policy or endorsement is sent to an insurer, when a claim is filed, or when an insured is contacted about providing missing information, the transaction is considered pending or incomplete. The agency must establish a follow-up procedure to ensure that the pending transaction is completed. Many different kinds of pending systems (often called suspense, diary, tickler, follow-up, or reminder) exist. The agency's size, the type of accounts it handles, and the type of active filing system it uses determine the appropriate pending system the agency should use.

Computerized pending systems have replaced manual systems in most agencies. Dates are entered into the computer, and a calendar is either displayed on the screen or printed for daily or weekly review. In many systems, processing a transaction, such as a claim or policy change, creates an automatic suspense item until all required information is received for that transaction and the pending file is closed. If necessary, an additional copy of the correspondence generating the suspense item is printed and sent as a reminder to the insurer or insured.

If an agency is not fully automated, the most common manual pending system consists of a "one to thirty-one" file, with copies of the suspense items filed according to the day of the month corresponding to their suspense date. An entire day's suspense items are pulled and followed up on if they have not been received or acted upon by the target date.

The fifth policyholder information system is maintained for expirations. The expiration filing system tracks policy expiration dates. Stringent controls must be maintained to ensure that renewals are ordered and coverage remains in force on any agency-billed policies. Therefore, the expiration filing system must provide an accurate and complete record of expiring policies and help ensure that renewals are processed on time.

E&O Alert!

A sound expiration filing system can dramatically reduce the possibility of an E&O claim against the agency for a late or missed renewal.

As a precaution, agencies should maintain expiration lists in two different agency areas. In addition to the list handled by CSRs, managers or department supervisors should have a list to verify that the renewal has been processed or that a binder has been issued by the current policy's expiration date.

The sixth system the agency needs to manage policyholder information is the policyholder accounting filing system. Accounting files must be maintained for all agency insureds. Usually, the accounting department handles this policyholder information, although CSRs generally handle the invoicing when processing a policy or endorsement.

Agencies may also retain a copy of the policyholder invoice in the active filing system (when it is a paper file) so a CSR or producer can have quick access to specific billing information when talking with a customer. Some agencies prefer not to maintain a copy but instead require the person who prepares the invoice or credit memo to make a notation in the file when the invoice is prepared.

Maintaining accurate and easily accessible information is extremely important and requires the use of all six of the policyholder information filing systems. This policyholder information must be retained over time. Appendix A provides an information retention schedule suggested by GE Insurance Solutions, an agents' errors and omissions insurer.

Preparing Documentation

The third major customer services function of insurance agencies is preparing documentation. This typically consists of creating or preparing form letters, binders, certificates of insurance, loss reports, proposals, and invoices.

Each of these types of documents may be fairly standardized within agencies in terms of form, language, and phrasing. However, their preparation requires a high degree of accuracy to avoid errors and omissions loss exposures. An agency must carefully consider which employees are best qualified to prepare these documents.

Using computerized templates that standardize common agency documents is often best for preparing policy-related documentation. For example, a CSR can use standard templates to quickly produce a form letter to the customer requesting policy renewal information and confirming policy change requests. Using such templates contributes to good customer service and reduces agency transaction costs.

Marketing Tip

An agency can use form letters not only to streamline agency operations but also to create a new sales opportunity every time the agency sends a new policy, a renewal policy, or an endorsement. For example, if the agency is expanding its product offerings to include financial planning and employee benefits products, it can take advantage of the customer contact to provide information about the products and about how to obtain additional information.

Key Word or Phrase

Define or describe the following word or phrase.

Cross-functional work team (p. 2.10)

Review Questions

1. What guidelines should agency managers consider when evaluating how well its customer services organizational structure supports the business plan? (p. 2.6)

2. What three tasks should an agency complete to create a customer services organizational structure? (p. 2.6)

3. Describe an advantage and a disadvantage of a customer services organizational structure organized by function. (p. 2.10)

4. What are three major service functions that should be handled by support staff? (p. 2.11)

REVIEW

5. What are two basic types of storage systems agencies use to store their information? (pp. 2.15–2.16)

6. What are some of the types of documents an agency's customer service staff can prepare using the agency's management system. (p. 2.20)

Application Questions

1. An agency manager has been given the responsibility of performing a customer services organizational structure analysis for the agency by the agency principal. Describe the four steps of an organizational structure analysis and explain why each step is important.

2. Although it can be argued that routine agency tasks should be handled by the persons with the least experience and technical training, some routine jobs are often delegated to experienced, technically trained persons. For each of the following, explain the advantages and disadvantages of having an experienced person perform the task.

    a.   Reception

    b.   Opening and distributing regular mail

Answers to Assignment 2 Questions

NOTE: These answers are provided to give students a basic understanding of acceptable types of responses. They often are not the only valid answers and are not intended to provide an exhaustive response to the questions.

Review Questions

1. When evaluating how well the agency's organizational structure supports its business plan, agency managers should consider the following guidelines:
   - Determine the customer service goals that are essential to success and build the organizational structure around them
   - Build linkages between customer services functions to coordinate delivery of customer services
   - Determine the degrees of authority necessary to manage each customer services function and to what extent authority is centralized and decentralized
   - Determine whether some customer services tasks can best be done by someone outside the agency (outsourced)

2. Three tasks an agency should complete to create an organizational structure for customer services are as follows:
   (1) Perform an organizational structure analysis—examine the tasks and services required of and performed by agency customer service staff
   (2) Select a customer service organizational method—structure by line of insurance or by function
   (3) Monitor the organizational structure—monitor work flows and revise procedures and job functions when necessary

3. One advantage to organizing an agency's customer services organizational structure by function is that CSRs develop specialized expertise in their functions. Employee training is also simplified because it is focused for each employee. A disadvantage of a functional structure is that processing customer transactions involving a life insurance policy can be entirely different from processing those involving a property or liability policy, and employees require different skills to handle these transactions efficiently.

4. Three major service functions that should be handled by support staff include the following:
   (1) Processing communications
   (2) Managing information
   (3) Preparing documentation

5. The two basic types of systems for storing agency information are (1) paper files and (2) electronic files maintained on agency management systems.

6. The types of documents that can prepared by an agency's customer service staff include the following:
   - Form letters

- Binders, certificates of insurance, and loss reports
- Proposals
- Invoices

Application Questions

1. The four steps of a customer services organizational structure analysis and their importance are as follows:

   (1) Perform a task identification. From the resulting list of tasks performed by the agency, the manager can determine the nature and scope of the agency's customer services. Various members of the customer services department should be involved in the task identification process to ensure that all tasks performed by the agency are captured during the analysis phase.

   (2) Group and rank the customer services tasks according to their importance in achieving the agency's overall goals and its specific customer services goals. The agency must be sure to focus on tasks that enable it to attain a competitive advantage in the marketplace and achieve agency goals, while operating efficiently and effectively.

   (3) Delegate the necessary authority so each customer services task can be effectively performed. Delegation of authority is an essential aspect of efficient and effective customer service. If individuals are not given authority to perform their assigned tasks, the completion of the tasks may be unnecessarily delayed or avoided, and other agency personnel may have to unnecessarily become involved in the task.

   (4) Coordinate job positions according to customer services tasks and communicate the responsibilities of those positions to support efficient work flow. If employees lack the information they need to properly perform their task, customer service suffers.

2. a.   The receptionist has one of the most important customer service positions because of its high visibility. Because a great deal of information is communicated by and to the receptionist, this position should not be handled by an inexperienced employee. Many telephone calls are requests for information, so the receptionist must be knowledgeable enough to give correct answers or refer the caller to the correct person. Also, the receptionist gives a first impression of the agency to prospects and customers. If the reception they receive is inadequate, business may suffer. A disadvantage of assigning an experienced person to the receptionist position may be the higher cost of that person's time. This cost can be offset by assigning the receptionist additional tasks that can be completed when he or she is not answering telephones or greeting guests.

   b.   The disadvantage of having an experienced person opening and distributing mail is the cost of time spent on a task as simple as opening a letter. However, many advantages outweigh that disadvantage. First, the experienced person is more likely to direct the mail to the appropriate person. Second, by seeing all the mail the agency receives, an experienced person, even someone in management, will have a better idea of the work flow among employees. Finally, some items received are confidential, and an experienced person is more likely to know what to do with such items and how to maintain their confidentiality.

TECHNICAL SERVICES FUNCTIONS

In addition to support services functions, managing customer services also involves managing technical services functions. This section describes the technical customer services functions of marketing and sales transactions, claims, and accounting. Determining which employee should perform each of these functions depends on the agency's size and customer services organizational structure and on the skills of the agency's staff. Agency principals and managers should consider which agency employee can most economically provide the best service in each function. Rather than assign each technical services function separately to different employees, it is becoming more common for agencies to have one person handle all or many of the technical services functions associated with a single account.

Marketing and Sales Transactions

The technical services function of marketing and sales transactions includes new business, renewals, and endorsements (policy changes) and adjustments. Many of these transactions involve similar tasks. For example, rating may be required on new business, renewal, and endorsement transactions. Likewise, invoices and credit memos must be prepared for each of these transactions. However, some agencies have found that they can facilitate these transactions by devoting certain days to handling each function exclusively, for example, handling renewals on Fridays.

New Business

New business accounts must be placed on the books continually both to replace those that have been lost and to provide for agency revenue growth. Agencies focused on producing new business accounts recognize this necessity and place top priority on prospecting new applicants and processing proposals.

Gathering information to underwrite and place new business begins with prospects. The producer must use an initial qualifying or screening process to ensure that certain individuals within a segmented market are potential insurance buyers. Once the individual or organization has been qualified through the agency's screening process, the producer may solicit its business. Many agencies maintain an electronic prospect database that contains specific information, such as the prospects' policy expiration dates, number of employees, payroll, sales, and key contact names. Solicitation letters to prospects are then prepared using the agency's database.

> **Marketing Tip**
>
> The agency should solicit new business from prospects that it has the greatest chance to convert into customers. Producers can do this by matching their prospects' needs with the products and services their insurer can provide.

Once the agency has qualified the prospect and the producer has completed the fact-finding (loss exposure identification) process with the prospect, the producer sends the submission to the underwriter to request coverages and premium quotes. Once these are obtained, the producer prepares the proposal. The proposal involves more than just providing a premium quote; it also includes a total services package and recommendations.

Efficiently managing the marketing and sales transactions function involves ensuring that a prospect's coverage needs are accurately determined. To do this, agency personnel must analyze a large amount of information about the prospect. In addition to completed applications, they must analyze a variety of reports and documents, including the prospect's inspection reports, financial statements, loss histories, and property appraisals. Decisions about needed coverages and policy limits, other needed services, and which insurers to approach are based on this analysis; therefore, all information must be accurate and detailed. Although the producer is most often responsible for obtaining the additional information, some agencies assign this task to CSRs. Having one person gather all the necessary underwriting information at one time eliminates the need for repeated prospect contacts.

Coverage requests with the necessary information must be directed to the proper insurers. Selecting insurers is extremely important because improper insurer selection wastes the underwriter's time as well as the time of agency personnel who must prepare, produce, and transmit underwriting information to multiple insurers. Understanding the dynamics of insurance marketing and which companies want certain types of business is a skill that must be continually developed by whoever places coverage for the agency.

Once each of the contacted insurers or brokers responds, the producer and others involved must decide which package of coverages and premiums is the best for the prospect and prepare a written proposal. For large accounts, several insurer quotations may be presented to the prospect. A spreadsheet included in the proposal can show prospects the similarities and differences between the quotations.

Marketing Tip

Many agencies use their IT management systems to prepare proposals and maximize proposal value. Data are first assembled with the appropriate applications as the insurance specifications. These are sent to various insurers. With only minor changes, this information becomes an insurance proposal. The document can also serve as an insurance review form; sixty days before renewal, the producer uses the document to update information and order the renewal. Because policy information is updated in the agency's database whenever it changes, these documents accurately reflect the status of the insured's account at any given time.

Processing new business continues when the producer receives the insurance placement order (with proposal changes, if any, as agreed upon) and binders are prepared. Many agencies prepare initial invoices to be delivered with these binders. Because the insurer, rather than the agency, issues most policies, especially commercial insurance policies, delivering actual policies may be delayed up to several weeks. Regardless of whether the business is new or a renewal, agencies efficiently manage new business by billing when the binder, rather than the policy, is issued to improve cash flow.

When the policies are received, CSRs must review them for accuracy by checking rating, classification, and coverage information against the original application, the proposal, and the binder. All policy limits and premiums should be reviewed and any errors corrected.

E&O Alert!

Many E&O claims against agents result from their delivering policies that do not provide all the insurance coverages outlined in the initial proposal. Although time consuming, a thorough review of each policy is an essential part of the customer services provided by the agency, and it also helps reduce E&O claims.

When the CSR determines that the policies are accurate and complete, an invoice or premium finance contract (discussed subsequently in this assignment) should be prepared unless one was prepared previously or unless the policy was direct billed. The policies are then ready for delivery.

Renewals

Renewals are another type of marketing and sales transaction. Placing new business on the books is almost always more expensive for an agency than renewing existing business. New business acquisition expenses (cost to pay staff for processing new business applications, higher first-year commission paid to producers compared to renewal commissions, and higher attrition rate among new business) account for much of this difference. Consequently, an agency's profitability is traditionally tied to the percentage of business renewed. Therefore, agencies must not ignore the importance of retaining existing business (that is, the agency's retention ratio) in the total sales effort.

The renewal process begins when policy expiration lists are generated and distributed, usually 90 to 120 days before the renewal date. Most personal insurance policies, including automobile and homeowners, are direct billed (discussed later in this assignment), and the insurers automatically issue these renewal policies. Other personal insurance policies and all commercial insurance should be reviewed before renewal. For most accounts, assigned agency staff should contact insureds before renewal, allowing adequate time to order and prepare policies.

E&O Alert!

Although personal auto and homeowners policies are generally renewed automatically, they still represent an E&O loss exposure. Most agencies, however, cannot afford to individually contact every personal insurance customer before renewing these policies every year. Agencies should use two procedures to help minimize the E&O loss exposure in this situation.

The first procedure relates to when the renewal policy is received. At this time, the CSR responsible for servicing that policy should compare the renewal to the expiring policy to ensure that no coverage changes have occurred. Changes in insurers' forms or processing systems can inadvertently change an insured's coverage. If the agency is operating with an agency interface, including upload/download capabilities, a data entry error may not be discovered until renewal. Agencies should check their insurer contracts to determine whether they are exposed to any such E&O liability and, if so, to what extent.

The second procedure is to contact customers directly every two or three years. When insureds develop new loss exposures that require coverage changes, many of them do not contact the agency to change coverage. When contacting insureds, a CSR should review their current coverages and ask them about new loss exposures. "Have you made any large purchases?" and "Have you made any home additions?" are good questions to ask. Following up with this kind of contact reduces the agency's exposure to E&O claims and may lead to additional business.

Depending on the agency, review of the accounts may be performed by the producer; the CSR; or a team consisting of the producer, the CSR, and the individual who places the renewal coverage. Generally, the producer should not be involved in reviewing small or noncomplex accounts in order to spend more time selling. If the insured has worked with a certain staff member during the year, that person can contact the insured about the account's renewal.

Producers and other designated salespeople typically should not be responsible for tracking expiration dates. The producer reviews the account and obtains renewal information, and the CSR responsible for tracking should speak with the producer about the renewal. If a team tracks expiration dates, the producer and the team should meet to discuss renewal procedures. The team should select one member to obtain renewal information from the insured.

Reviewing coverages with the customer before renewals can prevent errors and repetition of work. For instance, coverages may need to be added or deleted and policy limits changed. If the need for such changes is discovered after the renewal has been issued, the policy must be either endorsed or canceled and rewritten. Agency and insurer personnel must then spend additional time to execute the transaction again, adversely affecting productivity and customer service. Regular contact with the insured also helps maintain the goodwill created during the original sale.

Many agencies use checklists provided by insurers or trade associations to assist in renewal review. Some agencies have developed their own checklists as well as other communication tools, such as questionnaires that are sent to customers before initiating policy renewal. Agency personnel can obtain updated underwriting information from such questionnaires. Appendix B provides a sample homeowners checklist for a renewal review.

Checklists are also available from vendors, and they can be revised to suit particular agency needs. The International Risk Management Institute (IRMI) has prepared more than twenty checklists for analyzing insurance programs for major industries. These checklists are contained in a *Manual of Insurance Checklists* and are updated annually. They are available for sale in a number of formats including paper, CD-ROM, and online.[1] Some agencies enter the information from checklists into their coverage databases to generate automatic recommendations for policy coverages.

After the customer has been contacted and the renewal decisions have been made, the renewal policy is ordered from the insurer. Preparing a binder and an invoice may be necessary if the policy is not issued by the renewal date.

Some agencies have established a different set of procedures specifically for handling renewals that are being contested (the insured is seeking alternate price quotes). When an account is remarketed, the internal procedure more closely resembles a new business transaction because applications must be updated, loss runs obtained, submissions sent to insurers, multiple quotations managed, proposals prepared, and a sale made. Because so many additional steps are necessary compared to handling a straight renewal, many agencies treat this as a new business transaction and follow the procedures for securing a new account.

A final aspect of efficiently managing renewals is to establish and carefully follow expiration procedures to maintain control and avoid inadvertent nonrenewal of policies. The master expiration control list, periodically issued by the agency IT management system, must be updated at each step of the renewal process.

Broker of Record Letters

At some point during either the new business or renewal process, a producer may use a broker of record letter. A broker of record letter is a written statement signed by a policyholder or prospect advising an insurer that a particular producer (the broker of record) acts as the insured's representative in all dealings with that insurer. A producer may use such a letter when obtaining a new customer, to negotiate with an insurer on behalf of an existing customer, or to negotiate with an insurer on behalf of a prospect. Alternatively, a producer may lose a customer or prospect to a competitor who uses a broker of record letter that supersedes any previous broker authorization.

A broker of record letter is not a creation of statute or regulation, nor are there any formal producer notification procedures when broker of record letters are used. Broker of record letters are used by the insurance industry as a means of conducting business transactions. When a policyholder authorizes a new broker of record, the insurer usually notifies the former producer of the change.

Obtaining new and renewal business by broker of record letters may reduce producers' initial processing and administrative work because the producer may not have to create the new or renewal business submission in its entirety. However, if different premium quotes are offered to the same customer by the same insurer (one via the former broker and one via the new broker), the producer should take care that coverages offered are the same. Sometimes, coverages may change with a reduction in premium, and the new producer may not be aware of the coverage change from the previous broker's policy.

Endorsements and Adjustments

Endorsements and adjustments are another type of marketing and sales transaction. During the policy term, customers may request endorsements (policy changes) to their policies. For example, customers may acquire new homes and vehicles, change addresses, or require different coverages. Or, they may have a reporting form policy (requiring periodic reports on the policy's loss exposure basis, for example, payroll used to calculate the premium) or be subject to audits, both of which necessitate premium adjustments. Producers usually do not have to be involved in these marketing and sales transactions, but they should be informed of major account changes. If a change is significant, such as adding a new building to a policy or starting new operations, either the producer or a knowledgeable CSR should gather the necessary information. CSRs can handle most endorsements and adjustments.

When policy changes involve rating or require knowledge of coverages, an employee who has the necessary technical skills must handle them. Policy changes may involve a number of transactions, such as completing change request forms, sending form letters to the customer, issuing binders or certificates of insurance, and producing invoices. Technology allows one support person to process all these transactions quickly and efficiently.

Agencies that handle policy processing for some of their insurers usually prepare the policy or endorsement in-house and send a copy to the appropriate insurer. Otherwise, the agency must communicate policy changes to the insurer for processing, usually with a memo outlining what is required or with the universal ACORD change request form, and must follow up if they are not received within a reasonable period. Some insurers provide special change request forms or online access for communicating changes.

Because errors can occur in processing policies or endorsements, particularly those for commercial lines, they should be checked when they are received. Even policies or endorsements generated automatically can be wrong if the data are entered into the computer incorrectly.

When changes are made, the electronic file—and any paper file that may be maintained—should be updated. The procedures used to manage endorsement transactions should be standardized for the entire agency.

Claims

When a loss occurs, the customer expects prompt, efficient claim handling. This is why insurance is purchased—to have covered claims promptly processed and paid to protect the insured from financial loss. How claims are handled is the true test of customer service.

Marketing Tip

Treating third-party claimants well is also a good way to obtain new business. Third-party claimants are not the agency's customers but are other parties who have a claim as a result of the agency's customers' actions. Providing prompt and courteous service to these claimants gives the agency the opportunity to turn them into prospects or policyholders.

Some insurers have separate claim offices to which insureds report claims directly. In these cases, agency employees are not involved in any part of claim processing. Most direct writers and many exclusive agents have claim offices. Independent agencies and brokerages may also handle claims for certain types of insurance business, but typically they receive the initial claim report and forward it to the insurer for processing.

Agency managers should evaluate the following aspects of claims as part of managing customer services:

- How agency personnel view claims
- How the claim file is opened
- How the claim is adjusted and settled (handled)
- How the claim file is closed
- How loss experience affects pricing and coverage

How Agency Personnel View Claims

Those who handle claims must remember that customers submitting claims may be upset. Even minor claims are important to the insured or claimant. Good claim service requires treating each person who has a claim with sympathy and concern.

Producers need not be involved in most claims because other agency personnel can handle them efficiently. However, when the loss is large or complex, the producer should be advised and kept informed of the claim's status. Occasionally, producers may need to intercede with the insurer's claim representative on the insured's behalf. Exhibit 2-1 lists the types of claims in which a producer should be involved.

EXHIBIT 2-1

Claims in Which a Producer Should Be Involved

- Claims involving lawsuits
- Claims with questionable coverage
- Claims with a large dollar value (for example, over $10,000)
- Claims the insurer denies or disputes
- Claims with unique or questionable circumstances

How a Claim File Is Opened

How the agency opens a claim file is another aspect of claims that falls under customer services management. During the initial contact with the insured or claimant, the agency claim representative should obtain as much information about the loss as necessary to report it to the insurer. The claim representative should complete a loss report while talking to the involved parties to ensure that all the necessary items are discussed and recorded.

During the first contact, the applicable policy should be located and the coverage verified. For example, if the person is reporting a homeowners loss and the agency carries only automobile coverage for the customer, the customer should be directed to the proper insurer as soon as possible.

Marketing Tip

When the agency does not provide the policy for the insured, an alert agency claim representative can sometimes obtain an x-date and make a note to contact the insured about placing all of his or her business with the agency. Additionally, the claim representative may make a note to contact a claimant who was pleased with the agency's service.

> ### E&O Alert!
>
> Some agency owners believe that the insured must have an immediate definite indication about whether coverage applies to the reported claim. Others prefer to be more cautious and, unless the coverage issue is clear, suggest that the customer wait to hear officially from the insurer representative. What may appear to be a simple claim can sometimes be complicated, and many agencies prefer not to make a coverage commitment they cannot keep. Such an approach helps minimize the possibility of an E&O claim.

Whether or not coverage verification is initially made, the claim must still be submitted to the insurer. Written loss reports frequently use one of the ACORD Loss Notice forms. For some claims, the insurer is contacted by phone. This call is not a substitute for a written report, but it may accelerate the process by several days.

When the claim is serious or urgent, the agency should fax or e-mail the written report to the insurer. Some agencies may enter the claim information directly into their agency management systems and either send the printed hard copy to the insurer or transmit it electronically to save time.

Once the claim has been submitted, it is placed in the pending file for follow-up. Agencies using paper files usually include a claim summary sheet in the active policy file to indicate that a claim has been opened. Others wait until the claim is closed to update the file. Agency IT management systems automatically trace the claim's progress as data are added, and anyone accessing the customer's electronic file knows that a claim is in process.

Claim representatives should provide claim summaries when producers or others in the agency request them. Claim summaries include date of loss, policy number, insurer, type of loss, adjuster, reserves, status, date closed, and amount paid or reserved.

How the Claim Is Adjusted and Settled

In managing customer services, an agency manager should evaluate how the agency adjusts and settles (handles) claims. Claims are usually handled in one of the following ways:

- By the agency
- By the insurer
- By a specialty firm

Although the practice is unusual, some large commercial insurance agencies have received insurer authority to handle certain types of claims using their own staff. However, most insurers maintain a staff of claim representatives to handle the bulk of their claims. Frequently, these claim representatives specialize in certain types of losses. Some insurers maintain drive-in claim facilities to settle automobile physical damage (comprehensive or collision) claims quickly. The claim representatives in these facilities are experts trained in adjusting this type of loss.

The insurer may sometimes contract outside the company with independent adjusters if their claim representatives are overloaded with work, if the loss requires a particular expertise, or if a major disaster has occurred. Insureds can also retain their own adjusters, called public adjusters, to represent them in their dealings with the insurer.

There are many regional and local specialty adjusting firms that specialize in a particular type of losses, such as auto liability and no-fault, or in particular types of insurers, such as captive insurers. Also, several national firms have offices around the country to handle such losses.

How the Claim File Is Closed

How the agency closes the claim file should also be considered in customer services management. The agency claim file can be closed after the claim representative receives a check or draft for the insured, a copy of the insured's check or draft, or other insurer notification that the claim has been settled on behalf of all involved parties. Entering the information in the agency IT management system or customer's file and removing the claim from the suspense system closes the claim.

If the agency sends the claim payment on to the customer, it may include a letter explaining anything that may be unclear to the customer. If the insurer sends the payment, the agency can either call or write to the insured to confirm that the claim was handled satisfactorily.

Marketing Tip

For large losses, having someone, preferably the producer, deliver the claim payment shows that the agency is concerned about customer service. Such delivery may even provide an opportunity to sell another policy. The producer may also want to deliver a payment to a third party to show the agency's quality of service and possibly turn a satisfied claimant into a new prospect.

How Loss Experience Affects Pricing and Coverage

How loss experience affects pricing and coverage should be evaluated as part of managing customer services. For example, a special service an agency can provide is to monitor customers' claim experience and provide loss control advice. Agency personnel should become familiar with the underwriting criteria of the various insurers represented and know how losses affect future pricing and coverage. By informing the customer of the relationship between claims and premiums, particularly the effect that frequent, small claims have on premiums, the agency can help avoid premium increases and possible coverage terminations. By reviewing past claims with their insureds, producers can often help prevent or reduce future losses by recommending loss control techniques.

Some large brokerages and agencies provide loss control services for their large commercial customers. These firms either retain an outside loss control specialist to conduct inspections and perform consulting or hire their own staff specialists if they have enough work to warrant it. Often, this work is done for the customer for a fee. Reports of claims, especially if one type of claim occurs frequently, should be sent to a loss control representative on the insurer's or loss control specialist's staff. The representative should contact the customer to review the procedures or problems that caused the losses.

Accounting

Agency accounting need not be a complicated technical services function. By keeping accounting simple and current, the agency improves its chances of controlling its accounting expenses and increasing its profits. Simplicity saves time, thereby reducing expenses. Keeping current facilitates account collection, which increases profit. In considering its accounting function, an agency should remember that no sale is complete until the agency has recorded and collected the premium and commission for the business sold.

Traditionally, independent agents and brokers, as well as many exclusive agents and producers representing direct writers, were responsible for collecting all premiums from insureds and remitting them to insurers as required. This premium collection system is called agency billing. Technology introduced two other premium collection systems that have substantially changed the agency accounting function: (1) direct (or insurance company) bill, in which the insured sends the premium directly to the insurer and (2) premium finance plans, in which the insured sends the premium to a finance company. Both systems relieve the agency of the responsibility of premium collection, except for the initial premium or down payment. Agencies track their billings by monitoring accounting reports.

Agency Bill System

Independent agencies and brokerages still use the agency bill system for premium collection for a portion of their business, especially if they focus on large, commercial accounts. The **agency bill system** requires that the agency perform the following premium handling tasks:

1. Invoicing and crediting
2. Collecting premiums
3. Investing premiums
4. Remitting premiums (less any applicable commission)

The agency bill system begins with invoicing and crediting. In most agencies, the standard procedure for issuing invoices and credit memos (if a return premium is due) begins when invoice data are entered into the agency management system or an invoice is manually prepared. One or two copies of the invoice are then mailed to the customer. Some producers mail or deliver the bill with the policy or endorsement to reduce confusion and to eliminate the time and expense involved in preparing an additional mailing. For commercial accounts, some agencies mail the insurance bill separately to the person in the customer's firm who pays the bills.

In an agency that is not fully automated, another copy of the bill may be included in the backup expiration filing system. If the agency is fully automated, backup copies are not needed because the computer maintains all necessary information.

The next task in the agency bill system is collecting premiums. After the invoice (or credit memo) has been prepared, most of the other functions associated with the agency bill system become the responsibility of the accounting department unless the premium is overdue.

When payments are received, they must be matched with the invoices and applied to the customer's account. If payments are not received by the due date, a second notice must be sent or a phone call made to the customer in accordance with agency procedures. The first attempt to collect the overdue premium should begin as soon as the premium is overdue. Generally, the producer does not need to be involved at this point. However, if the premium has not been received after thirty days, most agencies ask the producer to take over. The producer generally has the ultimate responsibility to ensure that the premium is paid. Any unpaid premium may be deducted from the producer's future commissions.

If the premium is not received by a predetermined date (such as forty-five days after the due date), the agency should cancel the policy. The insurer involved is asked to send the insured direct notice of cancellation in accordance with the policy provision dealing with nonpayment of premium. Accounting department personnel may make this request, but it is made more often by the producer or CSR.

Agency bill system
An insurer billing system that requires the agency to perform certain premium handling tasks, including invoicing and crediting, collecting premiums, investing premiums, and remitting premiums, to companies (less any applicable commissions).

A good premium collection program is essential. If the agency does not follow up promptly and request policy cancellation as soon as possible, the agency could owe a considerable amount of earned premiums to the insurer. Earned premiums are the amount of written premiums recognized as revenue for the portion of the policy period that has already elapsed. The agency is responsible for paying the premium to the insurer even if it has not been collected from the insured. This is a major drawback of the agency bill system.

Investing premiums is another task of the agency bill system. Agency billing allows the agency to generate additional revenue from investing premium dollars while they are in the agency's possession. Insurers usually do not expect the agency to remit the premiums until thirty or forty-five days after policy or endorsement issuance. If the premiums are collected on time or even ahead of the effective date, the agency may invest premiums for as long as two months or more. This arrangement is called premium float. **Premium float** is an arrangement that allows an agency to collect insurer premiums; invest the premiums and generate earnings on the premiums payable to the insurer; and forward premiums, minus any earnings generated, to the insurer when the insurer account is payable.

Premium float
An arrangement that allows an agency to collect insurer premiums; invest the premiums and generate earnings on the premiums payable to the insurer; and forward premiums, minus any earnings generated, to the insurer when the insurer account is payable.

Premium dollars used in premium float do not belong to the agency. The premiums are entrusted to the agency; therefore, the agency has a fiduciary responsibility for them. Most states have regulations that require agencies to keep these funds in trust or escrow accounts to help protect them from misuse. Many insurers require escrow accounts even if state law does not require them. By keeping the premiums separate from operating funds, a trust or an escrow minimizes the possibility that the premiums will be used for something other than their intended purpose.

Even if they do require a trust account, most states allow agencies to invest premium dollars in relatively safe investments. Some large agencies add as much as 5 percent to their annual gross income through prompt collections and premium float investment.

Remitting premiums is the final task in the agency bill system. Once a month, premiums are paid to the insurers (minus any commissions due to the agency). The most common due date is the fifteenth of the month, although some insurers have set the due date at the end of the month. Premiums are occasionally sent at other times during the month, such as when coverage is placed with surplus lines brokers, who require payment to bind coverage.

Agencies use two methods to remit premiums to insurers: by an insurer prepared statement or by the agency's own statement, called an account current. Agencies should use the method that is the most accurate and economical for them and that is also acceptable to the insurers involved.

With either remittance method, agency personnel must verify that the insurer's and the agency's records agree. When the agency pays on its own statement, the insurer checks the statement against its records and sends notice of any discrepancies. Agency personnel, either in the accounting department or in customer service, must review and reconcile these accounting discrepancies. This is time consuming because the source of the discrepancy is often not clear. Accurate invoicing minimizes discrepancies and saves time. Many insurers now accept electronic transfer for premium payments.

Direct Bill System

In contrast to the agency bill system of collecting premiums, the **direct bill system** bills insureds directly, thereby relieving agencies of premium collection responsibility.

The direct bill system relieves agency personnel of the responsibility of invoicing, tracking, collecting, and remitting premiums, which can be both costly and time consuming. It also places the risk of an uncollectible receivable with the insurer rather than with the agency.

A disadvantage of the direct bill system is that it eliminates the premium float and can therefore affect an agency's cash flow. Additionally, a direct bill system can create extra work for agency personnel when it is not functioning properly or when insureds send their payments late. However, the time the direct bill system saves agencies probably outweighs its disadvantages, particularly if an agency has a large personal lines book of business.

The accounting function of the direct bill system differs significantly from that of the agency bill system. Using the direct bill system, the agency creates no invoices and makes no payments to insurers. Insurers send the agencies statements once or twice a month with checks for the commissions due. These statements are usually lengthy, and agencies that are not automated accept the insurer's records, recognizing that any discrepancies would not be material when compared to the amount of time required to examine every statement item.

In an automated agency, direct billed transactions are entered into the system in the same way as agency billed transactions. This enables the agency to reconcile the insurer's direct bill statement with its own records. For agencies capable of interfacing with their insurers, the insurer downloads direct bill accounting information directly into the agency's system when transmitting policies or endorsements. Many insurers also transmit direct bill commissions electronically.

Premium Finance Plans

Another premium collection system is the premium finance plan. Many insurers have established premium finance plans to assist insureds by allowing them to pay large premiums in installments. Banks and other financial institutions also have financing plans that are used to pay insurance premiums over time. In states where it is legal to do so, many agencies have set up their own premium finance plans. Independently owned premium finance companies also operate nationally or regionally. As premiums grow and cash flow becomes a greater concern, these plans are becoming more popular.

Direct bill system
An insurer billing system that bills insureds directly, thereby relieving agencies of premium collection responsibility.

At the time of sale (or sometimes as part of the proposal), the producer and customer decide whether the premium will be financed and then sign a contract. The premium financing plan may offer several alternatives for the size of down payments and length of the financing term. The producer and customer should select the plan that most closely matches the customer's needs and requirements.

Generally, the agency must collect the premium down payment and submit it to the insurer with the insurance application and premium finance plan contract. After that, the agency is no longer responsible for collecting premiums (unless it is an in-house finance plan) or remitting premiums to the insurer because the finance company handles these tasks.

Either the finance company or the insurer sends the commissions to the agency. Commissions may be paid up front for the entire year, or they may be sent as each premium installment is received. In either case, the accounting procedures and record-keeping problems are similar to those of the direct bill system. Also, investment income generated by the premium float is lost. However, relief from the responsibility of premium collections generally offsets this loss.

Accounting Reports

Generating accounting reports is an important aspect of the accounting function. Accounting reports are used for processing and recording financial transactions. The accounting records, on which accounting reports are based, are also used to generate financial and management reports. These reports are usually generated by the accounting department and given to principals and managers.

Although many of the reports do not directly affect the management of customer services, two standard reports do—the statement of account and the aged accounts receivable report.

Statement of account
A monthly statement providing the customer with a summary of the outstanding premiums owed to the agency.

The **statement of account** is usually prepared monthly and provides the customer with a summary of the outstanding premiums owed to the agency. Some statements are detailed and show every transaction and payment for the month as well as outstanding balances. Customers may have questions about or dispute their statements of account. Responding to questions and resolving disputes promptly and amicably are part of good customer service.

Aged accounts receivable report
A report used to determine which customers are behind in paying their premiums; usually generated in thirty-day past-due increments.

The **aged accounts receivable report** is used to determine which customers are behind in paying their premiums and is usually generated in thirty-day past-due increments. The aged accounts receivable report is not sent to the customer.

Analyzing aged accounts receivable can have a substantial effect on an agency's net income because collection problems can be identified before the agency develops bad debt on accounts that accrue earned but uncollectible premiums.

IMPROVING PRODUCTIVITY

An agency's workload is heavier at certain times of the year than at others. For example, many commercial insurance accounts renew in January to simplify insureds' tax accounting. Personal insurance activity generally increases in the summer when insureds are more likely to purchase new homes or cars. These periods place extra pressure on CSRs, but, if anticipated, they can be managed. A backlog can lead to carelessness and mistakes.

The easiest solution to a backlog is to hire additional staff. This may not always be the best solution, however, if the backlog is due to productivity problems rather than an insufficient number of employees. Agencies should periodically measure their customer services productivity and identify and eliminate the sources of productivity problems.

Measuring Productivity

Agency managers use a variety of approaches to measure productivity. Benchmarks can help determine whether the agency has too few or too many employees. A benchmark can be based on an average agency but, because every agency is unique, it may need to be adjusted to account for differences. Comparison with other agencies' benchmarks helps agency managers assess customer service quality and performance levels and target areas for improvement.

Some agencies use the number of accounts handled per CSR as a benchmark. Other agencies prefer to use commission generated per CSR or revenue per employee. Examples of average and high benchmarks found in the IIABA's *2005 Best Practices Study* include the following: personal property-casualty CSRs working in agencies with annual revenues between $1,250,001 and $2,500,000 service an average of $154,182 in commissions. However, the top 25 percent of agencies in the study have personal property-casualty CSRs servicing $206,771 in commissions.[2] Variations may be due to the number of accounts handled per CSR, the number of policies per account, or the average commission per account.

The *Best Practices Study* includes benchmarks for agencies within ranges and presents detailed profiles of agency productivity benchmarks. For example, the IIABA *2005 Best Practices study* provides a benchmark by which individual agencies can judge their overall productivity by examining revenue per employee—as applicable to the entire agency, not just CSRs.

Agencies With Revenues Between $1,250,001 and $2,500,000	
Revenue per Employee for Average Agency	$137,773
Revenue per Employee for Top 25% in Profit	$167,910
Revenue per Employee for Top 25% in Growth	$144,575

Adapted from the *2005 Best Practices Study Update*, copyright 2005, Independent Insurance Agents and Brokers of America, Inc., and Reagan Consulting.

These benchmarks should be tempered by business mix differences (for example, commercial commissions versus personal commissions) and territorial differences (insurance costs by state).

Solving Productivity Problems

Insurance agency productivity problems can arise from several major causes, including the following:

- Improper customer services organizational structure
- Unsuitable employees
- Poor training
- Insufficient direction and control
- Poor morale
- Inefficient processes
- Backlogs

An agency may experience low productivity because of an improper organizational structure. An agency that grows 15 percent annually will double in size in five years. When agency size (including staff, customers, and resource requirements) doubles, the customer services organizational structure may become ineffective. Agency managers should regularly reevaluate this structure and, when necessary, realign job positions to accommodate growth. Additionally, an organizational structure that requires employees to obtain approval for every action can reduce productivity. Productivity increases if managers give employees the authority and tools to perform their jobs independently. The customer services organizational structure should allow CSRs to use their best judgment in satisfying their customers' needs.

Low productivity can result when some employees are not qualified for the positions they hold or are in the wrong job positions. If this is the case, the agency should evaluate its employee screening, selection, and development processes. These processes, which should be continually reviewed by the agency principal and senior management, are an important part of human resources management.

An agency may experience low productivity because of poor training and education. Even if the right people are hired for the right positions, there is no guarantee that they will work to full capacity. Employees must be trained to handle their current responsibilities and given educational opportunities to assume new responsibilities.

Besides seminar attendance, classes, and workshops that deal with insurance, some employees may benefit from courses on such topics as time management, conflict resolution, customer service, and negotiating. A lack of people skills can adversely affect productivity and can adversely affect how an employee relates both to external customers and to other employees. All insurance agency functions are interdependent, and a problem with one individual can affect the entire agency.

Another reason an agency may experience low productivity is insufficient direction and control of employees. If activities are not sufficiently directed and results controlled through a sound performance evaluation system, duplication and wasted time can result.

Poor employee morale can also lead to low productivity in an agency. Morale problems arise from many causes. For example, the merger of two local agencies that were former rivals may cause discontent among some employees that could negatively affect productivity. One way to improve morale is to reward employees who are innovative and productive in performing their duties. Managers should encourage employees to find better ways to complete their tasks and reward this behavior. For example, many employees are motivated by oral or written recognition from their supervisor or manager or by public recognition, such as in the agency newsletter. Employees are an agency's most valuable resource. Consequently, managers should be alert for signs of poor morale, objectively evaluate the causes, and take steps to improve it.

Inefficient agency processes can lower productivity. When productivity is low or errors are frequent, managers may find it easier to find fault with staff than with processes. In reality, inadequate systems or inefficient processes may be the cause. Regardless of how dedicated an employee is to performing a task, a flawed or inefficient process can affect performance. For example, a process that requires routing paper files to producers to answer customer inquiries can result in less than optimal customer service. If, instead, the electronic file is used, inquiries can be answered more quickly, resulting in increased productivity and better customer service. Similarly, without standardized processes, CSRs may handle each transaction differently, rather than handle them routinely and procedurally.

Business process reengineering, which involves rethinking how work is performed, can improve productivity by eliminating redundancies and outmoded methods of doing business. Technology can help transform an insurance agency's business processes, leading to increased productivity, lower cost, and higher quality of output. When an agency changes its processes in order to better solve customer problems, customer satisfaction increases.

An agency may experience low productivity because of a backlog. The amount of aged (unprocessed) transactions in many agencies can be staggering. An intractable backlog can lower employee morale, cause customers to leave the agency because of service issues, and cause producers to stop generating new business because new customers may receive poor service.

Managers must provide everyone with an agency management system that eliminates backlog and prevents it from accumulating in the future. Managers should also support an organizational workflow (including policies and procedures) that is based on functionality, that achieves operational efficiency, and that contributes to the positive attitude of all employees.

REVIEW

Key Words and Phrases

Define or describe each of the words and phrases found in this assignment.

Agency bill system (p. 2.36)

Premium float (p. 2.37)

Direct bill system (p. 2.38)

Statement of account (p. 2.39)

Aged accounts receivable report (p. 2.39)

Review Questions

7. Identify an agency's three technical service functions. (p. 2.25)

8. What steps should an agency take in processing new business to ensure that a prospect's coverage needs are accurately determined? (pp. 2.25–2.27)

9. Under what circumstances should a producer become involved in claim handling? (p. 2.32)

10. Contrast the three types of claim handling (adjusting) systems. (p. 2.34)

11. What tasks does an agency perform when using the agency bill system? (p. 2.36)

12. What tasks must insurance agencies perform using the direct bill system? (p. 2.38)

13. What are the ways an agency can focus on improving productivity? (p. 2.40)

REVIEW

14. What are the major causes of low productivity in insurance agencies? (p. 2.41)

Application Questions

3. Pete, an agency owner, is training Patty, his agency's new producer, in the technical service function of marketing and sales transactions. "We have a terrific customer services department, which is important," Pete tells Patty. "It's almost always more expensive for me to pay producers like you for new business sales than it is to renew existing business. The combination of new business plus retention is what keeps me profitable."

   Justify Pete's comments.

4. Some independent agencies may believe the claim function takes up valuable time and personnel. Explain why this attitude is incorrect and describe potential benefits of having a claim department.

5. Explain why the slogan "Keep it simple and keep it current" is a good rule of thumb for agency accounting systems.

Answers to Assignment 2 Questions

NOTE: These answers are provided to give students a basic understanding of acceptable types of responses. They often are not the only valid answers and are not intended to provide an exhaustive response to the questions.

Review Questions

7. The following are an agency's three technical service functions:

   (1) Marketing and sales transactions

   (2) Claims

   (3) Accounting

8. When processing new business, an agency takes the following steps to ensure that a prospect's coverage needs are accurately determined:

   - Prepare a completed application
   - Prepare inspection reports
   - Analyze financial statements
   - Determine coverages and policy limits
   - Review loss history and property appraisals
   - Identify insurers to approach
   - Prepare a proposal (services, recommendations, and a premium quote)
   - When the new policy is received from the customer, prepare the binder and sometimes initial invoices
   - Prepare the policy and check for accuracy
   - Verify the policy (review rating, coding, and coverage information and check against original application and proposal; review limits and premiums)
   - Prepare an invoice or premium finance contract unless already done
   - Deliver the policy to the customer

9. A producer should be involved in the following claims:

   - Claims involving lawsuits
   - Claims with questionable coverage
   - Claims with a large dollar value (for example, over $10,000)
   - Claims the insurer denies or disputes
   - Claims with unique or questionable circumstances

10. The following are three types of claim handling:

    (1) Agency adjusting—CSRs or staff adjusters use draft authority granted by the insurer for handling claims.

    (2) Insurance company adjusting—Staff adjusters are specialists in certain types of losses. Some insurers use staff adjusters at drive-in claim facilities for fast settlement of auto physical damage claims.

(3) Specialty adjusting firms—Some insurers contract with outside independent adjusters if staff adjusters are overloaded with work or if the loss requires particular expertise. Public adjusters can also represent insureds in their dealings with the insurer.

11. The agency bill system requires the agency to perform the following tasks:
    - Invoicing and crediting
    - Collecting premiums
    - Investing premiums
    - Remitting premiums

12. The direct bill system requires the agency to perform the following tasks:
    - Enter direct bill policies into agency management system (automatic if the agency is interfaced).
    - Receive insurer's statements and commissions monthly or bi-weekly.
    - Direct bill accounting and policy information is automatically downloaded into the agency management system if the agency is interfaced.

13. An agency can focus on improving productivity by measuring productivity and solving productivity problems.

14. Major causes of low productivity in insurance agencies include:
    - Improper customer services organizational structure
    - Unsuitable employees
    - Poor training
    - Insufficient direction and control
    - Poor morale
    - Inefficient processes
    - Backlogs

Application Questions

3. Pete may tell Patty that it is almost always more expensive to pay producers for new business sales than it is to renew existing business because of business acquisition costs, such as paying first-year commissions (typically higher than subsequent years) to producers, the costs to pay staff for processing new business applications, and a higher attrition rate among new business accounts. Account renewal costs less, particularly if the accounts are on direct bill.

4. Good service in the claim department provides several benefits. First, a good attitude from agency claim personnel can make a customer under stress feel good about the agency. This should help retain this customer. Also, new sales are often generated by outstanding claim service in two ways. First, current customers who have only some of their insurance with an agency may be more interested in having that agency provide all their coverages after receiving excellent claim service. This is particularly true if their claim experience with the agency handling their other coverage had not been satisfactory. Second, when third-party claims are handled professionally, the third parties may consider switching their accounts to that agency. Proper claim handling is also important because a costly E&O suit can result from an unprofessionally handled claim. Even if an E&O suit is ultimately unsuccessful, it costs the agency time and money and damages its reputation.

5. Many agencies have an overly complex accounting process. Complexities can require more paperwork and increase the chance of errors. A simpler system is more efficient. Even more important is the system's ability to keep accounts current. Current accounts have the following three important benefits:

   (1) The producer does not have to contact the customer about overdue bills. The agency improves its customer relationships.

   (2) Current accounts do not become overdue (and uncollectible) accounts. The agency avoids extra collection expenses and bad debts.

   (3) Current accounts increase cash flow. The agency can invest the additional cash until premiums are payable to the insurers.

SUMMARY

An agency cannot achieve its business goals unless its customer services organizational structure supports its customer services functions, support services functions, and technical services functions. Over time and as their environment changes, agencies may need different customer services organizational structures. To determine what customer services organizational structure they need, agencies should complete the following three tasks:

1. Perform an organizational structure analysis
2. Select a customer services organizational structure
3. Monitor the customer services organizational structure

A customer services organizational structure analysis consists of four steps: (1) task identification, (2) grouping and ranking these tasks according to their importance in achieving the agency's goals, (3) delegation of necessary authority so each task can be effectively performed, and (4) ensuring that the various job positions responsible for the tasks are coordinated to support efficient work flow and communications.

Traditionally, agencies structure their customer services organization by either line of business or function. The line of business structure compartmentalizes customer services into divisions, such as personal insurance, commercial insurance, life insurance, health insurance, and employee benefits. Some agencies add other divisions, such as risk management, loss control, and claim administration. The function structure compartmentalizes customer services into sales, service, marketing, underwriting, and new business processing.

Agencies usually assign one person to monitor the customer services organizational structure. Within the structure, CSRs are generally assigned to one of three major support service functions:

1. Processing communications
2. Managing information
3. Preparing documentation

In addition to these support services functions, customer services involves technical services functions, such as marketing and sales transactions, which include processing new business, renewals, and endorsements and adjustments; and claims, which includes reviewing certain aspects of the claim handling process to facilitate work flow and optimize efficiency. Those aspects include the following:

*   How agency personnel view claims
*   How the claim file is opened
*   How the claim is adjusted and settled
*   How the claim file is closed
*   How loss experience affects pricing and coverage

Another technical services function, the accounting function, involves using an effective premium collection systems. Agencies may use the agency bill system, the direct bill system, or premium finance plans for premium collection.

In an agency bill system, agencies perform such functions as invoicing and crediting, keeping track of outstanding premiums, recording payments, collecting overdue premiums, advising customers of account status, holding collected premiums, and remitting premiums to insurers. In a direct bill system, the insurer bills the agency's customers directly, relieving the agency of the responsibility of collecting premiums. Agencies can also use premium finance plans established by insurers and banks that allow customers to pay policy premiums in installments. Accounting reports, such as a statement of account and an aged accounts receivable report, allow agencies to process and record financial transactions.

Agencies measure their own productivity by comparing it to benchmarks. Once productivity is measured, agencies improve productivity by identifying and eliminating the sources of productivity problems. Reasons for low productivity vary and can include improper customer organizational structure, unsuitable employees, poor training, insufficient direction and control, poor morale, poor processes, and work backlogs.

Sound management of customer services ensures not only efficient and effective customer service but also that an agency is profitable. Agency financial management is discussed in the next assignment.

ASSIGNMENT NOTES

1. *IRMI Insurance Checklists*, 2006 (Dallas, Tex: International Risk Management Institute, Inc., 2006).
2. *2005 Best Practices Study Update*, copyright 2005 Independent Insurance Agents and Brokers of America, Inc., and Reagan Consulting (Alexandria, Va., 2005).

Appendix A

Suggested Policyholder Information Retention Schedule

SUGGESTED POLICYHOLDER INFORMATION RETENTION SCHEDULE

Customer Information on File	Time Frame for Maintaining Information
Agent of record letter	permanent
Applications	see policies
Appraisals	until superseded
Binders	until superseded by policy
Customer data sheet, personal lines	5 years after loss of account
Claims reports	until superseded by draft
Policies, personal lines	1 policy period past expiration[1]
[2]Policies, commercial lines	5 policy periods past expiration[1]
Expiration records	until superseded
Expiration records, policies not taken	1 year after not taken
Fact finder, commercial accounts	until superseded
Rating worksheets	until superseded
Claim drafts	permanent
Modification letters	until 1 year after superseded
Recommendations	until 1 year after accepted
Survey reports	until 1 year after superseded
Transmittal letters	do not retain

1 Subject to the provisions of your state Insurance Code.

2 Occurrence and products liability policies with unlimited tail—permanent

Accounting and Financial Information on File

Account payable invoices	3 years
Account payable ledger	permanent
Account receivable invoices	1 year
Account receivable ledgers	permanent
Audit reports	permanent
Audit working papers	3 years
Balance sheets	permanent
Bank deposits	3 years
Bank statements	3 years
Budgets	3 years
Cash receipt record	7 years
Check register	permanent

Continued on next page

Checks, payroll ....3 years

Checks, voucher ....5 years

Cost accounting records ....5 years

Depreciation schedules... permanent

Dividend register .... permanent

Employee withholding records ....7 years

Expense reports ....3 years

Financial statements, certified.. permanent

General ledger records .... permanent

Note register... permanent

Payroll register...3 years

Petty cash records..3 years

Profit and loss statements .... permanent

Sales representatives' commission reports..3 years

Travel expense reports ....3 years

Tax bills and statements .... permanent

Tax returns.. permanent

Trial balances...2 years

Corporations/Partnership Records

Annual reports...permanent

Buy and sell agreements .... until superseded

Capital stock ledger ....permanent

Charter, constitution, bylaws...permanent

Contracts .... 20 years after termination

Corporation election records..permanent

Incorporation records ....permanent

Licenses.. until superseded

Minutes of stockholders and directors meetings..permanent

Partnership agreement ....permanent

Property deeds ....permanent

Purchase or lease agreements ....permanent

Stock transfer records ....permanent

Personnel Information on File

Accident reports, injury claims, settlements.. 30 years after settlement

Annuity or deferred compensation plans.. permanent

Applications for employment not acted upon.. do not retain

Applications for employment by persons hired...................................6 years after termination

Attendance records...7 years

Employee activity filed ....2 years or until superseded

Employee contracts ....6 years after termination

Group insurance records .... permanent

Health and safety bulletins... permanent

Job description .... until superseded

OSHA Form 100 .... 5 years following end of calendar year

OSHA Form 101 (or equivalent) .... 5 years following end of calendar year

OSHA Form 102 .... 5 years following end of calendar year

Solicitor agreements ....6 years after termination

Terminations ....6 years

Time cards ....3 years

Agency/Company Information on File

Agency contract... permanent

Contingency agreement .... permanent

Correspondence .... variable

Initial letter of appointment.. permanent

Prohibited lists ....until 1 year after superseded

Underwriting guidelines and instruction........................until 1 year after superseded

Adapted with permission from GE Insurance Solutions, May 2006.

Appendix B

Homeowners Checklist

HOMEOWNERS CHECKLIST

1. What are your legal names?
2. What is the address of the property?
3. Is your home under 40 years of age?
4. What is the year of construction of your home?
5. What bank holds the mortgage?
6. What is the type of construction?
7. Does a single family inhabit your home?
8. Does your home have smoke detectors?
9. Do you have a burglar alarm?
10. Do you have a fire department fire alarm?
11. Do you have automatic sprinklers?
12. How many rooms in your home?
13. Do you have a woodstove?
14. Has your woodstove been inspected?
15. Do you have a central heating system?
16. How do you heat your home?
17. Have you had any insurance losses in the last five years?
18. Do you or any household member smoke?
19. Do you desire a $250 or $100 deductible?
20. Do you own a dog? What breed?
21. Do you own a boat, trailer or camper?
22. Do you live near a pond, river or large body of water?
23. Are you in a flood zone?
24. Is your home under construction or being remodeled?
25. Do you have any boarders that are not family members?
26. Do you have tenants?
27. Do you furnish any belongings in the part of the premises you rent?
28. Would you like replacement cost on your contents?
29. Would you be interested in an inflation guard built into your policy?
30. Do you want earthquake coverage?
31. Do you have any children away at school
32. Will your home be vacant more than 30 days?
33. Do you own an aircraft?
34. Do you or your family members have any belongings owned by others in your care custody or control?
35. Do you keep any belongings in any other residence owned by you?
36. Do you rent any structure on your property?
37. Do you use any structure on your property for business use?
38. Do you own a personal computer? Is it used for business use?
39. What is the estimated worth of your software?

Section I Coverages

1. Do you or anyone in your household own a single item of jewelry, watches, furs, or precious or semiprecious stones worth more than $1,000?

2. Does the total value of your jewelry, watches, furs or precious or semiprecious stones exceed $1,000?

3. Do you own firearms worth over $2,000?

4. Does the value of your silverware, silver-plated ware, goldware, gold-plated ware, or pewter, exceed $2,500?

5. Do you keep any belongings in your home that are used in any manner for business use worth more than $2,500?

6. Do you belong to any association of property owners responsible for something owned collectively?

7. Do you have articles of value such as antiques, stamp or coin collections, fine arts, furs, golf equipment, musical instruments, silverware, china or the like, which you would like to insure on a scheduled per-item basis?

Section II Coverages

1. Would you like a limit of liability higher than $100,000?

2. Would you like a higher amount of coverage for medical payments than the $1,000 limit?

3. Do you own any other residence?

4. Do you rent the other residence?

5. Do you conduct any farming on your premises?

6. Is farming your principal occupation?

7. Do you own a snowmobile?

8. Would you like to be covered for libel, invasion of privacy or false arrest for an additional $13 a year?

9. Would you be interested in a personal umbrella policy covering you for $1 million above and beyond the liability coverages you carry on your home and auto?

Signature of Applicant _____ Date _____

Signature of Agent _____ Date _____

Reproduced, with permission, from Insurance Marketing & Management Services (IMMS).

Direct Your Learning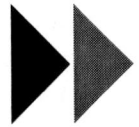

Agency Financial Management

Educational Objectives

After learning the content of this assignment, you should be able to:

1. Explain who is assigned financial management responsibility in agencies.

2. Describe the steps in the financial management process.

3. Given an insurance agency case, explain how the agency can control revenue by implementing proper handling procedures for the following:

   a. Premiums received

   b. Unearned commission reserve accounts

   c. Return commission on brokered policies

4. Given an insurance agency case, explain how the agency can control expenses using the following:

   a. Accounts receivable control

   b. Internal controls

   c. Expense measurement

   d. Expense analysis

   e. Expense reduction

5. Explain how an agency's legal form of ownership can affect its taxation.

6. Describe common employee benefit plans.

7. Explain how various tests of agency profitability, liquidity, and efficiency are used to evaluate an agency's financial performance, and be able to calculate them.

8. Describe the methods used to determine an agency's value, including the factors that affect valuation.

9. Define or describe each of the Key Words and Phrases for this assignment.

ASSIGNMENT

Develop Your Perspective

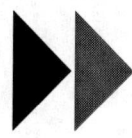

What are the main topics covered in the assignment?

Agency principals and management staff are typically responsible for the agency's financial management. By using the financial management process and other tools, they can control revenue and expenses and any tax implications arising from their operations. Agency financial managers also supervise the implementation of employee benefit plans and use various financial ratios to evaluate the agency's performance.

Describe the ways agencies can control revenues and expenses.

▶ What steps can an agency take to uphold its legal and fiduciary responsibility to the insurer regarding premiums it collects on behalf of the insurer that are payable to the insurer at some future date?

▶ Why would an agency want to develop and adhere to accounts receivable procedures?

Why is it important to learn about these topics?

Agencies that make good financial management decisions and control revenues and expenses are able to increase profitability.

Explain how agency profitability can be measured.

▶ Does the agency have sufficient cash to pay its bills on time?

▶ Should the policy be written when compared to the cost of handling the particular account?

How can you use what you will learn?

Picture yourself as an insurance agency's chief financial officer reviewing the agency's expenses. Analyze the elements of accounts receivable control.

▶ Has the agency developed a practices and accounts receivable policy?

▶ Are accounts receivable goals in place?

▶ Are premium financing plans available for customers?

Agency Financial Management

Outline

Agency Financial Management

Producers and agency owners cite two main reasons for being in the insurance industry: to provide financial security for their customers and to make a profit. Many factors can affect agency profitability. Some are internal, such as organizational structure, and others are external, such as the underwriting cycle. The underwriting cycle is a pattern of insurance pricing and profitability that affects underwriting results. When insurers are earning underwriting profits, they often decrease their rates and offer broader coverage (known as a soft market), which expands their market share but causes underwriting losses. When insurers are experiencing underwriting losses, they often increase rates and restrict the availability of coverage to promote underwriting gains (known as a hard market). It is critical for agencies to understand the current phase of the underwriting cycle and its influence on the products they sell. With this understanding, an agency can make financial management decisions that result in profits regardless of underwriting cycles.

FINANCIAL MANAGEMENT

Financial management is the effective management of assets, liabilities, capital structure, revenues, and expenses. It is a key element in helping an agency achieve its strategic plan.

Although financial management information originates from accounting records, financial management involves more than merely gathering and processing accounting information. It also involves analyzing this information and using it to make financial decisions. Agencies make financial decisions by assigning financial management responsibility and using the financial management process.

Assigning Financial Management Responsibility

In small agencies, the owner typically has financial management responsibility, usually with the assistance of a bookkeeper. However, some owners, who may also be their agency's primary producer, may not have the skills and experience necessary for financial management. Additionally, time spent handling financial matters takes time away from sales, the producer's primary responsibility. Therefore, in small agencies, owners must find ways to effectively manage finances while making sales.

Financial management
The effective management of assets, liabilities, capital structure, revenues, and expenses.

Large agencies may employ a chief financial officer (CFO), vice president of finance, or controller. Those who handle financial management functions, regardless of the job title, manage the receipt and disbursement of funds (accounts receivable and payable), coordinate investments, and provide financing reports to management. Allocating funds to current and fixed assets, obtaining the best mix of financing alternatives, negotiating with vendors, and making investment decisions are also functions the financial manager performs. Less routine financial management functions include selling stock and other assets and handling capital budgeting for major expenditures.

Financial management goals should support the agency's strategic goals as specified in its strategic plan. To accomplish financial management goals, agencies can use the financial management process.

Using the Financial Management Process

The financial management process involves the following four steps:

1. Identify the current financial position
2. Analyze results of operations
3. Implement any necessary corrective actions
4. Monitor and revise the process

Identify the Current Financial Position

Balance sheet
A financial statement that indicates assets, liabilities, and owners' equity as of a particular date.

An agency begins the financial management process by using a balance sheet to identify its current financial position. A **balance sheet** is a financial statement that indicates the agency's assets, liabilities, and owners' equity as of a particular date.

Assets are what the agency owns, such as cash, accounts receivable, and property. Liabilities are claims against the assets, such as premiums payable to insurers, accrued taxes, and long-term debt. Owners' equity is total assets minus total liability, or net worth. Exhibit 3-1 provides an example of an agency's balance sheet.

Analyze Results of Operations

Income statement
A financial statement that indicates revenues and expenses over a specified period.

After identifying the agency's current financial position, financial managers use an income statement to analyze the results of operations. An **income statement** is a financial statement that indicates the agency's revenues and expenses over a specified period, such as one month, three months, or one year.

Income is calculated as revenues minus expenses. For an agency, revenues include commission payments, interest income, and other income. Expenses include salaries, employee benefits, rent, and depreciation. Exhibit 3-2 provides an example of an agency's income statement.

EXHIBIT 3-1

XYZ Agency, Inc., Balance Sheet—December 31, 200X

Assets

Current Assets

Cash	$ 709,832	
Accounts receivable	1,339,584	
Less: Reserve for bad debts	40,763	1,298,821
Total Current Assets		2,008,653

Fixed Assets

Property & equipment	$ 209,646	
Less: Reserve for depreciation	90,055	119,591
Other Assets		14,128
Total Assets		$2,142,372

Liabilities and Owners' Equity

Current Liabilities

Current maturities of long-term debt	$ 47,814
Premiums payable to insurers	1,808,080
Accrued taxes and other current liabilities	65,201
Total Current Liabilities	1,921,095
Long-term debt (minus current portion)	87,914
Total Liabilities	2,009,009

Owners' Equity

Common stock—no par value

Issued and outstanding 100 shares	10,000
Retained earnings	123,363
Total Owners' Equity	133,363
Total Liabilities and Owners' Equity	$2,142,372

To effectively analyze revenue and expense data, financial managers must classify them. Data classification should be detailed enough to enable agency managers to identify patterns. Consistent financial data classification also provides a basis for comparing financial results over time. Once data are classified, they can provide information about premiums, total income, commissions, or other financial items that managers measure. Such information can also be used to calculate financial ratios, which are discussed later in this assignment.

EXHIBIT 3-2

XYZ Agency, Inc., Income Statement
January 1, 200X to December 31, 200X

Revenue

Personal lines commissions	$275,063	
Commercial lines commissions	391,575	
Contingency income	59,435	
Life/health commissions	68,656	
Interest income	12,543	
Other income	3,497	
Total Revenue		$810,769

Expenses

Sales expenses

Entertainment	6,029	
Automobile	13,237	
Advertising	11,562	
Commission to nonowners	210,013	
Other sales expenses	8,501	
Total Sales Expenses		$249,342

Office and General Expenses

Salaries	181,575	
Payroll taxes and benefits	46,640	
Employment costs (owners)	21,148	
Information technology	13,910	
Professional services	7,814	
Printing and supplies	11,316	
Postage	8,446	
Rent	35,985	
Depreciation	45,809	
Telephone	12,829	
Dues, seminars, travel	8,162	
Insurance	13,894	
Donations	1,979	
Bad debts	5,985	
Interest	11,257	
Utilities	4,012	
Other expenses	6,016	
Total Office and General Expenses		$436,777
Net Income Before Taxes		124,650
Income Taxes		25,316
Net Income		$ 99,334

The income and other financial statements can be used to compare actual financial results to the agency's financial goals and to the internal and external benchmarks that were established in the planning process.

External benchmarks are standards of comparison set by other agencies or firms in other industries. These benchmarks may be determined by state agents' associations that have conducted financial studies of their members or other groups and business organizations that serve the property-casualty industry, such as educational organizations, trade associations, consultants, and publishers. For example, the Independent Insurance Agents and Brokers of America (IIABA) and the National Association of Professional Insurance Agents (PIA) have conducted national financial studies of their agency members. Similar studies have been completed by technology firms that perform agencies' accounting using their accounting data.

The *2005 Best Practices Study*,[1] conducted by the IIABA, contains several useful external benchmarks. The study is divided into sections based on agency net revenue to enable agencies to compare their financial information with that of similarly-sized agencies. The study lists averages for all respondents and highlights the top 25 percent (top-performing) study respondents. An agency can use the external benchmarks to identify the areas of financial management that need the most attention.

For example, the *2005 Best Practices Study* shows that average agencies with net revenue between $1.25 million and $2.5 million report an operating pre-tax profit of 6.9 percent. (Operating pre-tax profit equals pre-tax profit minus contingent commissions, bonuses, and investment income.) The top 25 percent, however, have an operating pre-tax profit of 20.2 percent. An agency can use either or both of these benchmarks to compare its own profitability and determine what, if any, action is needed.

The *Rough Notes Company* biennially publishes studies on agency revenues, expenses, and profit in six revenue size categories in *What It Costs*.[2] Similar studies are available from some insurers and insurance management newsletters. Any of the information from these studies can be adopted as benchmarks. Additionally, agency managers may review several studies to evaluate variations among benchmarks. Such evaluations may have implications for profitability. For example, high performing agencies may do better than average agencies at controlling certain operating expenses, such as supplies and printing due to economies of scale.

Internal benchmarks are standards of comparison set within the agency. They may be based on past agency performance and from past budgets. Past performance benchmarks are the most frequently used internal benchmarks. The agency's performance during a current period is compared with that of the same period for the prior year. For example, an agency may base its benchmark for agency bill commissions on a percentage of its prior year's revenue. Similarly, agencies may set benchmarks for all or a portion of their operating expenses based on the prior year's budgets.

Comparing actual results to the projected results and benchmarks identifies how the agency is performing, what revenue and expense trends exist, and what specific areas need attention in light of the agency's goals. Variances should trigger inquiries and further analysis. For example, if total actual expenses are high compared to projected expenses or compared to internal or external benchmarks, then the financial manager may opt to perform further analysis by comparing individual expense components as necessary. Likewise, if revenue is deficient, data can be analyzed further to determine how the deficiency developed.

Implement Any Necessary Corrective Action

In the third step of the financial management process, an agency implements any necessary actions to correct the problems identified in the results analysis. Implementing corrective action requires the assistance of all agency employees and is successful only if implementation plans, including the reasons for the plan and the implementation methods, are clearly communicated. Employees must also know how their performance affects successful implementation and how achievement of the target financial goals affects them.

Monitor the Process and Revise as Needed

Finally, an agency must monitor its financial management process and make revisions as needed. Monitoring requires regularly comparing actual results with projected results and indicates whether and to what extent an agency needs to adjust its implementation plan.

REVENUE CONTROL

Revenue control is an important aspect of agency financial management. Agencies that practice revenue control are complying with legal and regulatory requirements as well as practicing sound agency financial management. Agencies control revenue by establishing proper handling procedures for premiums received, unearned commission reserve accounts, and return commissions on brokered policies.

Premiums Received

Premiums have two components: the commission, which the agency earns, and in which it has an interest, and the remainder of the premium, which is due to the insurer for providing insurance coverage. The agency's insurance company contract determines when the insurer's portion of the premium is due to the insurer. Premiums may be due immediately upon receipt or within a specified period, such as thirty, forty-five, or sixty days after the end of the month in which the insurance became effective.

For agency-billed business, the agency collects and holds on deposit premiums paid by customers until payment is due to the insurer. Some agencies make no attempt to segregate the insurer's share of the premium from the agency's share and use the entire amount for agency operations, if allowed by state law.

Some states have enacted **anticommingling laws** that prohibit depositing funds (premiums) due to insurers into agency operating or personal accounts, that is, commingling of funds. Some agency contracts with insurers also prohibit such commingling of funds.

Courts have interpreted an agency's legal responsibility for premiums held until they are due to the insurer in two different ways. One interpretation is that agencies are acting in a fiduciary capacity for funds held. A **fiduciary** is a person or entity that holds a position of trust, manages another person's or entity's affairs or funds, and has a duty to that person or entity to act in a trustworthy manner.

If the agency is the insurer's fiduciary, it is a trustee of the funds (not the owner). Some state laws may *require* that agencies handle funds as a fiduciary. If a choice is available, putting funds into fiduciary accounts offers the agency the advantage of having creditor protection and increased Federal Deposit Insurance Corporation (FDIC) protection, discussed subsequently. Another interpretation is that agencies are insurers' debtors. Treating premiums as funds for which the agency acts as an insurer's debtor gives the agency greater flexibility in cash management. However, agencies that take this approach incur more work in managing the funds. As they review their revenue control requirements, they should be aware of their states' anticommingling laws.

Anticommingling laws
State laws that prohibit depositing funds (premiums) due to insurers into agency operating or personal accounts, that is, commingling of funds.

Fiduciary
A person or entity that holds a position of trust, manages another person's or entity's affairs or funds, and has a duty to that person or entity to act in a trustworthy manner.

E&O Alert!

Agency principals can encounter severe problems if they combine agency and insurer funds into a single account—even when the insurer funds are easily identifiable. Assume market conditions change and an agency's new business sales and renewals decrease, and customers who renew their policies are slow to pay their premiums. The agency principal may be tempted to use premiums due to the insurer to temporarily cover operating expenses. However, when premiums subsequently become due to the insurer, sufficient funds may not be available to satisfy the debt. This can negatively affect the relationship with the insurer, result in a lawsuit, or cause an agency's bankruptcy. Additionally, many errors and omissions policies exclude claims resulting from commingling of funds.

Fiduciary Obligation

As previously mentioned, anticommingling laws prohibit an agency from commingling the insurer's share of premiums with agency funds. These laws specifically state that the agency has a fiduciary obligation to the insurer for such funds.

Consequently, some state laws require that premiums be deposited in a premium trust account at an approved bank. Accurate records of any deposits made to and checks drawn against the trust account must be kept. Separate trust accounts are usually not required for each insurer, but any funds held in the trust account for different insurers must be ascertainable from the agency's records. Checks drawn against the trust account are permitted to the extent that the remaining balance is at least equal to the total of net premiums collected and owed to insurers, whether or not payment is immediately due. If the trust account balance is lower than required, the agency is said to be "out of trust."

Compliance

The procedures for compliance with anticommingling laws are straightforward. The agency establishes two bank accounts: an operating account and a trust account. All premiums collected are deposited in the trust account. When premiums are remitted to the insurer, a check equal to the commission is also written and deposited in the operating account. The operating account is used to pay agency expenses, such as payroll, insurance, and office supplies. The trust account (or fiduciary account) is used to make refunds to customers and to pay insurers, managing general agents, and surplus lines brokers. Therefore, the agency never uses any money belonging to insurers for agency operations. Even if not required by law, this is a prudent revenue control technique.

Protection From Creditors

Funds in trust accounts are segregated to protect them from claims by agency creditors. For example, assume an agency owes on an overdue bill for office repairs. A bank may offset this claim against funds in an agency's operating account but may not offset against funds in a trust account. If the agency commingles funds in a personal or business account, then the bank is unable to distinguish the agency's personal or business funds from premium funds and may offset the claim against such funds.

Forced Money Management

Anticommingling laws help agencies in their financial management efforts. By preventing the use of funds owed to insurers, the laws force agencies to collect their accounts receivable vigorously in order to have adequate operating funds available. Compliance with anticommingling laws helps agencies prevent financial difficulties that result from temporarily using insurer funds that may be difficult for the agencies to reimburse.

Federal Deposit Insurance Corporation (FDIC) Insurance

Another advantage of a trust account is added protection in the event of bank insolvency. The FDIC insures bank deposits up to $100,000, and FDIC rules stipulate that the $100,000 FDIC insurance applies to each insurer to whom premiums are owed. However, the failed bank's records must clearly reflect the existence of any and all insurer fiduciary relationships. Also, the FDIC has sole discretion in determining whether the failed bank's records are sufficiently clear to apply the $100,000 limit to multiple insurers for whom the insurance agency was holding the trust funds. Therefore, agencies should be careful to maintain trust funds within the $100,000 FDIC limits. Large balances in trust accounts may need to be split into separate accounts to ensure adequate protection. Also, if the insurer maintains funds at the same bank as the agency, the $100,000 limit could be exceeded because it applies on a per entity basis. The agency's financial manager should check with the agency's banker to determine exactly how trust accounts are handled.

Unearned Commission Reserve Accounts

Producers usually treat commissions as earned revenue when a policy is written or an initial premium is paid. This overstates income, however, because producers are generally required to refund commissions to insurers on return premiums to insureds, which may be due whenever policy endorsements generate a credit or a policy is canceled before expiration. Small return premiums may not create problems. However, if a policy with a large premium is canceled or if an insurer terminates an agency's large book of business, large return premiums are due.

To prevent problems associated with refunded commissions, agencies can use conservative accounting. Conservative accounting requires creating an unearned commission reserve account, similar to the unearned premium reserve account that appears on insurer balance sheets. Insurers are legally required to include the entire unearned premium in the unearned premium reserve account. However, for the unearned commission reserve account, agencies need only create an account equal to the probable amount of commissions that may have to be refunded to insurers because of endorsements or cancellations.

The amount of unearned commission reserve maintained depends on the following three factors:

1. Total amount of unearned commissions—indicates the maximum amount at risk
2. Ratio of return commissions to total commissions for several years—shows the average experience over time
3. Total amount of commissions on large accounts—recognizes that these commissions are more susceptible to competition than accounts for personal insurance or small commercial accounts and that they represent a greater loss exposure regarding unearned commission

Taking these factors into consideration, the principal and financial manager use their judgment to determine the amount of the unearned commission reserve. Unless the reserve is to equal the entire unearned commission, no set formula for determining its amount exists.

Return Commissions on Brokered Policies

In most states, brokers are not required to refund return commissions. The law regards a broker as earning the commission at the time of the policy sale.

This presents a problem for an insurance agency that has accepted brokered business. The agency is almost always contractually obligated to refund all its unearned commissions on a return premium regardless of whether it can obtain a refund of the commission paid to a broker. To help control revenue, agencies should require brokers to sign brokerage agreements stipulating return commission policies.

EXPENSE CONTROL

Most organizations understand the need for expense control as a part of financial management. Although many insurance agencies prefer to increase profit by increasing revenue, controlling expenses is also an effective method of increasing profit. Saving a dollar in expenses is equivalent to making a dollar of pre-tax net income. Some agencies try to control expenses only when disbursements are made. This approach does not really control expenses because the money has already been spent.

The decision to institute expense control measures in an agency should be effectively communicated to all staff. Analyzing the expense items in the agency's income statement can help managers choose the appropriate areas in which to focus expense control.

Agencies can control expenses through accounts receivable control, internal controls, expense measurement, expense analysis, and expense reduction.

Accounts Receivable Control

Accounts receivable
A current asset representing monies owed to a business by customers for goods or services rendered.

Controlling accounts receivable is vital to an agency's expense control. **Accounts receivable** are a current asset representing monies owed to a business by customers for goods or services rendered. For most agencies, accounts receivable are the largest current asset. If accounts receivable are uncollectible, then agencies incur bad debt. However, many agencies have no formal program to control accounts receivable.

Some insurers, such as direct writers, require premium payment with the insurance application and therefore do not have accounts receivable. Direct-billed premiums do not present any collection risk to the agency (except that, in such situations, many insurance agencies believe they need to extend credit to customers to facilitate sales). Therefore, this discussion of accounts receivable applies only to agency-billed premiums.

One method used to analyze accounts receivable, the average collection period ratio, indicates how long it takes an agency, on average, to collect its accounts receivables. Insurance agencies generally have between thirty and forty-five days after the end of the month to pay premiums to insurers. For example, premiums on policies written in March are due to the insurer on May 15. An agency's collection period of greater than forty-five days indicates that the agency is extending more credit to its insureds than it has from the insurer.

The following formula is used to calculate the average collection period:

$$\text{Average collection period} = \frac{\text{Average accounts receivable balance}}{\text{Total agency-billed premium}} \times 365.$$

For example, assume that XYZ Agency has $2.4 million in annual agency-billed premiums. Its average accounts receivable balance is $493,000. The collection period for XYZ can be calculated as follows:

$$\text{Average collection period} = \frac{\$493,000}{\$2,400,000} \times 365 = 75 \text{ days.}$$

The seventy-five-day ratio indicates a lax collection policy because the agency must typically pay the insurer within thirty to forty-five days. To pay insurers, the agency would have to either borrow funds or use its operating funds. Accounts receivable can be determined from year-end accounting records but are better averaged from month-end totals to reflect the current collection period.

Because accounts receivable directly affect an agency's ability to control expenses, they must be effectively managed. To effectively manage accounts receivable, agencies must do the following:

- Evaluate accounts receivable cost factors
- Develop an accounts receivable policy
- Set an accounts receivable goal
- Arrange for premium financing

Evaluate Accounts Receivable Cost Factors

Successful and well-managed agencies recognize and can evaluate the cost factors of accounts receivable and take steps to control such factors and minimize their effects on agency expenses.

Agencies must evaluate the following accounts receivable cost factors:

- Surrendered opportunity cost of accounts receivable funds
- Increased accounts receivable collection cost
- Cost of borrowing to finance accounts receivable
- Increased bad debt expense
- Potential commission losses from failure to extend credit

Opportunity cost refers to the advantage forgone as a result of accepting an alternative. For example, accounts receivable are an opportunity cost to the agency because interest can be earned on accounts receivable funds. If an agency has, on average, $150,000 of its own funds tied up in accounts receivable, the opportunity cost is $4,500 annually, assuming a 3 percent interest rate. Therefore, agencies must evaluate the effects of opportunity costs related to accounts receivable on its expenses.

Opportunity cost
The advantage forgone as a result of accepting an alternative.

All agencies with agency-billed premiums have accounts receivable collection expenses. Lax accounts receivable policies, however, increase those expenses. Effort devoted to collecting aged receivables can affect agency expenses in several ways. For example, the agency must consider the amount of time spent on the collection process and the compensation of the individuals involved. Some agencies employ a person whose sole job function involves collecting overdue accounts, thus increasing annual agency expenses by the amount of that person's salary.

According to the IIABA *Best Practices* study, agencies overwhelmingly indicate that producers are primarily responsible for collection of accounts receivable. If producers spend time collecting overdue accounts, agencies incur not only the direct cost of the producer's time but also the opportunity cost of the sales that would have occurred had the producer been focused on production.

Some agencies have to borrow from outside sources to finance large accounts receivable balances. If an agency consistently borrows $150,000 to finance overdue accounts, the annual cost at 6 percent interest would be $9,000. The borrowing cost can be eliminated if the agency's average collection period ratio is maintained within insurers' credit terms.

Bad debt
Any account receivable that is considered uncollectible.

Agencies may also have increased bad debt expenses. A **bad debt** is any account receivable that is considered uncollectible. Determining when an account receivable becomes uncollectible is based on an agency's credit policy. For example, some producers believe they can still collect a debt well after the point at which a customer or former customer is willing to pay. In such cases, the debt remains on the agency's books as an account receivable when it should be declared a bad debt. Ideally, agency credit policies should specify when an account becomes a bad debt and identify the responsible party. When an account receivable is designated as a bad debt, it is typically eligible for special tax consideration for that year, as a business bad debt "write-off."

Bad debt expense varies directly with the age of accounts receivable. Reducing the collection period should sharply reduce bad debts. This is particularly true for agencies whose contracts permit them to avoid responsibility for premium payments by notifying the insurer of uncollectible premiums within a certain period (usually thirty to forty-five days). Under this arrangement, the agency transfers the bad debt risk to the insurer, and the uncollectible premiums are removed from the agency's accounts receivable total. Agencies should be aware that they surrender their right to commissions on any such accounts receivable collected by the insurer. Agencies should also be careful not to use the insurer's collection mechanism as a substitute for a sound credit policy.

Finally, insurance agencies have traditionally hesitated to institute strict collection policies because they believed they would lose sales. The fallacy in this belief can be revealed by comparing the total cost of the credit extension to the total potential income from the account receivable. When all the previously mentioned cost factors are evaluated, an agency may discover that extending liberal credit terms may actually result in losing money on a new account. In addition, an evaluation of all these factors helps agencies determine the total cost of carrying accounts receivable balances.

E&O Alert!

With E&O claims on the rise, it is important for every agency to analyze any incidents, losses, or claims submitted in order to determine whether an account involved is a bad debt account. Some customers may represent an E&O hazard to the agency if coverage is not in force at the time of a claim but a certificate of insurance has been issued on a canceled account, if a claim report is taken after coverage has terminated, or if an insured is told that coverage can be reinstated when it cannot.

Develop an Accounts Receivable Policy

Effective management of accounts receivable requires an accounts receivable policy that specifies the terms under which credit will be extended. The policy, which should be written and communicated to all employees, should assign responsibility for implementing the credit terms. It should state who will make collection calls and the circumstances under which the account will be turned over to a collection agency.

Appendix A describes the steps agency financial managers can take to develop an effective collection system as well as the importance of setting collection goals. Establishing collection systems that include goals such as reducing average accounts receivable can result in significant savings. The actual savings and their relative significance vary among agencies.

An agency should consider several possible accounts receivable policies before choosing one to implement. Exhibit 3-3 discusses eleven tactics agencies can incorporate in their policies to gain control of problematic accounts receivables.

Some agencies do not implement formal accounts receivable policies until unpaid balances cause the agency significant financial stress. Many agencies have a poor accounts receivable position because their management's attitude is that customers will eventually pay or that the insurer is responsible for collecting the debts. Some agencies actually budget for significant levels of bad debts in the belief that they have little control over accounts receivable. Such attitudes must be changed at the highest management levels, and accounts receivable goals should be set high in order to minimize bad debts.

EXHIBIT 3-3

11 Surefire Tactics to Gain Control of Receivables

by Ken Buehler

If you have a receivables problem, now is the best time to contain it. Most agencies with receivables problems believe they appeared suddenly, but in reality the problem had existed for some time.

Controlling receivables is nothing more than training your customers and your producers and the staff persons who support the producers in your policy.

Monitoring should be ongoing, and that requires discipline.

Here are 11 tactics that will get receivables under control and keep them that way.

1. Have a formal, written collections policy and enforce it.

2. If you have a receivables problem, meet with each producer every few days until they find the source of the problem. For those problems you are unable to solve right away, require a signed note if the customer is willing. When the customer is unwilling, start cancellation and collection proceedings.

3. If a particular producer has a problem, conduct a person-to-person review of the receivables. Set weekly goals to complete until the producer has receivables under control. When you meet with the producer each week, make the goal the first item on the agenda. Start with the accounts that are more than 90 days past due, and once those are under control, start working on the ones more than 60 days past due.

4. Charge receivables back to the producer when they reach over 90 days past due, unless the producer is willing to guarantee them personally.

5. Don't make exceptions, and make that part of your agency's collections policy.

6. Designate a person in the agency your "Collection Manager," (CM) and design a demand letter to send to past-due customers, which calls for some action from the customer before a deadline. The letter should also include customer contact with the CM to make payment arrangements. Then, if the customer does not respond, make arrangements with an attorney to send a letter. If the customer again does not respond, then have the attorney tell the customer that legal action is impending. If that fails, start the legal action. Making these tough decisions now will assist in resolving the problem permanently.

7. Make it your agency's policy to not bind anything without either a premium up-front or a signed financial agreement accompanied by an appropriate deposit premium.

8. Make receivables control an office-wide project, involving all staff and producers. Communicate this policy to everyone.

9. Train your producers to set an agreement on payment terms as a part of the proposal presentation, whether it is on a new account or a renewal account. Include payment terms in the written proposal to the customer.

10. Determine each of your carrier's positions on uncollectible audits. Whether they allow turn-backs (to the insurer) or not, be sure each of your producers and customer service representatives understands the carrier's position. One way to do this is to have each carrier and their terms displayed on a matrix, which is accessible either on your system or in printed form. Then hold staff accountable for monitoring what happens. Use your information technology system to create a report of outstanding and uncollected audits. If the carrier does not permit audit turn-backs, you'll want to consider not placing auditable policies with them. If you use the carrier anyway, then you want to feel comfortable that your premium base is adequate for the risk. On a new account, you may consider interim audits to monitor progress.

11. Use direct-billed plans on accounts that have had payment problems. Forewarn the customer that the company will probably not reinstate coverage canceled for nonpayment of premium, or that the company will reinstate coverage only once after a nonpayment cancellation.

Receivables control is an absolute necessity for agencies. You can get in immediate financial trouble if you don't control them.

Strictly adhere to a set policy. Agencies will have time for more productive activities if less time is spent on outstanding accounts receivable.

Adapted with permission from Insurance Marketing & Management Services (IMMS).

The accounts receivable policy should specify that premium payment arrangements should be made when the customer accepts the insurance, whether for renewal or new business. The policy should also specify that all insurance proposals should include payment options, such as premium financing, in order to avoid agency financing. Clearly specifying payment options and expectations is vital to expense control and improves the long-term relationship between the agency and the customer because the payment terms are agreed to in advance.

Conducting credit checks on applicants should also be part of the accounts receivable policy. Although some agencies do not take the time or expense to review a customer's credit record, credit checks can help minimize the agency's exposure to accounts that are slow to pay and to bad debts.

If an agency denies a customer credit after a credit check, the producer may appeal to the person in charge of agency credit on the customer's behalf, if extenuating circumstances apply. The agency's policy should state the circumstances under which exceptions to the credit policy will be made. For example, the policy may state that if an exception is made and the customer fails to pay, the producer may be held liable for the debt.

Once developed, the accounts receivable policy should be communicated to all agency personnel and adhered to by all employees, including principals and producers.

Set an Accounts Receivable Goal

The accounts receivable policy should set a goal for keeping accounts receivable under control. The goal can be stated in terms of the collection period, which, as discussed previously, shows the average number of days of outstanding uncollected accounts.

The agency can adopt an external benchmark as its accounts receivable goal, such as that included in the *Best Practices* study or *What It Costs*. The top 25 percent of agencies with annual revenue between $1.25 million and $2.5 million included in the study report the following aged receivable figures:[3]

> Receivables aged past 60 days were 3.0% of accounts receivables.

> Receivables aged past 90 days were 1.7% of accounts receivables.

In comparison, agencies classified as average in the study reported 9.4 percent of receivables aged past sixty days and 5.5 percent aged past ninety days. An agency could use either of these figures as benchmarks for measuring performance and determining whether improvements should be made.

Arrange for Premium Financing

Although insurance agency financial managers have always valued the administrative ease of managing customers who prepay insurance premiums in cash, alternate methods of paying premiums have become important because customers are reluctant to tie up operating capital in prepaid insurance premiums. Customers may be more willing to purchase insurance products when presented with flexible payment methods for premium financing.

All concerned parties benefit from premium financing. The insurers receive prompt premium payment, the producers can sell more insurance, and customers can make convenient payments on their insurance as they do on other purchases. However, the agency must always have enough money collected to cover earned premiums.

Agencies can use any of the following five premium financing methods:

1. Agency financing
2. Bank financing
3. Insurer financing
4. Premium finance company financing
5. Captive finance company financing

With agency financing, agencies use their own in-house premium financing. One variation of agency financing is that premiums are paid in installments without a service or finance charge. For example, the customer might pay one-third of the premium as a deposit, a second third in thirty days, and the final third in sixty days, without having to pay a finance or service charge. This system allows the customer to pay in cash without producing the full amount of the premium at the policy's inception. The agency receives the full premium before the account becomes payable to the insurer. This variation of the agency financing method does not extend to the agency the benefit that the time value of money provides when the full premium is obtained and invested at policy inception.

Another variation of the agency financing method imposes a finance or service charge on the unpaid premium balance. Laws in some states prohibit finance or service charges or stipulate the maximum percentage that can be charged. An agency's premium financing method must adhere to applicable state laws.

Some agencies treat the service charge as an income source and encourage customers to use this method. However, this method ignores the time value of money and the additional work it creates. It also encourages customers to pay slowly. The real purpose of the service charge should be to encourage customers to pay when coverage begins rather than to generate income.

Bank financing is a premium financing method in which a bank enters into a premium finance agreement with the insured. This agreement, which must be signed by both the insured and the agency, sets the guidelines for the transaction. The insured is required to make a down payment (typically 20 percent) and to pay installments until the unpaid balance and the finance charges are paid. When all parties have signed the agreement, the bank advances the full premium to the insurer or the agency.

Bank financing can be **recourse financing** (the lender can recover from a borrower and any parties secondarily responsible for the borrower's bad debt) or **nonrecourse financing** (the lender is barred from recovering from the borrower and any parties secondarily responsible for the borrower's bad debt). Recourse financing is the most common, and the burden for a customer's nonpayment or bankruptcy can ultimately reside with the agency.

Agencies should be aware that bank financing can reduce the insured's and the agency's overall credit line, and the bank's financing terms may contain recourse provisions disadvantageous to the agency.

Insurer financing is another premium financing method. Many property-casualty insurers offer premium financing for policies exceeding a minimum premium. Often, only annual policies qualify for financing, and they require a down payment of 20 to 30 percent, with the balance paid over nine, ten, or eleven months. If the insurer also finances semiannual policies, the down payment is typically 50 percent; the other 50 percent is paid in three monthly payments. Many insurers offer installment financing with only a small installment charge.

If premium-bearing endorsements are added during the policy period, the additional premium may be added to the existing finance agreement. However, the producer may be required to collect a down payment on the endorsement. If only a few payments are left on the existing finance agreement, the endorsement's premium is paid in a lump sum or is refinanced.

Premium finance company financing is similar to bank financing. At policy inception, the premium finance company pays the insured's total premium to the insurer or agency. The agency has the benefits of prompt commission payment, reduced billing expense, reduced collection expense, lower accounts receivable, and use of the money until payable to the insurer.

As with the other premium financing methods, the insured pays a down payment to the premium finance company and the balance through one of many available installment options. The variety of options for premium financing are perhaps its greatest advantage. Some individuals and businesses have irregular or seasonal income sources, and premium finance companies are known for their ability to address such situations. Premium finance companies also offer the advantage of confidential borrowing that will not affect the insured's credit line.

If an insured defaults on any installment payments, the premium finance company requests that the insurer cancel the policy. Any unearned premium is returned to the premium finance company as collateral. The premium finance agreement contains a limited power-of-attorney clause that allows the company to request that a policy be canceled when the insured has not made a scheduled payment. Often, this request for cancellation provides only five days' notice to the insured, rather than the standard ten-day notice of cancellation for nonpayment of premium. This is probably the most important provision in the premium finance agreement because it protects the premium finance company's interest.

Recourse financing
A type of financing in which a lender can recover from a borrower and any parties secondarily responsible for the borrower's bad debt.

Nonrecourse financing
A type of financing in which a lender is barred from action against the borrower and any parties secondarily responsible for the borrower's bad debt.

Captive finance company financing is another premium financing method. Captive finance companies are owned and controlled by insurance agencies or agency networks and are operated according to their needs or demands. Only policies written by the insurance agency are accepted for premium financing. The amount to be financed must exceed a minimum dollar amount. For most captive finance companies, premium financing is available only for annual or semiannual policies.

A captive finance company operates in nearly the same way as a premium finance company in terms of payments. Down payments of 20 and 30 percent are typically required on the financed amount for the annual and semiannual policies, respectively. The annual policies are typically financed over a nine- or ten-month period, but the semiannual policies must be paid within 120 days. Delinquent accounts are usually given a grace period before cancellation. If a policy is canceled, the insurance agency credits its captive finance company with the unearned premium.

E&O Alert!

Competent management of a captive finance company can greatly increase an agency's profitability. However, operating a finance company also involves substantial additional work for the agency's management and should not be undertaken without careful consideration. Agency principals must also determine whether operating a captive finance company is legal in their states and whether the errors and omissions loss exposures presented by such business operations are included under the agency's E&O policies.

Internal Controls

In addition to controlling accounts receivable, agencies can control expenses by establishing effective internal controls for cash, cash equivalents, and negotiable securities, which constitute a large part of any insurance agency's assets. Such controls include both personnel controls and accounting controls.

Personnel Controls

Agencies, like all organizations, implement internal controls to prevent the theft of cash, cash equivalents, and negotiable securities. Personnel controls include screening job applicants and prosecuting dishonest employees.

Employment applications should contain questions that help agency management screen employees. All such questions must adhere to various state and federal employment laws, and agency management should consult with a lawyer or a human resources professional before preparing employment applications.

Agencies should always verify the job applicants' prior employment and check their references. Although former employers may be reluctant to divulge detailed information, a general indicator of an applicant's suitability can often be obtained by speaking with the employee's prior supervisor and asking whether the supervisor would rehire the former employee.

In addition to personnel control for job applicants, agencies should implement personnel control for employees. Agency employees should know that they will be prosecuted if they steal from the agency. However, discharging employees is not enough to prevent further occurrences of theft and can even result in more losses due to dishonesty. Failure to prosecute when in possession of conclusive evidence of dishonesty establishes a precedent within the agency that may encourage others to commit dishonest acts. Therefore, agencies should have written policies that specify the actions the agency will take in the event of employee dishonesty.

Accounting Controls

Accounting controls include the organizational plan, procedures, and other records that are concerned with the safeguarding of assets and the reliability of financial records. They are designed to provide reasonable assurance of the following:

- Transactions are executed in accordance with management's general or specific authorization and control.
- Transactions are recorded as necessary to maintain accountability for assets and liabilities.
- Access to assets is permitted only with management's authorization.

Examples of internal accounting controls include requiring segregation of duties, such as assigning the reconciliation of bank statements to someone not authorized to deposit or withdraw funds; and requiring two signatures on checks for amounts above a specified limit.

In addition to internal accounting controls, an external independent certified public accountant (CPA) can be engaged to perform one of three levels of service in preparing agency financial statements: a compilation, a review, or an audit.

In a compilation, the CPA compiles and reports data provided by agency management in the form of financial statements without rendering an opinion on the financial statements. In a review, the CPA also does not provide an opinion on the financial statements. However, a review does provide a limited negative assurance by indicating nothing has come to the CPA's attention to suggest that the financial statements are materially misstated. During an audit, the CPA performs enough work to be able to express an opinion that, with a reasonable level of assurance, the financial statements taken as a whole present a true and fair representation of the agency's financial position and the results of its operations for the period audited.

Expense Measurement

Agencies can use expense measurement as a practical way to quantify the effect of expense control measures. For example, assume that an agency is writing $2 million in annual premiums at an average commission of 13 percent, generating gross commissions of $260,000. Assuming management earns 50 percent of gross commissions before taxes, the agency yields a pre-tax net income of $130,000. Also assume that the agency can reduce expenses by $130,000. The reduction in expenses goes directly to pre-tax net income. Therefore, a $130,000 reduction in expenses has the same effect as $2 million in additional annual premiums for the agency. Consequently, this expense measurement indicates that expense reduction has about fifteen times the effect of an increase in premium volume. This relationship varies with the commission rate. At 10 percent commission, $1 of expense reduction has the same financial effect as twenty times as much premium volume. Exhibit 3-4 illustrates how expense measurement indicates the effect of expense reduction compared to increased premium volume for various commission rates under the same assumptions.

EXHIBIT 3-4

Expense Measurement Illustration

At a commission level of	A $1 reduction in expenses is as profitable as this increase in premium volume
20%	$10.00
18%	$11.00
16%	$12.50
14%	$14.29
12%	$16.67
10%	$20.00

Expense Analysis

Expense analysis is another way agencies can control expenses. Agencies using expense analysis develop expense benchmarks and analyze results to assess agency performance and target specific areas for improvement.

What It Costs and the *Best Practices* study, discussed previously, are good external sources of expense benchmarks. Additionally, national and state agents' associations often publish compilations of expense benchmarks gathered from their members. These expense benchmarks are grouped by agency size and location. Percentages of total revenue to expenses are given for comparison.

Each of the published benchmarks has the weakness of being an average. The best benchmark is established by developing a profit goal, establishing a budget, and using cost accounting, discussed in the next section, to determine expense control measures.

Regardless of the benchmark selected, actual expenses should be compared with the benchmark regularly. Each item in the income statement, not just expenses, should be compared. If the agency's performance is worse than the benchmark, action should be taken. Additionally, the financial manager must determine why the agency's results varied from the benchmark.

Expense Reduction

Expenses can be reduced by implementing sound time management practices and cost accounting. Time management can eliminate the expense resulting from employees' taking too much time to complete tasks and devoting less than optimum time to activities that generate revenue and/or reduce expenses. Cost accounting helps agencies associate costs with their sources.

Time Management

An employee's time is like any other valuable agency resource—it must be used efficiently. Any time spent by agency staff on any agency activity has a dollar value. Time wasted has a dollar value as an expense. If not recognized, cumulative wasted time could cause an agency to consider hiring additional staff to meet its goals. Additionally, time wasted is time not spent generating new sales or supporting renewals.

Expenses can also be reduced by setting specific work standards so that personnel know what is expected of them. Clear expectations save time by reducing the need to undo or redo work. Additionally, eliminating unnecessary steps in the work process and streamlining processes through technology can save time, thereby reducing expenses. Invariably, agencies can improve efficiency in all areas of agency operations, from sales and customer service to claims and accounting. Many sources of information on business process reengineering are available.

Cost Accounting

In addition to using sound time management, agencies can reduce expenses through cost accounting. **Cost accounting** tracks, records, and analyzes an organization's expenses relative to its associated products, activities, and departments.

An insurance agency typically handles more than one line of insurance, but the agency manager may not know how costs are distributed among the lines of insurance. The income statement indicates revenue, expenses, and net income for a given period but does not provide information relating to profitability by specific product line or even by a general class of business, such as personal or commercial.

Cost accounting
The systematic tracking, recording, and analyzing of an organization's expenses relative to its associated products, activities, and departments.

Accurate cost information is crucial for management to make informed decisions. However, because of the expense of implementing cost accounting systems and the burden of additional work for agency staff, many agencies have rejected cost accounting systems as impractical. As competition among agencies and the use of technology increase, the need for cost information will also increase. Fortunately, the expense and burden of obtaining such information have decreased. Therefore, agencies should seriously consider the benefits of cost accounting.

Most cost accounting techniques are beyond the scope of this text but can be found in managerial accounting texts. A simple cost accounting technique is to determine the cost of the agency's time. This can be calculated by dividing the total payroll (including all employee benefits) by the number of employees (part-time employees count as one-half). Tasks are then examined based on how long they take to perform. By determining the cost of an hour, or even a minute, an agency can determine the cost of any single transaction.

Key Words and Phrases

Define or describe each of the words and phrases found in this assignment.

Financial management (p. 3.5)

Balance sheet (p. 3.6)

Income statement (p. 3.6)

Anticommingling laws (p. 3.11)

Fiduciary (p. 3.11)

Accounts receivable (p. 3.14)

Opportunity cost (p. 3.16)

Bad debt (p. 3.16)

Recourse financing (p. 3.21)

REVIEW

Nonrecourse financing (p. 3.21)

Cost accounting (p. 3.25)

Review Questions

1. How do agencies make financial decisions? (p. 3.5)

2. What are the four steps in the financial management process? (p. 3.6)

3. Describe the following benchmarks: (p. 3.9)

   a.   External benchmarks

   b.   Internal benchmarks

4. What are two reasons an insurance agency might establish anti-commingling procedures? (p. 3.11)

5. Describe three factors agencies use to determine the appropriate size of an unearned commission reserve account. (p. 3.13)

6. When has a broker earned commission generated from a sale, according to the law? (pp. 3.13–3.14)

7. What cost factors must agencies evaluate in order to set realistic collection policies? (p. 3.15)

8. What are three issues that an agency's accounts receivable policy should address? (pp. 3.17–3.19)

REVIEW

9. What types of accounting controls do agency financial managers use to assist in managing the agency's assets? (p. 3.23)

10. How do agencies use expense measurement? (p. 3.24)

11. Describe cost accounting and explain why it is useful in an agency. (pp. 3.25–3.26)

Application Questions

1. Sandy, the owner of XYZ Insurance Agency (XYZ), is reviewing her agency's financial statements. She notes that on the monthly income statement, the line item for commercial insurance commissions, budgeted at $20,000, is only $10,000. The $20,000 budgeted figure was based on using the agency's previous year's totals for the same month as an internal benchmark ($15,000) and projecting the commission growth generated by the addition of a new agency producer ($4,000) and the development of existing accounts ($1,000). After noting this income variance, describe Sandy's next actions, using the steps in the financial management process.

2. Accounts receivable are a challenge for many agencies.

   a.   What are four accounts receivable issues agencies must manage?

   b.   What issues should an accounts receivable policy address to achieve its goals and why?

   c.   Identify other ways in which an agency can help insureds finance premiums and how this affects the agency's accounts receivable.

3. When collecting premiums, an insurance agency acts in a fiduciary capacity.

   a.   Explain the role of a fiduciary.

   b.   What responsibility does the agency have for premiums it has collected?

REVIEW

c. Explain how the agency must treat these funds while they are
    in its possession.

Answers to Assignment 3 Questions

NOTE: These answers are provided to give students a basic understanding of acceptable types of responses. They often are not the only valid answers and are not intended to provide an exhaustive response to the questions.

Review Questions

1. Agencies make financial decisions by assigning financial management responsibilities and by using the financial management process.

2. The four steps in the financial management process are as follows:
   (1) Identify the current financial position
   (2) Analyze results of operations
   (3) Implement any necessary corrective actions
   (4) Monitor and revise the process

3. a. External benchmarks are standards of comparison set by other agencies or firms in other industries using accounting data, such as operating pre-tax profit.
   b. Internal benchmarks are standards of performance set within the agency, such as past performance standards, which compare the agency's performance during a current period with the same period for the previous year, and budgeted standards, which compare the agency's performance during a current period with a well-designed budget that will meet goals.

4. Insurance agencies may establish anticommingling procedures for the following reasons:
   (1) Some states have enacted anticommingling laws to prohibit depositing money due insurers into agency operating accounts or personal accounts.
   (2) Some agency contracts with insurers prohibit commingling of funds.

5. Agencies use the following three factors to determine the appropriate size of an unearned commission reserve account:
   (1) The total of unearned commissions indicates the maximum amount at risk.
   (2) The ratio of returned commissions to total commissions for several years shows the average experience over time.
   (3) Total commissions on large accounts are more susceptible to competition than personal insurance or smaller commercial insurance accounts and represent a greater exposure for unearned commission.

6. According to the law, a broker earns commission generated from a sale at the time of the sale.

7. The following cost factors must be evaluated to set realistic collection policies:
   • Surrendered opportunity cost of accounts receivable funds
   • Increased collection activities cost
   • Cost of borrowing
   • Increased bad debt expense
   • Perceived commission losses from failure to extend credit

8. An agency's accounts receivable policy should address the following three issues:

   (1) Management attitude—Many agencies have poor accounts receivable because management believes customers will eventually pay or the insurer will collect the debts. Such attitudes must be changed at the highest management level and communicated to staff.

   (2) Premium payment—Premium payment arrangements should be made when the customer accepts the insurance, whether the acceptance is for new or renewal business. Payment terms between the customer and the agency must be clearly understood and agreed to in advance.

   (3) Credit checks—Credit checks should be used by the agency to minimize its exposure to accounts that are slow to pay and to bad debts.

9. Agency financial managers use the following accounting controls to assist in managing the agency's assets:

   - Segregating duties

   - Assigning the reconciliation of bank statements to someone not authorized to make deposits or withdrawals

   - Requiring two signatures on checks over a specified limit

   - Requiring an annual audit, a compilation, or a review

10. Agencies use expense measurement as a practical way to quantify the effect of expense of expense control measures.

11. Cost accounting is the systematic tracking, recording, and analyzing of an organization's expenses relative to its associated products, activities, and departments. Cost accounting is useful because management can use it to make informed decisions to control expenses.

Application Questions

1. The difference between the commercial insurance commissions should generate inquiry and analysis on Sandy's part. For example, were renewal commissions in line with her budgeted projection of $15,000? Did the new producer achieve his monthly production goal of $4,000? Did account development of the current commercial book generate an additional $1,000 of commission?

   Sandy should then implement corrective action. For example, if the producer is not meeting certain production goals, his production plan should be reviewed to determine whether it is realistic. If the producer requires additional training in order to be effective in agency sales, Sandy can arrange for him to receive such training. Sandy and her staff can examine retention issues relating to the renewal book of business and account development increases. It is possible that an insurance rate increase did not take effect as anticipated or a key insurer restricted its underwriting. Sandy and her staff can implement an account development and account retention plan, focusing on cross-selling personal and commercial insurance coverages to existing accounts.

   Finally, Sandy should monitor and revise the process as needed. She should frequently monitor the commercial insurance commissions line item and respond to any variance by implementing changes to her budgets and plans as necessary.

2. a. Four accounts receivable issues agencies must manage are as follows:

(1) Evaluating accounts receivable cost factors

(2) Developing an accounts receivable policy

(3) Setting an accounts receivable goal

(4) Arranging for payment

b. An accounts receivable policy should address the following issues to achieve its goals:

- Management attitude—If agency management believes either that customers will eventually pay or that the insurer will collect bad debts, the agency is unlikely to develop a strong and effective accounts receivable policy.

- Payment arrangements must be made when the business is written because if terms are not clear at the time of the sale then it is often more difficult for the producer to return after the sale and collect premiums that are in dispute.

- Credit checks should be used to help minimize the agency's exposure to accounts that are slow to pay bills and to bad debts. Although a customer with a good credit score can have cash-flow problems, typically an individual or business with an unfavorable credit rating will have a greater than average risk of generating a bad debt.

c. An agency can help insureds finance premiums in the following ways:

- Agency financing—This method must adhere to any applicable state laws and may affect the agency's receivables.

- Bank financing—This method of assisting the insured in paying premium can free up the agency's receivables.

- Insurance company financing—The insured's premium is paid through the insurer's finance company and clears the agency's receivables.

- Premium financing—Financing the insured's premium through a premium finance company clears the agency's receivables.

- Captive financing—The captive finance company pays the insured's premium. This method may or may not clear the agency's receivables depending on who owns the captive and what the legal relationships are.

3. a. A fiduciary holds a position of trust, manages another person's or organization's affairs or funds, and has a duty to that person or organization to act in a trustworthy manner.

b. Because the agency owns only the commission portion of the premium, the balance is held in trust for the insurer. The agency must safeguard this money and repay the insurer if the money is lost or destroyed.

c. Most states have laws against mingling agency money and company money held in a fiduciary capacity. The agency should establish a separate account for these fiduciary funds. The agency cannot spend this money, but, in most states, the agency can keep any interest earned while it controls the funds.

INCOME TAX CONSIDERATIONS

All agencies want to maximize their annual profit and the overall value of their agencies. Agency principals can help accomplish this by maximizing their legally allowable tax-deductible agency expenses in light of their legal form of ownership. This section discusses important tax considerations for insurance agencies, including the following:

- Legal form of ownership
- Tax-advantaged employee benefit plans
- Lease arrangements

Legal Form of Ownership

An agency's legal form of ownership affects many phases of its operations, including taxation. Consequently, the decision of the agency's principal(s) to organize the agency as a sole proprietorship, partnership, limited liability company, corporation, or S-corporation is important. Many firms that start as proprietorships or partnerships incorporate later. This step is taken for many reasons, but one of the most common is that employee-owners of a corporation receive some distinct benefits not available to nonincorporated owners, such as freedom from personal liability and tax-free benefits such as group life insurance.

The corporate form of ownership is not without disadvantages. Sole proprietors or partners can determine how much of their agencies' revenue they want as salary. However, for corporations, the Internal Revenue Service (IRS) compares the compensation of owner-employees (corporate executives) with that of corporate executives in comparable businesses and decides whether it is reasonable or excessive. Amounts found to be excessive are not deductible as business expenses by the corporation. The corporation also pays taxes on its net income, and owner-employees pay taxes on their salaries. Consequently, owner-employees are subject to taxation at the corporate level and at the personal level.

This double taxation can be avoided by electing Subchapter S status. Income from Subchapter S corporations is not taxed at the corporate level but is passed to stockholders in much the same way as partnership income. However, some of the tax advantages of a typical corporation (for example, tax-free group life insurance) are not available in a Subchapter S corporation.

A relatively new form of business ownership, called a limited liability company (LLC), offers some of the tax advantages of both corporations and partnerships.

Agency principals should consider the advantages and disadvantages of the various forms of legal ownership and the tax implications of those forms of ownership for their agencies. Employee benefit plans also have tax implications for agencies.

Employee Benefit Plans

Employee benefit plans provide agencies with a means of rewarding employee performance and attracting and retaining quality employees. No employee benefit plan fits every situation, and a variety of plans have been created to meet different organizations' needs. Each type of plan varies in complexity and in its tax implications. This section describes and discusses the advantages to both the agency and employees of the following six common employee benefit plans:

1. Bonus plans
2. Qualified profit sharing plans
3. Employee stock ownership plans (ESOPs)
4. Deferred compensation plans
5. Section 401(k) plans
6. Stock option plans

For further details, producers are encouraged to talk with tax experts and employee benefit specialists.

Bonus Plans

Bonus plans reward employees when they achieve their goals and/or the agency makes a certain amount of profit. The sooner a bonus is paid after goals are achieved or a profit is made, the greater its motivational effects. If performance can be measured monthly, monthly bonuses should be used because they are more effective than an annual bonus. Bonuses based on overall agency or work group performance tend to encourage teamwork and may help make the staff work more harmoniously. Cash bonuses are typically taxable to the employees when the bonus is received and are tax deductible by the agency as business expenses.

Qualified Profit Sharing Plans

Qualified profit sharing plans are plans by which an employer makes special deferred sums based on the profits of the business available to all employees. Profit sharing is widely used in the insurance business and typically averages between 15 and 25 percent of an agency employee's total compensation. Qualified profit sharing plans can unite employees in a common goal and encourage teamwork and cooperation. The employer is allowed a tax deduction for contributions to the plan, and employees pay no taxes on the plan assets until the assets are distributed to them. The earnings on the plan assets are also tax deferred.

Employee Stock Ownership Plans (ESOPs)

An ESOP is a qualified (eligible for special tax considerations for both the employer and employee) retirement plan that provides employees with employer stock. ESOPs allow employees to participate in their agency's growth as investors. They are often structured either as a stock bonus plan or as a combination bonus plan and pension plan. When an employee is entitled to a distribution in accordance with the terms of the ESOP, such a distribution is made to the employee in employer stock. However, if an employer's stock is not tradable on an established market (for example, if the agency is not publicly traded), the employee has the right to sell the stock back to the employer for its fair market value.

Deferred Compensation Plans

Deferred compensation plans are plans by which an employer agrees to pay an employee in the future for work performed today. For valued employees with sufficient current income, some agencies defer a portion of salary or bonuses, agreeing to pay the employee in the future under specified conditions when the employee presumably is in a lower income tax bracket. The IRS imposes restrictions on such deferrals to allow employees to defer taxation. For example, an employee who agrees to defer a bonus until retirement must agree to forfeit the deferred bonus to the employer if he or she quits. Otherwise, the amount deferred is immediately taxable to the employee. Employers receive special tax considerations on deferred compensation in the year(s) employees include the payments in their taxable income.

Section 401(k) Plans

Section 401(k) plans allow employees to authorize their employers to reduce their salary and contribute the salary reduction to an employer-sponsored qualified retirement plan. Employee contributions are made on a pre-tax basis. Employers may match a certain portion of the employees' contributions and deduct their contributions as business expenses.

Stock Option Plans

Stock option plans are benefit plans that are tied to an agency's stock value and that reward certain employees based on the increase in the value of the agency's stock. In a typical stock option plan, employees are given the right to purchase stock at a specified price within a specific time period. For example, 100 shares at $40 per share may be purchased at any time within a five-year period. If the employee exercises the option and the market price at time of purchase is higher than what the employee actually pays for the stock (options price), then the difference in prices (gain) is taxable income to the employee. Likewise, if the employee sells the stock and the sale price is higher than the option price, the difference in prices (gain) is also taxable income to the employee. The employer receives a corporate income tax deduction for compensation expense when the employee realizes compensation income from the stock plan. Because most insurance agencies are closely held and no independent market value can be determined, these types of plans are rare, except in very large agencies or public brokerages.

Lease Arrangements

Besides providing employee benefits, agency principals may consider other methods of decreasing income tax liabilities. One common method is to lease certain fixed assets, such as computer equipment, rather than purchase them. Leasing permits tax deduction of the full cost of leasing the asset (including land and residual values). Leasing also provides tax advantages to the asset owner by allowing deductions for asset depreciation to be accelerated as compared to deductions for asset depreciation of owned assets. Finally, leasing permits 100 percent financing, making financing charges tax-deductible business expenses and conserving cash and working capital. Many agencies find that leasing fixed assets provides the following additional benefits:

- Leasing permits rapid changes in equipment and reduces the risk of obsolescence.

- Leasing may be more flexible because lease agreements may contain less restrictive provisions than debt agreements.

- Leasing does not add debt to a balance sheet and does not affect financial ratios; therefore, it may increase borrowing capacity.

- Leasing can shift agency income to family members or key agency members who own the assets that are leased to the agency.

Although owning an asset may often be preferable to leasing it, leasing usually offers these advantages without corresponding tax disadvantages.

FINANCIAL ANALYSIS

Financial analysis involves using financial tests (or ratios) to evaluate an organization's financial performance and to compare organizational performance to industry benchmarks. Information from financial statements is used to calculate these ratios. Although financial analysts have developed many ratios in a number of categories, the following discussion is limited to ratios in three categories: profitability, liquidity, and efficiency.[4] (The average collection period ratio, discussed previously, evaluates asset use.)

Profitability Ratios

Profitability ratios are used to measure the firm's ability to earn an adequate return on sales, total assets, and invested capital.

Many problems related to profitability can be explained, in whole or in part, by a firm's ability to use its resources effectively. Profitability ratios are calculated using an agency's income statement and balance sheet. To be meaningful, they must be compared to industry or other external benchmarks. Profitability ratios appropriate for agencies include the net profit margin ratio, the return on assets (ROA) ratio, and the return on equity (ROE) ratio.

Profitability ratios
Tests of profitability that measure a firm's ability to earn an adequate return on sales, total assets, and invested capital.

Net Profit Margin Ratio

Profit margin ratios are used to assess the ability of the firm's management to control the various expenses involved in generating sales rather than the expenses involved in cost of goods sold. Because insurance agencies, unlike manufacturers, do not have cost of goods sold on their income statement, they generally use net profit margin to evaluate expenses. Net profit margin is calculated as follows:

$$\text{Net profit margin} = \frac{\text{Net income}}{\text{Sales}}.$$

Return on Assets (ROA) Ratio

The return on assets (ROA) ratio measures the firm's net income in relation to the assets invested to generate that net income. This ratio is useful in evaluating the overall effectiveness of the firm's management.

Return on assets is calculated as follows:

$$\text{Return on total assets} = \frac{\text{Net income}}{\text{Total assets}}.$$

Return on Equity (ROE) Ratio

The return on equity (ROE) ratio measures how the firm's net income compares to the owners' equity. The owners are interested in maximizing return on the money they have invested in the firm. Return on equity is calculated as follows:

$$\text{Return on equity} = \frac{\text{Net income}}{\text{Owner's equity}}.$$

Liquidity Ratios

Liquidity ratios
Tests of liquidity used to measure a firm's ability to satisfy short-term debt obligations as they are due.

Liquidity ratios help answer the question, "Does the firm have sufficient cash and near-cash assets to pay its bills on time?" Near-cash includes assets such as savings accounts, certificates of deposit, and marketable securities that can easily be converted to cash. **Liquidity ratios** are used to measure a firm's ability to satisfy short-term debt obligations as they are due. Liquidity ratios appropriate for agencies include the current ratio, the acid test ratio (insurance agency), and the accounts receivable and cash ratios.

Current Ratio

Current ratio
A ratio comparing a business's current assets to its current liabilities.

The primary measure of a firm's liquidity is the **current ratio**, so named because it compares the business' current assets to its current liabilities. The higher the firm's current ratio, the more easily the business can meet current obligations using current assets. The current ratio is calculated as follows:

$$\text{Current ratio} = \frac{\text{Current assets}}{\text{Current liabilities}}.$$

An agency's current ratio is considered good if it equals two or higher. An agency with a ratio of 2 has twice as many current assets as current liabilities.

Acid Test (Quick) Ratio

The **acid test (quick) ratio** is a commonly used balance sheet ratio. It measures not only a firm's liquidity position but also the safety margin of cash or near-cash assets that management maintains to allow for fluctuations in cash flow.

This ratio is often called the "quick" ratio because it deals with assets that can be quickly converted to cash. The acid test ratio is calculated as follows:

$$\text{Acid test ratio} = \frac{\text{Current assets} - \text{Inventory}}{\text{Current liabilities}}.$$

Current assets for most firms consist of cash, near cash, accounts receivable, and inventory. Because insurance agency inventory is usually negligible, an agency's current assets consist primarily of cash, near cash, and accounts receivable. The acid test ratio for an insurance agency is calculated as follows:

$$\text{Acid test ratio (insurance agency)} = \frac{\text{Cash} + \text{Accounts receivable} + \text{Near cash assets}}{\text{Current liabilities}}.$$

Acid test ratio interpretation should consider the proportion of various types of current assets. An agency with a high percentage of current assets in cash is more liquid than one with a high percentage of current assets in accounts receivable. The accounts receivable ratio and the cash ratio should, therefore, be used in conjunction with the acid test ratio.

Accounts Receivable and Cash Ratios

Assume that an agency collects $1.2 million in annual premiums, evenly distributed throughout the year ($100,000 in premiums per month) and that the agency's cash balance is $166,000. Further assume an average commission rate of 13 percent, accounts receivable of 4 percent of annual premiums (fifteen days), and an accounts current payable to the insurance company in sixty days (two months). Based on these assumptions, the agency will have $48,000 (0.04 × $1.2 million) in accounts receivable, $166,000 in cash, and accounts payable of $174,000 ($200,000 of premium minus 13 percent commission). Exhibit 3-6 shows the results of the accounts receivable, cash, and acid test ratios used in this example.

Acid test ratio, or **quick ratio**
A commonly used balance sheet ratio that measures a firm's liquidity position and the safety margin of cash or near-cash assets that management maintains to allow for fluctuations in cash flow.

The ratios cited for the agency in Exhibit 3-5 are excellent. Unfortunately, in some less successful agencies, the cash and accounts receivable figures are reversed, with outstanding receivables (the percentage of total assets in accounts receivable) being greater than that in cash. Under these conditions, the ratios would be as shown in Exhibit 3-6.

The acid test ratio is the same in both cases, but the agency in Exhibit 3-5 has much stronger liquidity. If an agency considers only its acid test ratio, it could be unaware of a severe accounts receivable problem. The agency illustrated in Exhibit 3-6, for example, has $166,000 in accounts receivable in a collection period of over fifty days.

EXHIBIT 3-5

Liquidity Ratios for the Example Agency

$$\text{Accounts Receivable Ratio (RR)} = \frac{\text{Accounts receivable (AR)}}{\text{Current liabilities (CL)}} = \frac{\$48,000}{\$174,000} = 0.28.$$

$$\text{Cash Ratio (CR)} = \frac{\text{Cash (C)}^*}{\text{Current liabilities (CL)}} = \frac{\$166,000}{\$174,000} = 0.95.$$

$$\text{Acid Test Ratio (A)} = \frac{C + AR}{CL} = \frac{\$166,000 + \$48,000}{\$174,000} = 1.23.$$

$$RR + CR = A; 0.28 + 0.95 = 1.23.$$

*Cash includes marketable securities and other near-cash assets.

EXHIBIT 3-6

Reversed Liquidity Ratios

$$RR = \frac{AR}{CL} = \frac{\$166,000}{\$174,000} = 0.95.$$

$$CR = \frac{C}{CL} = \frac{\$48,000}{\$174,000} = 0.28.$$

$$A = \frac{C + AR}{CL} = \frac{\$48,000 + \$166,000}{\$174,000} = 1.23.$$

$$RR + CR = A; 0.95 + 0.28 = 1.23.$$

Efficiency ratios
Tests of efficiency used to measure a firm's ability to use its resources.

Efficiency Ratios

Efficiency ratios indicate how well a firm is using its resources. They can reveal that even profitable agencies may not be efficient. Consequently, agencies should analyze their profitability ratios in conjunction with their efficiency ratios. The efficiency ratios appropriate for agencies include the cost per account ratio, the revenue per employee ratio, the retention ratio, and the expense ratio.

Cost Per Account Ratio

The cost per account ratio is calculated by dividing office or sales costs by the number of accounts the agency handles. Cost per account ratios can be expressed as either office cost per account or sales cost per account and are calculated as follows:

$$\text{Office cost per account} = \frac{\text{Office costs}}{\text{Number of accounts}}.$$

$$\text{Sales cost per account} = \frac{\text{Sales costs}}{\text{Number of accounts}}.$$

These ratios can be misleading because they ignore the fact that agency costs are mostly fixed. Therefore, most agencies can write additional accounts without increasing either sales or office costs. Writing additional accounts decreases the average cost per account. This does not mean that management should seek accounts that generate small premiums. Instead, the agency manager should examine actual costs of writing any account, large or small. Low-premium accounts can be profitable if the handling costs are low, and high-premium accounts can be unprofitable if handling costs are high.

Cost accounting, discussed previously, is necessary to determine whether a policy should be written when the premium is compared to the cost of handling the particular account.

Revenue Per Employee Ratio

The revenue per employee ratio also measures efficiency. The 2005 *Best Practices Study* shows a wide range of revenue per employee levels for agencies. For example, for agencies with revenues between $1.25 million and $2.5 million, the average revenue per employee was $124,059. For the top 25 percent of agencies in profitability, however, revenue per employee was over $165,000. This ratio varies based on agency size and focus (for example, personal versus commercial accounts). Exhibit 3-7 summarizes the results of the 2005 *Best Practices Study*. Revenue per employee is calculated as follows:

$$\text{Revenue per employee} = \frac{\text{Total revenue}}{\text{Number of employees}}.$$

EXHIBIT 3-7

Revenue Per Employee

Agency Size (by net revenue)	Average Agency	Top 25% Profitability	Top 25% Growth
Less than $500,000	$ 91,610	$118,078	$87,521
$500,000–1,250,000	124,059	127,452	121,322
$1,250,000–2,500,000	137,773	167,910	144,575
$2,500,000–5,000,000	141,027	162,525	150,155
$5,000,000–10,000,000	148,393	164,736	134,557
$10,000,000–25,000,000	157,192	177,473	142,503
Over $25,000,000	164,633	192,758	159,969

Adapted from the 2005 Best Practices Study. ©2005 Independent Insurance Agents and Brokers of America, Inc., and Reagan Consulting.

Retention Ratio

The retention ratio, also called retention rate, measures the rate at which the existing book of business is renewed during a particular period, usually a calendar year. Account retention rates can be determined by employee or department and are calculated as follows:

$$\text{Retention rate} = \frac{\text{\# of existing accounts at end of period*} - \text{\# of new business accounts written}}{\text{\# of existing accounts at beginning of period}}.$$

*Not including any new business written

Retention rates are influenced by the competitiveness of the agency's carriers, the quality of customer service, economic conditions, an insurer's willingness to write certain classes and lines of business, and other factors. The higher the retention ratio, the more efficient the agency operations.

Expense Ratio

The expense ratio for insurance agencies is calculated as follows:

$$\text{Expense ratio (insurance agencies)} = \frac{\text{Total agency expenses}}{\text{Commissions} + \text{Fee income}}.$$

In addition to commissions and fee income, the expense ratio could use net written premiums or total agency revenue as the denominator (bottom number in ratio). However, commissions and fee income more closely measure an agency's efficiency.

Some industry analysts believe that because the income statement measures the use of all assets, total agency revenue should be used. However, including contingent commissions, real estate commissions, and other income items may be misleading because it lowers the agency expense ratio.

Expenses in themselves have little meaning, but the ratio of expenses to revenues puts them in a perspective that can be used in decision making. If an agency principal wants to reduce the expense ratio, revenues must increase more than expenses, or expenses must decrease more than revenues.

VALUE OF AN AGENCY

Because an insurance agency has little physical inventory, its value is based largely on intangibles. The goodwill the agency has established in the community over time and the potential to renew the existing customer base are difficult items to set a precise value on. However, their values are among the things a buyer needs to know when considering purchasing an insurance agency.

The precise methods used to set a value on a particular insurance agency are beyond the scope of this text. When considering the sale or purchase of an agency, the potential seller or buyer should consult finance experts, agency consultants, legal counsel, and accountants who specialize in such matters. The following discussion highlights the items a prospective buyer should consider when evaluating an agency for purchase. These items include the following:

- Organization and operations
- Financial information
- Nonfinancial valuation factors
- Valuation methods

Organization and Operations

An agency's organization and operations are significant factors to consider in relation to an agency's value. An agency that is well-organized and efficiently operated efficiently has a greater value than an agency that is not. Prospective buyers examine certain aspects of an agency's organization, including its legal form of ownership and its operational organization.

An agency's legal form of ownership affects its value to a prospective buyer. For example, if a corporation is buying a partnership and wants to convert the partnership into a corporation, the corporation must consider any extra legal expenses involved in such a conversion. A prospective buyer should also consider the compatibility of the existing agency's organization with the buyer's desired operational organization. Business plans, policies, and procedures may have to be changed. Information technology (IT) and filing systems may not be compatible. The more operational organization changes that must be made, the less value the agency has to the prospective buyer. Furthermore, because employees sometimes resist change, making major operational changes can be expensive and time consuming.

Many different aspects of an agency's operations affect the agency's value. The following are some issues of primary concern to prospective buyers:

- *Companies represented.* A purchaser of an independent insurance agency is likely to place greater value on an agency if it represents the type of insurers the buyer is seeking and has good relations with those insurers. Sometimes agencies are purchased solely because of the insurers they represent.

- *Type of billings.* A buyer looking for insurer representation with a direct billing system might pay more for an agency that has a high percentage of direct-billed business. In contrast, an agency that has a high percentage of agency-billed business might be more valuable to a buyer seeking the higher commission levels and short-term investment opportunities usually associated with agency-billed business.

- *Relations with customers.* Customer relations are important. If one agency owner or producer controls a large block of business, that business may move to another agency if that individual leaves the agency. Some sales agreements stipulate that key personnel must remain with the agency for a certain period or the remaining purchase payments may be reduced.

  Average customer age is also a factor. For example, new producers may have trouble identifying with older customers. Additionally, older customers of personal insurance may be less likely to renew because of changing needs or because of a higher mortality rate within that group of customers than with other groups. The likelihood that the purchaser will renew existing business is a major consideration in agency valuation.

- *Errors and omissions.* A factor closely related to customer relations that also indicates the quality of an agency is the number of errors and omissions claims filed against it. A high number of errors and omissions claims lowers the agency's value.

- *New business potential.* One-policy customers are more likely to move their business to another agency than are multiple-policy customers. However, one-policy customers offer agencies a great opportunity to generate new business through the sale of additional insurance. Also, if the agency is located in a growing area and has a good community reputation, the potential for new business is increased.

Financial Information

An agency's financial information is a major consideration in determining agency value. Agency financial information includes information from the agency's balance sheet and income statement, as well as from additional sources.

Balance Sheet

The balance sheet is composed of assets, liabilities, and owners' equity. The agency's assets have a book value, or value shown on the balance sheet. Sometimes, book value is a valid measure, and sometimes it is not, as the following discussion about assets illustrates:

- *Cash and short-term investments.* Cash is the most liquid asset. The value of cash on hand and in the bank is its book value, which is its true value. Similarly, short-term investments are also usually worth their book value.

- *Accounts receivable.* The value of accounts receivable to a prospective buyer depends largely on how likely they are to be collected. If an agency has a significant portion of its assets in accounts receivable and a large percentage of the receivables are more than sixty days old, the value of the receivables drops dramatically. An aggressive collection policy and an average receivables age of fifteen days or less would, on the other hand, increase the value of receivables up to a maximum percentage of their book value.

- *Other assets.* Many other assets may affect an agency's value. An office equipped with modern and well-maintained facilities, communication equipment, and furnishings, increases the agency's value. An owned office building in a good location for the book of business written is also a positive factor, as is an up-to-date IT system that easily interfaces with other similar systems.

The value of real estate and other tangible property is shown on the balance sheet as the original purchase price minus any accumulated depreciation (for tax purposes). The book value then does not match the property's market value. A building, for example, is probably worth much more than the value shown on the balance sheet, but a five-year-old IT system is probably worth little, even though a value is included on the balance sheet.

Any current and long-term agency liabilities decrease the agency's value if the purchaser assumes the liabilities. For example, the accounts current, if assumed by a purchaser, decrease the agency's value because they must be paid relatively soon after agency purchase.

Finally, the book value of owners' equity is not normally equivalent to the actual agency value. An agency's purchase price includes its goodwill value of renewal business. This is likely the agency's greatest asset, even though it is not listed on the agency's balance sheet, because it yields income for years to come.

Income Statement

Income statements provide additional financial information that should be considered when determining an agency's value. The agency's income statement is probably the most important financial document used to determine its value because the agency's income-producing ability is the most important feature to a prospective purchaser. The income statement begins with revenues and deducts expenses to determine income.

The sources and quality of revenue are also very important to a prospective buyer. Sources of revenue include commissions, investment income, and other revenue.

- *Commissions.* Commissions are probably the largest revenue source, but not only the size of commissions is important. The percentage of commissions to written premiums and the trend of both actual commissions and commission percentages are also important. If an agency has a history of significant growth in the past five years and commissions as a percentage of written premiums are reasonably stable over the same period, that source of revenue is more valuable than a decreasing commission percentage.

  Also taken into consideration is any earned contingent commission. Because contingencies are typically based on the loss ratios and/or premium growth of the agency with the insurers represented, stable or growing contingency commissions are more valuable than a variable contingency commission. Some industry analysts, because of the variability of contingent commissions and agencies' lack of control over them, do not consider them when calculating agency value.

- *Investment income.* If an agency has a history of steady investment gain as a result of investing premiums from their receipt until payment to insurers, this revenue source can increase agency value.

- *Other revenue.* Other sources of revenue are fees for service, rentals, and real estate commissions. The value placed on these items depends on the prospective buyer. If a prospective buyer is interested in continuing fees for service, they are valuable. Similarly, if real estate sales commissions or other sources of miscellaneous revenue are to be a continuing part of the operations after purchase, they too are considered valuable assets.

An agency's expenses are a valuation factor to the extent that the prospective buyer considers them uncontrollable. For example, if clerical salaries are considered excessive, but the prospective buyer believes some employee positions can be consolidated or revenue can increase to cover expenses, the prospective buyer may not be concerned.

Additional Financial Information

Five types of additional financial information should be considered when determining an agency's value, as follows:

1. Cash flow
2. Billings
3. Mix of business
4. Loss ratio
5. Tax factors

Cash flow information includes cash flow size and timing. Many agencies make purchases based on their expected cash flows. In determining value, the significance of cash flow is based on the size and the timing of cash available to make payments to previous owners. Buyers naturally prefer large amounts of cash to be immediately available. Conversely, an agency with a substantial amount of accounts receivable over sixty days old has a reduced value because of the increased costs to carry the receivables and the increased risk of bad debts.

Billing transactions also affect an agency's value. The cost to bill a customer for a $25 installment payment is approximately the same as the cost to bill for a $5,000 annual payment. Therefore, the fewer the billings based on premium volume the better. Such billings reduce the agency's value. Additionally, the more billings the agency processes, the less efficient it is. For example, if each policy could be billed once instead of twice, the agency staff could handle a larger volume of business. A large number of billings may indicate that the agency finances a large percentage of business. The agency may find it difficult to have those financed customers pay on a cash-only basis.

Mix of business can also affect an agency's value. An agency that has 70 percent of its business in personal insurance is more attractive to a purchaser interested in an agency that sells primarily personal insurance; a purchaser seeking a new block of commercial business would place a lower value on this agency.

A purchaser may be looking for a volume of a specific type of business, such as homeowners. Examples of the mix of business buyers may want include the following:

* Property-casualty/life/employee benefits
* Commercial/personal
* General liability/commercial auto/workers' compensation
* Package/monoline
* Contractors (or any type of customer)/other commercial

Another type of financial information that should be considered when determining an agency's value is loss ratios. Loss ratios that are historically high (above 80 percent, for example) decrease agency value. An agency's loss ratio affects the size of its contingent commissions as well as its relations with insurers. However, a one- or two-year high ratio, in itself, can be insignificant because nearly every agency is subject to an occasional catastrophe loss.

Tax factors should also be considered when determining an agency's value. The selling price of most agencies is based partly on a noncompete agreement. A noncompete agreement, sometimes called a **covenant not to compete**, is an agreement in a sales contract made by the seller not to engage in insurance sales in the same geographic area as the agency for a specified period, such as three or five years.

Covenant not to compete
An agreement in a sales contract made by the seller not to engage in insurance sales in the same geographic area as the agency for a specified period, such as three or five years.

The selling price is also based on a valuation for the expiration list and agency goodwill. For example, a $1 million selling price might be apportioned as follows:

Noncompete agreement	$ 250,000
Expiration list	600,000
Goodwill	150,000
	$1,000,000

These three items, and others, are included in the IRS definition of "Section 197 intangibles." Section 197 intangibles, which are acquired in a transaction that results in a significant change in ownership and that are used in a trade or business, receive special tax treatment, detailed in IRS *Publication 535 Business Expenses*.[5] Because this information is subject to change and greatly affects an agency's value, it is best to check with a tax professional before any sale or purchase.

Nonfinancial Valuation Factors

Prospective buyers should also consider nonfinancial valuation factors when evaluating an agency for purchase. Although the list of nonfinancial factors is potentially endless, the most important are the employees, key employees, geographic representation, and subjective variables.

Employees

A well-compensated, motivated, highly productive group of employees is invaluable. Salary levels and fringe benefits should be at least competitive with other agencies in the area yet at a level the buyer can afford to maintain.

The employees' education, training, and production experience and potential are also important. Are the employees willing to accept education, and are they willing to try to sell more insurance? A "yes" answer can mean a higher agency value.

One major indication of the merits of current employees, in addition to compensation, is the turnover rate. If turnover is excessive, management problems may exist. If turnover appears high, a buyer should meet with the prospective seller to determine the nature and extent of any management or morale problems. People are so important to the success of an insurance agency that severe morale problems significantly lower the agency's value.

Key Employees

If key employees do not remain with an agency after its sale, then noncompete agreements in the sales agreement may not protect the new purchaser. The greater the likelihood of losing key employees, the lower the agency value. For example, a buyer may want to review whether any producers with large books of business have employment contracts with the agency. If not, there would be no reason for such a producer to remain with the agency after a sale. Additionally, a key administrative or operations staff member may be essential to the agency's daily operations. Such details would be important for a prospective buyer to identify prior to the sale.

Geographic Representation

Some buyers, particularly national brokerage firms, pay higher prices for agencies in geographic areas where they want to open an office. For example, an agency may want to acquire an office in an area with significant economic and business development, where new home construction is on the rise. Conversely, agencies may be worth less in areas where numerous national firms already have offices.

Subjective Variables

To a large extent, an agency's value is subjective and, in many cases, based on the buyer's needs. A well-managed agency with solid planning and organization, staffed with quality employees, directed by an efficient management team, and with excellent controls carries a higher value than one without those attributes. Similarly, a financially sound agency with few collection problems and a history of profitability is a valuable firm. But an agency's true value or what a prospective buyer is willing to pay is largely determined by the agency's profit potential as perceived by its buyer. If a buyer is not involved in determining an agency's value, the value should be determined by an expert. The actual terms of purchase are so varied that a discussion of them is beyond the scope of this text.

Valuation Methods

Several methods can be used to value insurance agencies. Many consultants offer specialized valuation services. Three commonly used valuation methods—the traditional method, the discounted present value method, and the publicly traded brokers multiple of earnings method—are discussed next.

Traditional Method

Traditionally, insurance agencies were valued using a multiple of commissions rather than net earnings. Agencies were said to be worth from one to two times annual commissions. This simplistic approach to valuation has two major shortcomings. First, it fails to focus on profitability. An agency that is highly profitable has the same value under this method as one that is losing money if both have the same amount of commission income. Second, it fails to discount payments. A sale at two times commission paid out in five years at little or no interest is treated the same as an all cash payment. Nevertheless, when adjusted for the factors discussed in this section, the traditional method provides a rough estimate of agency value and is still used in many transactions. Trade publications frequently carry advertisements of agencies for sale with the price stated in a multiple of commissions, and agents frequently discuss sale prices in those terms.

The 2003 edition of *What It Costs* shows that the average property and casualty commission revenue (not including life and health commissions, fees, contingent commission, or investment income) for agencies with $3 million to $5 million in revenues is $3,112,023.[6] Therefore, under the traditional method, the agency values would range from $3,112,023 to $6,224,046.

Discounted Present Value Method

The discounted present value method involves estimating the revenue the agency's book of business will generate over a specific period. For example, to determine the appropriate price to pay for a group of accounts, a buyer would estimate how much commission income that book of business would produce over a period of years. The amount of commission revenue would then be discounted because the actual payments would not be received immediately. This evaluation method is based on the general principle that a dollar to be received a year from now is worth less than a dollar received today.

Publicly Traded Brokers Multiple of Earnings Method

A publicly traded broker is one whose stock is currently listed on any of the stock exchanges. The publicly traded brokers multiple of earnings method of agency valuation is based on a selected multiple of the brokerage's stated earnings. Although publicly traded brokers are much larger than the average insurance agency, they are in some ways an assemblage of large local agencies. However, unlike a small agency, these firms often include such operations as third-party administration, risk management, and claim handling services. These significant differences between large brokerages and the typical agency make this valuation method the least appropriate.

Key Words and Phrases

Define or describe each of the words and phrases found in this assignment.

Profitability ratios (p. 3.39)

Liquidity ratios (p. 3.41)

Current ratio (p. 3.41)

Acid test ratio, or quick ratio (p. 3.42)

Efficiency ratios (p. 3.43)

Covenant not to compete (p. 3.49)

Review Questions

12. List two reasons a business organization might start as a proprietorship and later incorporate. (p. 3.37)

REVIEW

13. Describe six common employee benefit plans. (pp. 3.38–3.39)

14. What are six reasons that leasing fixed assets can be advantageous for an agency? (p. 3.40)

15. Compare the current ratio with the acid test ratio, or quick test ratio. (pp. 3.41–3.42)

16. Identify ways to calculate each of the following efficiency ratios: (pp. 3.43–3.46)

    a.   Cost per account

    b.   Revenue per employee

c.   Retention ratio

d.   Expense ratio

17. Describe the items a prospective buyer should consider when
    evaluating an agency for purchase. (pp. 3.46–3.53)

18. What are the commonly used methods of establishing the value of
    an agency? (pp. 3.52–3.53)

Application Questions

4. The Callaway Insurance Agency (Callaway) is considering purchasing another insurance agency, Danford Insurance (Danford). Fred, Callaway's owner, is evaluating Danford's financial performance. Assume the following for Danford:

Accounts receivable $ 50,000

Current liabilities $175,000

Cash $160,000

a.   Calculate Danford's accounts receivable ratio.

b.   Calculate Danford's cash ratio.

c.   Calculate Danford's acid test (quick) ratio.

d.   Based on your calculations in (a), (b), and (c), should Callaway continue its exploration of Danford as a possible acquisition target?

REVIEW

5. Determining the value of an agency when it is being considered for purchase is a very difficult task. Many factors must be considered, and there are no generally accepted principles for developing exact valuation. For each of the following, describe how it should be analyzed for valuation purposes.

   a. Income statement items

   b. Organization and operations

   c. Employees

Answers to Assignment 3 Questions

NOTE: These answers are provided to give students a basic understanding of acceptable types of responses. They often are not the only valid answers and are not intended to provide an exhaustive response to the questions.

Review Questions

12. The following are two reasons a business organization might start as a proprietorship and later incorporate:

    (1) Freedom from personal liability

    (2) Tax-free benefits, such as group life insurance

13. The following are six common employee benefit plans:

    (1) Bonus plans reward employees for profitable or positive performance.

    (2) Qualified profit sharing plans are special deferred sums the employer makes available to employees based on the business's profits.

    (3) Employee Stock Ownership plans (ESOPs) are qualified retirement plans designed to invest primarily in employer stock.

    (4) Deferred compensation plans are plans by which employers agree to pay employees in the future for work performed today.

    (5) Section 401(k) plans allow employees to authorize employers to reduce salary and contribute the salary reduction to an employer-sponsored qualified retirement plan.

    (6) Stock option plans are tied to agency's stock value and reward certain employees based on increases in the stock's value.

14. Leasing fixed assets can be advantageous for an agency for the following reasons:

    • Leasing permits tax deduction of the full cost of leasing the asset (including land and residual values) and provides tax advantages to the asset owner through acceleration of deductions.

    • Leasing permits 100 percent financing, thus conserving cash and working capital.

    • Leasing permits rapid changes in equipment and reduces the risk of obsolescence.

    • Leasing may be more flexible because lease agreements may contain less restrictive provisions than debt agreements.

    • Leasing does not add debt to a balance sheet and does not affect financial ratios; therefore, it may add to borrowing capacity.

    • Leasing can shift agency income to family members or key members of the agency that own the assets that are leased to the agency.

15. The current ratio is a primary measure of a firm's liquidity because it compares the current assets of a business to its current liabilities. The higher the firm's current ratio, the more easily it can meet current obligations using current assets. The acid test is a balance sheet ratio. It not only measures a firm's liquidity position but also includes assets that can quickly be turned into cash. A standard formula for the acid test ratio compares current assets less inventory to current liabilities.

16. Efficiency ratios are measured in the following ways:

a.
$$\text{Office cost per account} = \frac{\text{Office costs}}{\text{Number of accounts}}.$$

and

$$\text{Sales cost per account} = \frac{\text{Sales costs}}{\text{Number of accounts}}.$$

b.
$$\text{Revenue per employee} = \frac{\text{Total revenue}}{\text{Number of employees}}.$$

c.
$$\text{Retention ratio} = \frac{\text{Number of existing accounts at the end of period* + New business written during period}}{\text{Number of existing accounts at beginning of period}}.$$

*not including any new business written

d.
$$\text{Expense ratio} = \frac{\text{Total agency expenses}}{\text{Commissions + Fee income}}.$$

17. A prospective buyer should consider the following items when evaluating an agency for purchase:

- Organization and operations indicate the agency's efficiency.

- Financial information, including balance sheets, income statements, and financial ratios, provide information useful in determining an agency's value.

- Nonfinancial factors: Employees and key employees can indicate employee stability and competency; the agency's geographic representation and other subjective variables can also affect agency value.

- Valuation methods, such as the traditional, discounted present value, and multiple of earnings methods, are commonly used to value insurance agencies.

18. Commonly used methods of establishing the value of an agency include the following:

- The traditional method uses a multiple of commissions rather than net earnings.

- The discounted present value method estimates the revenue that the book of business will generate over a specific period.

- The publicly traded brokers multiple of earnings method uses a selected multiple of the earnings of publicly traded brokers.

REVIEW

Application Questions

4. a.
$$\text{Accounts Receivable Ratio (RR)} = \frac{\text{Accounts receivable (AR)}}{\text{Current liabilities (CL)}} = \frac{\$50,000}{\$175,000} = 0.28.$$

b.
$$\text{Cash Ratio (CR)} = \frac{\text{Cash (C)*}}{\text{Current liabilities (CL)}} = \frac{\$160,000}{\$175,000} = 0.91.$$

* Cash includes marketable securities and other near-cash assets.

c.
$$\text{Acid Test Ratio (A)} = \frac{C + AR}{CL} = \frac{\$160,000 + \$50,000}{\$175,000} = 1.2.$$

$$RR + CR = A; 0.28 + 0.95 = 1.23$$

d.   Based on the liquidity ratios measured in (a), (b), and (c), Danford should remain a target for possible acquisition by Callaway. It is keeping its receivables at a low ratio in proportion to its cash ratio. Additionally, its acid test ratio reinforces its liquidity in relation to its accounts receivable management.

5. The analysis of the following factors should be considered for agency valuation:

a.   Income statement items—It is important to analyze commission income and the trend in the average percentage commission. Levels of contingent commissions and investment income are also key factors. Some firms receive a significant amount of revenue from other sources, such as fees for service, rentals, and real estate commissions. These sources of income should be carefully investigated. Expenses are also important to examine, especially those that seem excessive or that the agency cannot control.

b.   Organization and operations—The type of organization has legal implications for the purchase. How the organization is operated and any changes in operations or staffing that will have to be made are also important characteristics. One important factor is the list of insurers that the agency represents. Other key factors are the agency's relationship with its customers and the general attributes of the customers. Finally, the new business potential of the agency is important, including its geographic range of operations.

c.   Employees—Well-compensated, motivated, and highly efficient employees are probably the best asset that can be purchased. If employee turnover has been low and if the employees seem willing to take on new challenges, the purchase should be profitable. This is particularly true of key employees, including producers with large books of business. The purchase should probably not be made if the employees are not considered a favorable factor.

SUMMARY

Financial management is the effective management of assets, liabilities, capital structure, revenue, and expenses. Agencies make financial decisions by assigning financial management responsibility and using the financial management process. Financial management seeks to maximize the value of the agency, and agencies can accomplish this goal by using the following steps in the financial management process:

1. Identify the current financial position
2. Analyze results of operations
3. Implement any necessary corrective action
4. Monitor the process and revise as needed

Revenue control is an important aspect of agency financial management. Agencies practice revenue control to comply with legal and regulatory requirements. Anticommingling laws are related to revenue control and frequently govern how agencies manage their operating accounts and personal accounts. Agencies achieve revenue control by examining the following areas:

- Accounting of premiums received
- Unearned commission reserve accounts
- Return commissions on brokered policies

Expense control is another important aspect of financial management. If an agency can control its expenses, its value and profitability can increase. Agencies control expenses through accounts receivable control, internal controls, expense measurement, expense analysis, and expense reduction, including time management and cost accounting.

For most agencies, accounts receivable comprise the largest portion of current assets, yet many agencies have no formal accounts receivable policy. The cost factors involved in establishing or evaluating an accounts receivable policy include the following:

- Surrendered opportunity cost of accounts receivable funds
- Increased accounts receivable collection cost
- Cost of borrowing to finance accounts receivable
- Increased bad debt expense
- Perceived commission losses from failure to extend credit

Agencies should develop accounts receivable policies because reducing average agency accounts receivable can result in significant savings and increase agency value. Agencies should evaluate the opportunity costs (advantages foregone as a result of accepting alternatives) associated with such policies.

To maximize their annual profit and overall value, agencies need to minimize their taxes. The legal form of an agency can affect its taxation. For example the decision of the agency's principal to be a sole proprietorship, partnership, limited liability company, corporation, or S-corporation affects how the agency is taxed.

Tax-advantaged employee benefit plans also help agencies minimize taxes. Employee benefit plans can provide incentives and reward employees for good performance. No employee benefit plan fits every situation, and taxation of plans varies. Producers and principals are encouraged to discuss such plans with tax experts and employee benefit plan specialists. Examples of employee benefit plans include the following:

- Bonus plans
- Qualified profit sharing plans
- Employee stock ownership plans (ESOPs)
- Deferred compensation plans
- Section 401(k) plans
- Stock option plans

Financial tests (or ratios) are used to measure an agency's financial performance and compare that agency's performance to industry benchmarks. Data derived from financial statements are used for these comparisons. The ratios calculated for a particular agency can be compared to selected industry benchmarks as a measure of performance and value.

Profitability ratios measure an agency's ability to earn an adequate return on sales, total assets, and invested capital. Profitability ratios include the following:

- Profit margin ratio
- Return on assets (ROA) ratio
- Return on equity ratio

Liquidity ratios measure an agency's ability to pay short-term debt obligations as they are due. Liquidity ratios include the following:

- Current ratio
- Acid test ratio, or quick ratio
- Accounts receivable and cash ratios

Efficiency ratios measure an agency's ability to use its resources efficiently. Efficiency ratios include the following:

- Cost per account ratio
- Revenue per employee ratio
- Retention ratio
- Expense ratio

Because an insurance agency has little physical inventory, an agency's value is based largely on intangibles, such as the agency's goodwill standing in the community. Therefore, factors that can affect an agency's valuation include:

- Organization and operations
- Financial information
- Nonfinancial valuation factors
- Valuation methods

Among the ways an agency's value can be determined are the traditional method, based on the agency's annual commission earnings; the discounted present value method, which estimates that the agency's current book of business revenue changes over time; and the publicly traded brokers multiple of earnings method, which estimates agency value using a multiple of the earnings of publicly traded brokers.

Understanding financial management is vital to an agency's survival. The next and final assignment in this segment discusses additional topics essential for producers to understand in order to conduct their business operations in an ethical and professional manner, including insurance regulation, the specifics of errors and omissions insurance, and producer ethics and professionalism.

ASSIGNMENT NOTES

1. Independent Insurance Agents and Brokers of America of America, Inc., and Reagan Consulting, Inc., *2005 Best Practices Study: Executive Update to the Best Practices of the Leading Independent Insurance Agencies in the United States* (Alexandria, Va.: Independent Insurance Agents and Brokers of America, Inc., 2005), www.iiaba.org (accessed March 17, 2006).

2. *What It Costs* (Carmel, Ind.: Rough Notes Co., 2003 [biennial]).

3. IIABA, *2005 Best Practices Study*.

4. Adapted, in part, from Stanley B. Block and Geoffrey A. Hirt, *Foundations of Financial Management* (New York: Mc-Graw-Hill/Irwin, a business unit of the McGraw-Hill Companies, Inc., 2005), pp. 2.4–6.5.

5. *What It Costs* (Carmel, Ind.: Rough Notes Co., 2003), p. 22.

6. Available on line at the Internal Revenue Service Web site, www.irs.gov (accessed April 25, 2006).

Appendix

Collections

COLLECTIONS

The purpose of a collection system is to collect money owed to the agency without alienating the insured. In this section, we will answer the following questions:

- Who should do the collecting?
- What are the steps to developing an effective collection system?
- When should you collect?
- Why must every agency set a goal concerning collections?

OVERVIEW

Who should do the collecting?

One staff person should be responsible for the collection system. This person should be the bookkeeper, financial manager, or another individual in the accounting department.

Do not involve the producer in collecting unpaid premiums. It takes away from the producer's time to devote to sales.

What are the steps to developing an effective collection system?

1. Appoint a responsible collection manager.
2. Establish a list of key accounts (the agency's largest and best accounts), which are not subject to automatic collection rules. These accounts receive special attention by telephone from the collection manager.
3. Establish an agreement with CSRs and anyone who processes new and renewal policies that a policy inception date cannot go by without a binder and a billing.
4. Proceed to get payment within 15 days of the renewal date, or issue a notice of cancellation directly to the insured (with the exception of previously agreed-upon key accounts). Use either an automated aged-accounts receivable printout or your manual bookkeeping system.
5. Educate all producers, agency staff people, and insureds regarding the collection policy of the agency.
6. All existing past-due accounts must be called, then followed up by a letter that advises them to pay the balance due within 10 days or pay a substantial deposit and sign an installment notice for the balance. If you have some bad accounts, it's wiser to cancel them and turn the balance over to an attorney immediately for collection. Waiting only makes matters worse from a collection standpoint.

When should you collect?

New and Renewal Business. The producer must tell the insured exactly what the collection policy of the agency is, how it works, and that company credit procedures do not allow the agency to make exceptions.

The producer must collect at least 25% or more of the premium with this binder. (Make sure insureds understand what is meant by needing this amount now to "bind the contract.")

If the binder is mailed with invoice attached, be sure to explain the need for the deposit "by return mail, to bind the contract" You may wish to type on the binder "If payment is not received within 15 days after effective date, this coverage will be rescinded."

In the event that the insured cannot pay the full premium within 15 days of the effective date, suggest premium financing.

If the balance is not paid within the time frame given, send a direct notice of cancellation if you have the authority to do so; if not, request that the company send direct notice. (Companies usually ask for a written request.)

Recommend to the insured that a due date on the first of the month might be advantageous because:

- For the insured, this simplifies payroll reporting, and makes for timely installment billings and uniformity of handling.
- For the agency, there's an average of 15 days of additional investment income, it's easier to collect, and it conforms to agency accounting procedures.

Endorsements, Audits, Installments. Since the credit period your agency receives to collect this type of additional premium is usually shorter than that given on a new or renewal premium, it is imperative that the request for payment be stated very clearly when an endorsement, audit, or installment is sent out or delivered to the insured.

Remember:

- Audits are fully earned and often cannot be turned back to the company for direct collection.
- Installments, if not collected when due, can result in an earned premium larger than the deposits when you finally do cancel. These may not be collectible.
- Endorsements, if not collected when charged, may end up being due at the end of the policy period, when it's likely they cannot be collected.

Why must every agency establish a goal concerning collections?

There are three reasons why this is important:

1. Bad debts are bottom-line losses.
2. Large account receivable balances reduce interest income.
3. Unpaid accounts turned back to the company indicate bad management practices to the company, often resulting in canceled contracts or stricter underwriting attitudes.

Let's look at the steps that occur during a 30-day cycle:

1-31 DAYS: Producer orders invoice

Policy inception date

15 DAYS: Reminder letter sent

Direct notice of cancellation or picks up policies to return to company for flat cancellation

30 DAYS: Date agency responsible for paying premium

These reminder letters may be sent to an insured who has not paid within five days after policy inception.

Used with permission from Insurance Marketing & Management Services (IMMS).

Direct Your Learning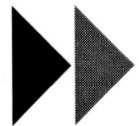

Producers' Legal and Ethical Responsibilities

Educational Objectives

After learning the content of this assignment, you should be able to:

1. Describe the purpose of each of the federal and state regulations governing insurance.

2. Describe the causes of insurance errors and omissions (E&O) claims.

3. Describe the sources of an insurance agent's legal responsibilities.

4. Describe an insurance agency's common-law duties to its customers, insurers, and others.

5. Describe the measures used to control E&O loss exposures.

6. Describe the coverage features commonly available to producers through agents and brokers professional liability insurance.

7. Explain why certain coverage variations should be considered when selecting agents and brokers professional liability insurance.

8. Describe the nature of ethics, ethical decision making, and codes of ethics.

9. Describe the seven characteristics that make a producer a professional.

10. Define or describe each of the Key Words and Phrases for this assignment.

 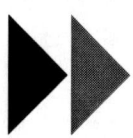

Develop Your Perspective

What are the main topics covered in the chapter?

The business of insurance is primarily subject to state regulation. However, federal regulations, common law, and potential errors and omissions (E&O) loss exposures also create significant frameworks within which producers and agencies must operate. Beyond laws and regulations, Codes of ethics and characteristics of professionalism define the ideal behaviors of producers and agencies.

Compare insurance functions governed by federal regulations to those governed by state regulations.

▶ In general, what types of business or insurance activities fall within these two governing bodies?

▶ How are the regulations from these governing bodies separate and distinct?

Why is it important to learn about these topics?

Compliance with regulation is a crucial operating function in insurance because insurance serves the public interest. Producers who maintain a high level of professionalism and ethical behavior can enhance the image of insurance practitioners and the entire insurance industry.

Examine how ethical and professional practices transcend compliance to federal and state insurance regulation.

▶ Why is ethical behavior difficult to define and why does it involve gray areas of conduct?

▶ Why is ethical and professional behavior characteristic of an insurance professional?

How can you use what you will learn?

Consider your approach if you were asked to mentor a new insurance producer regarding legal and ethical responsibilities.

▶ What state and federal regulations are most likely to affect the producer's activities immediately?

▶ What activities should the producer perform to prevent E&O claims?

▶ Explain how a producer can incorporate the seven characteristics of professionalism into his or her daily activities.

Producers' Legal and Ethical Responsibilities

Outline

- ▶ **Insurance Regulation**
  - A. Federal Regulations Affecting Insurance Producers
    1. Securities and Exchange Commission (SEC)
    2. Federal Emergency Management Agency (FEMA)
    3. Department of Transportation (DOT)
    4. Fair Credit Reporting Act
    5. Gramm-Leach-Bliley Act
    6. Electronic Signatures in Global and National Commerce Act (ESIGN)
    7. USA Patriot Act
    8. Sarbanes-Oxley Act
    9. CAN-SPAM Act
    10. Telemarketing and Consumer Fraud and Abuse Prevention Act and the Do Not Call Implementation Act
    11. Telephone Consumer Protection Act
  - B. State Regulations Affecting Insurance Producers
    1. Licensing Laws
    2. Unfair Trade Practices Acts
    3. Unfair Claims Settlement Practices Acts
    4. Handling Premiums
    5. Dealing With Suitable Insurers
- ▶ **Errors and Omissions (E&O)**
  - A. Causes of Errors and Omissions Claims
    1. Common External Causes
    2. Common Internal Causes
  - B. Sources of an Insurance Agent's Legal Responsibilities

- C. Agency's Common-Law Duties
    1. Agency's Common-Law Duties Owed to Customers
    2. Agency's Common-Law Duties Owed to Its Insurer
    3. Agency's Common-Law Duties to Others
- D. Controlling E&O Loss Exposures
    1. Measures to Prevent E&O Losses
    2. Measures to Help Defend Against E&O Claims
- E. Agents and Brokers Professional Liability Insurance
    1. Coverage Features
    2. Variations Among E&O Policies
- ▶ **Ethics and the Producer**
  - A. Nature of Ethics
  - B. Ethical Decision Making
  - C. Codes of Ethics
- ▶ **Professionalism**
  - A. Commitment to High Ethical Standards
  - B. Attitude of Altruism
  - C. Mandatory Educational Preparation and Training, and Mandatory Continuing Education
  - D. Membership in a Formal Association or Society
  - E. Independence of Action
  - F. Public Recognition as a Profession
- ▶ **Producer as a Professional**
- ▶ **Summary**
- ▶ **Appendix A**
- ▶ **Appendix B**
- ▶ **Appendix C**

Producers' Legal and Ethical Responsibilities

The major legal and ethical responsibilities of insurance producers fall into three categories. First, producers have a responsibility to obey the laws and regulations that govern their business activities. Failure to meet this legal responsibility may cause loss of license and other penalties. The first part of this assignment deals with regulation of insurance on the federal and state levels. The laws and regulations pertaining to insurance provide minimum standards of acceptable behavior with which agency personnel should comply. (Note that in this assignment the terms "producer," "agent," and "broker" all represent a seller of insurance to a customer on an insurer's behalf. Depending on various legal and contractual factors present in the relationship, the specific terms may be used interchangeably. Unless otherwise noted, this assignment uses the term "producer" to describe sellers.)

Second, producers have a responsibility to avoid errors and omissions (E&O) that could cause a loss to the customers or insurers they represent. After examining a sample of the types of errors and omissions losses that can occur, this assignment explores ways to control E&O loss exposures and examines E&O insurance—an essential coverage for agencies.

Third, producers have a responsibility to behave ethically, according to a standard of conduct higher than mere adherence to the law and avoidance of errors and omissions. Codes of ethics specify minimum ethical behavior standards for insurance practitioners who subscribe to them. The codes of ethics discussed in this assignment also provide an established set of behavior standards that individuals not bound by the codes may use as a guide.

Professionalism goes beyond adopting a set of behavior standards. The final section of this assignment describes the nature of professionalism and the characteristics of a professional.

INSURANCE REGULATION

Unlike regulation of other interstate businesses, regulation of insurance rests with the states rather than the federal government. This is largely the result of the McCarran-Ferguson Act (Public Law 15), a federal law passed in 1945.[1] In passing the act, the United States Congress expressed the belief that continued state regulation of insurance was in the public interest. Therefore, no act of Congress is to be "construed to invalidate, impair, and supersede any law enacted by any state for the purpose of regulating the business of insurance, or which imposes a fee or tax upon such businesses."[2] Federal laws apply to insurance only to the extent that state regulations do not apply.

Federal Regulations Affecting Insurance Producers

No federal legislation enacted since 1945 has attempted to specifically regulate the relationship between policyholders and privately owned insurers (including the Gramm-Leach-Bliley Act of 1999, which reaffirmed the McCarran-Ferguson Act). Nevertheless, many federal regulations of several federal agencies affect the daily activities of insurance producers.

Securities and Exchange Commission (SEC)

The Securities and Exchange Commission (SEC) is a federal regulatory agency for the securities industry whose responsibility is to protect investors and maintain the integrity of the securities markets. Because of an exception in the securities laws, the SEC does not have regulatory authority over the sale of most life insurance. However, the Supreme Court has ruled, for regulatory purposes, that variable life insurance and variable annuities are "securities" rather than insurance policies. To sell these products legally, a producer must hold a federal securities license and abide by federal regulations. Property-casualty insurance does not have any investment features that would subject it to federal securities laws.

Federal Emergency Management Agency (FEMA)

The purpose of the Federal Emergency Management Agency (FEMA), a part of the Department of Homeland Security's Emergency Preparedness and Response Directorate, is to prepare the nation for all hazards that can potentially cause major loss of life and of property and to effectively manage federal response and recovery efforts after any national incident. FEMA also initiates mitigation activities, trains first responders, and manages the National Flood Insurance Program (NFIP) and the U.S. Fire Administration. In administering the NFIP, FEMA sets the insurance rates, coverage limits, and eligibility requirements for flood insurance. Any licensed producer may place insurance through the NFIP, either directly or indirectly, using private insurers as servicing companies.

Department of Transportation (DOT)

The Department of Transportation (DOT) is a federal department established to ensure a fast, safe, efficient, accessible, and convenient transportation system in the U.S. The department does not regulate insurance producers. However, DOT regulations affect insurance because they specify limits of insurance that commercial truckers must carry in different cargo and usage circumstances. The Motor Carrier Act of 1980 substantially increased the effect of these regulations on insurance sales. A producer who insures commercial vehicles must be aware of applicable DOT regulations and provide a trucker with all prescribed insurance.

Fair Credit Reporting Act

The Fair Credit Reporting Act of 1970 is a federal law enforced by the Federal Trade Commission. The law's purpose is to protect consumers from the disclosure of inaccurate and arbitrary personal information held by consumer reporting agencies and to establish procedures for reporting and correcting credit record mistakes.[3] The act requires an insurer to inform an insurance applicant in advance if it intends to order various consumer reports. In addition to credit and claim history, these reports may also contain information about an applicant's lifestyle, habits, personal character, and reputation. When an insurer acts based on information contained in these reports, the applicant has the right to ask the insurer which company provided the information. The consumer reporting company must then inform the applicant of its findings. The applicant can challenge the information. The applicant's version of the information must be added to the file by the reporting company and given to those who inquire about that individual.

Because insurance agencies and brokerages submit insurance applications, the producer may be responsible for providing appropriate notice to the applicant that various consumer reports may be obtained as part of the application process. Most insurance applications contain written disclosure notices and require the applicant to acknowledge the notice.

E&O Alert!

Although insurance producers are subject to federal laws regarding consumer information, some states have their own fair credit reporting acts with more stringent disclosure requirements than the federal law. Producers must comply not only with federal law but also with state laws. Some consumer reporting companies have developed training courses for producers that detail consumer protection requirements imposed by state law and the Fair Credit Reporting Act.

Gramm-Leach-Bliley Act

The Financial Services Modernization Act of 1999, also called the Gramm-Leach-Bliley Act, is a federal law that promotes affiliation and diversification in the nation's financial banks, insurers, and brokerages and protects consumers' personal financial information held by financial institutions.[4] The act allows banks, insurance agencies, and brokerages to have ownership interest in one another, a right that did not exist previously in all states. Additionally, the act requires all financial institutions, including insurance agencies, to establish policies about how to collect and disclose nonpublic personal financial information about customers.

Gramm-Leach-Bliley also strongly urged that a minimum of twenty-nine states adopt reciprocity agreements to process nonresident producer licenses within three years of the act's passage or that an alternative mechanism be established to accomplish that goal. Reciprocity provisions were included in the National Association of Insurance Commissioners (NAIC) Producer Licensing Model Act (PLMA) of 2000. By January 2002, thirty-nine states had adopted either the PLMA or other nonresident producer reciprocity licensing laws, making federal government intervention unnecessary.

Electronic Signatures in Global and National Commerce Act (ESIGN)

The Electronic Signatures in Global and National Commerce Act (ESIGN) of 2000 is a federal law designed to facilitate the use of electronic records and signatures in interstate and foreign commerce by ensuring the validity and legal effect of contracts entered into electronically.[5] ESIGN declares the validity of electronic signatures for interstate and international commerce (including insurance transactions), prohibits denial of the legal effect of certain electronic documents and transactions signed with an electronic signature, and clarifies the circumstances under which an electronic record satisfies any statute or regulation that mandates a record in writing.

USA Patriot Act

The USA Patriot Act of 2001, enacted after the September 11, 2001, terrorist attacks, makes it harder for terrorists, other criminal entities, and individuals to engage in money-laundering activities.[6] The law requires financial institutions to establish anti-money-laundering programs by assigning a compliance officer, training employees to detect money laundering, conducting annual independent audits, and establishing policies and procedures to identify money-laundering risks and minimize opportunities for abuse. Property-casualty and health operations of insurers, insurance agents, and brokers are exempt from the Patriot Act's anti-money-laundering regulations. The reporting and compliance requirements apply to life insurers but not directly to life insurance agents. However, life insurers may integrate agents into their compliance programs.

Sarbanes-Oxley Act

The purpose of the Sarbanes-Oxley Act of 2002, officially called the Corporate and Auditing Accountability, Responsibility, and Transparency Act, was to introduce reforms to enhance corporate responsibility, enhance financial disclosures, and combat corporate and accounting fraud.[7] The act applies to companies listed on U.S. stock exchanges; companies otherwise obligated to file reports under the Securities and Exchange Act; and officers, employees, contractors, subcontractors, and agents of those companies. These categories include most insurers and a few large insurance agencies and brokerages. The act addresses accounting and financial reporting abuses by tightening internal accounting controls and holding company executives responsible for financial misdeeds. The act is also designed to reduce conflicts of interest between external audit firms and the companies they audit, as well as to increase the independence of board members.

CAN-SPAM Act

The CAN-SPAM Act of 2003 (Controlling the Assault of Non-Solicited Pornography and Marketing Act) addresses the problem of unsolicited commercial e-mail (spam). The act applies to "any electronic mail message whose primary purpose is to commercially advertise or promote a commercial product or service."[8] Such e-mail messages, unless exempt from the act, should include a notice that the message is an advertisement or solicitation, a notice of the opportunity to opt out of future commercial messages, and a valid physical postal address of the sender. The act exempts messages to a firm's customers that facilitate, complete, or confirm a commercial transaction. Insurance producers who have already established business with current customers and are electronically corresponding regarding insurance transactions or the general insurance relationship are exempt from the act. However, customer correspondence that is obviously an advertisement for a new product not previously discussed should comply with the act and include the opt-out notice.

Telemarketing and Consumer Fraud and Abuse Prevention Act and the Do Not Call Implementation Act

The Telemarketing and Consumer Fraud and Abuse Prevention Act of 1994 is the primary federal law governing telemarketers.[9] Its regulations include prohibiting repeated calls or prolonged conversation, limiting calls to between 8 AM and 9 PM daily, and requiring telemarketers to reveal their identities and the purpose of the call.

Under authority granted to the Federal Trade Commission (FTC), the Telemarketing Sales Rule portion of the Telemarketing Consumer Fraud and Abuse Prevention Act was amended in 2002 to include national do-not-call regulations. The Do Not Call Implementation Act of 2003 authorizes the FTC to implement and enforce the do-not-call provisions of the Telemarketing Sales Rule and to impose fees on telemarketer violations to pay for the national do-not-call registry.[10] The FTC maintains a do-not-call registry in which consumers can enroll to indicate their unwillingness to accept unsolicited telemarketing calls. Businesses are prohibited from calling a consumer listed in the registry for the purpose of selling a product or service. Exceptions are made for established business relationships. Many states have implemented separate do-not-call registries for consumers that may be subject to rules different from the federal rules. Insurance agencies that make cold calls to prospects should carefully research these federal and state laws.

Federal Laws That Affect Insurance Producers

McCarran-Ferguson Act (Public Law 15)

Establishes that insurance regulation rests with the states rather than the federal government.

Fair Credit Reporting Act

Protects consumers from the disclosure of inaccurate and arbitrary personal information held by consumer reporting agencies and establishes procedures for reporting and correcting credit record mistakes; enforced by the Federal Trade Commission.

Financial Services Modernization Act of 1999/Gramm-Leach-Bliley Act

Promotes affiliation and diversification in the nation's financial banks, insurers, and brokerage firms and includes privacy requirements that protect consumers' personal financial information held by financial institutions.

Electronic Signatures in Global and National Commerce Act (ESIGN)

Facilitates the use of electronic records and signatures in interstate and foreign commerce by ensuring the validity and legal effect of contracts entered into electronically.

USA Patriot Act

Makes it harder for terrorists, other criminal entities, and individuals to engage in money-laundering activities.

Sarbanes-Oxley Act

Criminalizes many corporate acts, including accounting abuses, that were previously relegated to various regulatory authorities.

CAN-SPAM Act

Addresses the problem of unsolicited commercial e-mail (spam).

Telephone Consumer Protection Act

The "Junk Fax Law" addresses the problem of unsolicited ads sent to a telephone facsimile machine or computer.

Telephone Consumer Protection Act

The Telephone Consumer Protection Act of 1991, also known as the "Junk Fax Law," deals with the issue of unsolicited advertisements sent to telephone facsimile machines, computers, or other devices.[11] The key word is "unsolicited," because not all ads sent to fax machines are unsolicited. The law defines an unsolicited advertisement as any material advertising the commercial availability or quality of any property, goods, or services that is transmitted to any person without that person's prior express invitation or permission.

The act, enforced by the Federal Trade Commission (FTC), requires any message sent to a fax machine to display the following information on the first page or on each page:

- Identity of the sender
- Date and time of transmission
- Telephone or fax number of sender

Producers should ensure that their solicitations comply with the act and that any fax advertisements include an opt-out or do-not-call provision.

State Regulations Affecting Insurance Producers

Insurance activities in each state are regulated by a state insurance department. The names for the state regulatory agencies vary. In some states, the insurance regulatory unit is combined with the regulatory unit for another industry, such as banking. In this text, state regulating agencies are called insurance departments, and the individuals who head those departments are called commissioners.

Insurers and insurance producers are often subject to state regulatory constraints. Five areas of state regulation that directly affect producers are the following:

1. Licensing laws
2. Unfair trade practices acts
3. Unfair claims settlement practices acts
4. Regulations governing the handling of premiums
5. Regulations governing dealing with suitable insurers

Licensing Laws

Producers must be licensed in each state in which they transact business. Those who operate without a license are subject to civil and, possibly, criminal penalties. Those states that have adopted the NAIC's Producer Licensing Model Act have replaced the license classifications of agent and broker with the single license classification of producer. Some states issue separate agent, broker, and solicitor licenses; others issue only agents' licenses, in which case brokers become agents of the particular insurer involved in each transaction. Still other states issue combined agent/broker licenses, and the status of the transactor is determined by an agency agreement. Most states require separate licenses for insurance agencies that operate as corporations, partnerships, or other legal entities.

E&O Alert!

The definition of "transact" varies by state. However, most jurisdictions require a license to conduct the following activities:

- Solicit applications for insurance

- Negotiate before a contract of insurance is executed

- Execute a contract of insurance

- Transact any insurance matters subsequent to executing the original contract

Agencies have been fined for failing to license producers and other agency support personnel who are considered to "transact" business, as defined by the state's insurance code.

All states require producers to pass an examination sponsored by the insurance department that is administered either by the department or by an independent testing service. States differ in the difficulty of their exams and the number of exams an applicant must pass to sell particular lines of insurance. Some states require applicants to complete some classroom training before taking the license examination. Some states waive the exam for applicants who take an exam similar to the department exam after completing an approved course or who hold certain professional insurance designations. Some states have reciprocal agreements whereby that state's exam is waived for producers who have met the requirements in other states. However, those states that have implemented the PLMA have standards for who should be licensed, license classifications, lines of authority, and license applications.

Licenses generally have a term of one or two years but are usually renewed with payment of a fee. Most states, however, have introduced mandatory continuing education or reexamination requirements that producers must satisfy to renew their licenses. In 1978, the NAIC adopted a model regulation establishing continuing education requirements, but states requiring continuing education set their own standards.

Countersignature laws
Laws that require all policies covering subjects of insurance within a state to be signed by a resident producer licensed in that state.

All but a few states have eliminated their **countersignature laws**, which required all policies covering subjects of insurance within a state to be signed by a resident producer licensed in that state.

Management Tip

Although required continuing education is a controversial issue—due, in part, to the time and expense involved in relation to the perceived benefit—producers who want to be viewed as professionals should not rely on the state to determine the proper level of training and education. Continuing, goal-oriented professional development should be part of every agency employee's job and is more important than ever in today's competitive environment.

Provisions of countersignature laws may require that the resident producer be paid some fraction (usually 25 to 50 percent) of the total commission. These laws are facing strong challenges and are being eliminated because some regulators believe they are archaic and unnecessary, and some courts believe them to be unconstitutional restrictions on interstate commerce.

Specific regulations affecting producer licensing vary by state. This text does not describe all these regulations. Licensed producers should know the applicable licensing regulations affecting their business operations.

E&O Alert!

Every agency and brokerage should have a current copy of the state insurance code or know where to find it on the Internet. This code is an important reference tool for determining acceptable actions and agency procedures. Many state insurance departments have Web sites where producers can access the current insurance code and download both the text of the law and any applicable regulations.

Unfair Trade Practices Act

Other state regulations that directly affect producers involve unfair trade practices. **Unfair trade practices** are methods of competition or advertising or procedures that tend to deprive the public of information needed to make informed insurance decisions. Individuals engaging in any unfair trade practices may be subject to cease and desist orders, loss of licenses, or heavy fines.

The NAIC has developed a model act relating to unfair trade practices in the business of insurance. All states have laws based on the model Act. A portion of this act is found in Appendix A of this assignment.

Exhibit 4-1 defines unfair trade practices common to the NAIC Model Act and many state laws. Although states vary in how they address these practices, the Model Act represents a consensus regarding practices in which producers should not engage and for which they may incur penalties. All producers transacting insurance in a particular state must carefully examine the provisions of that state's unfair trade practices act.

Unfair trade practices
Methods of competition or advertising or procedures that tend to deprive the public of information necessary to make informed insurance decisions.

EXHIBIT 4-1

Common Unfair Trade Practices

Misrepresentation and/or False Advertising   An insurer's written or oral statement that does not accurately describe an insurance policy's coverage or benefits.

Defamation   A false, malicious, or abusive written or oral communication that harms another's reputation or character.

Boycott, Coercion, or Intimidation   The act of compelling an insurance consumer to purchase from a particular producer or insurer.

Twisting   The unethical act of persuading a policyholder to cancel or replace a policy solely to sell another policy, without regard to possible negative consequences to the policyholder.

Rebating   The act of providing the buyer of an insurance policy a portion of the amount of the policy premium he or she paid (or the producers' commission) or anything of significant tangible value in return for purchasing the policy (permitted in some states, such as California and Florida, under certain conditions).

Unfair Claims Settlement Practices Acts

Another kind of regulation that directly affects producers is unfair claims settlement practices regulation. Both the NAIC Model Act and state unfair trade practices acts contain a separate section dealing with unfair claim settlement practices, and most states have adopted versions of them. The purpose of these laws is to protect insureds and claimants during the claim filing, investigation, and settlement process. Although many of these laws concern insurers and their claim representatives, they also affect insurance producers. Most unfair claims practices regulations set specific time frames for communicating with claimants and policyholders. These time frames are binding on producers as well as on insurers. Improperly handling claims can expose the agency to regulatory penalties as well as to errors and omissions claims. Exhibit 4-2 summarizes the unfair claims settlement practices to which state laws commonly apply.

Handling Premiums

Premium handling regulations also directly affect producers. A producer collects insurance premiums on the insurer's behalf and acts as the insurer's fiduciary for these premiums. In many states, the premiums must be kept in a separate trust account and must not be commingled with other personal or business funds. Failure to comply with this requirement can subject the producer to civil and criminal penalties, including fines, loss of license, and imprisonment.

EXHIBIT 4-2

Common Unfair Claims Settlement Practices

- Knowingly misrepresenting policy provisions to a claimant or insured at the time of the claim
- Failing to promptly acknowledge pertinent communications about a claim
- Failing to adopt and use reasonable standards for settling claims
- Attempting to settle claims late and/or unfairly when the insurer's liability has become reasonably clear
- Failing to affirm or deny coverage of a claim within a reasonable period after receiving a proof of loss statement
- Attempting to settle a claim for less than could be reasonably expected, according to public advertising material
- Failing to offer a reasonable and accurate explanation for denying a claim
- Compelling policyholders to file suit to recover amounts due them by offering them substantially less than the amounts that could be recovered by litigation
- Refusing to pay claims while conducting a reasonable investigation based on all available information
- Engaging in activities that result in a disproportionate number of complaints against the insurer received by the state insurance departments
- Failing to provide necessary claim forms promptly, including explanations about how to use the forms effectively

E&O Alert!

Although most of the issues addressed by claims settlement practices acts involve insurers rather than producers, any action or inaction on the producer's part that impairs the insurer's ability to handle a claim may cause an E&O loss for the agency or brokerage.

Consider these real-life scenarios: A producer was found guilty on federal charges after a routine audit by the department of insurance revealed that premiums were being diverted for the producer's personal use. In addition to sanctions by the department, the producer was sentenced to a federal prison term. In another incident, a producer who collected premiums from customers but failed to remit them to the insurer had his license revoked. The misappropriation of premiums and breach of the agent's fiduciary duty will invariably cause severe penalties as well as loss of customers and damaged business reputation.

Dealing With Suitable Insurers

State regulations governing relations with suitable insurers also directly affect producers. The purpose of these regulations is to prohibit producers from writing insurance with insurers not licensed or admitted to do business in the state, unless the producers have special licenses to do so, or unless they broker the insurance through an individual or entity that is licensed. Producers involved in an insurance transaction without complying with this licensing requirement can be held personally liable and can also lose their licenses.

E&O Alert!

All states have regulations regarding the authority of insurers to operate in that state. In some states, producers placing business with approved, or "admitted," insurers or with authorized unapproved, or "nonadmitted," insurers are relieved of legal liability to their customers if the insurer subsequently becomes insolvent. This regulation is based on the premise that the insurance department is responsible for determining the financial stability of the insurer before allowing it to do business in the state. However, if a producer places business with an unauthorized insurer, the insurer's insolvency could prompt an E&O claim against the producer. Producers should be aware of their states' regulations regarding admitted and nonadmitted insurers.

Producers should use due diligence before recommending an insurer to a customer. One definition of due diligence is the diligence an individual can reasonably expect to exercise in discharging a duty or an obligation and the diligence that, in turn, can reasonably be expected from that individual.

In an insurance context, a producer's responsibility in using due diligence includes determining the insurer's legal status, analyzing the insurer's financial ability to provide the purchased coverage, and evaluating the insurer's suitability for the customer and the customer's loss exposures. Failure to use due diligence could expose a producer to an E&O claim.

ERRORS AND OMISSIONS (E&O)

Like other professionals, insurance producers face legal action when their customers or others believe that producers have not met the accepted legal standards for professional conduct. The characteristics that can be ascribed to a "professional" producer are described later in this assignment. However, the fact that all states require an insurance producer to be licensed before transacting insurance implies that the producer has the expert knowledge necessary to provide the public with the complex product of insurance.

Courts have said that, because of the increasing complexity of insurance and the specialized knowledge required to interpret policy forms and provisions, individuals in the insurance industry present themselves to the public as experts who can assist customers in understanding these complexities.

Therefore, it is in the public's best interest that producers be held liable for their negligence, as would any other professional who is found negligent.

The amounts involved in a claim against a producer can be substantial. Agencies routinely process insurance policies involving limits of hundreds of thousands or even millions of dollars. Few agencies can absorb such large losses. Agents and brokers professional liability (E&O) insurance is considered a business necessity today because of the increasing frequency and severity of E&O claims.

Fortunately, E&O loss exposures can be treated by using risk management. Risk management is a process of making, implementing, and monitoring decisions that minimize the adverse effects of risk on an organization. It consists of the following six steps:

1. Identify loss exposures
2. Analyze loss exposures
3. Examine the feasibility of risk management techniques
4. Select the appropriate risk management techniques
5. Implement the selected risk management techniques
6. Monitor results and revise the risk management program

The following errors and omissions discussion covers many aspects of the risk management process. It identifies and analyzes causes of errors and omissions claims in some detail, along with the sources of an insurance agent's legal responsibilities and the common-law duties of an agency. Agencies can control their E&O loss exposures by using the risk management process, including examining alternative risk management techniques. It is essential that agencies purchase E&O insurance to finance losses that occur despite the controls. However, typically, insurers will not offer E&O insurance to agent and broker customers unless they are assured that a form of E&O risk management is in place.

The processes of implementing and monitoring risk management decisions relating to the E&O loss exposure are not significantly different from the processes used with other loss exposures and do not receive separate attention here.

Causes of Errors and Omissions Claims

E&O claims can be caused by acts of commission as well as acts of omission. An agent may intend to do the right thing but may nevertheless make a mistake, for example, by performing a task incorrectly. Or an agent may neglect to undertake a transaction, also leading to an E&O claim. Whether caused by a failure to perform correctly (an error) or failing to perform at all (an omission), E&O claims can result from external and internal causes.

Common External Causes

Errors and omissions claims generated by external causes are increasing in frequency. Producers often have little control over these causes. Common external causes of errors and omissions claims include changes in products, customer relationships, company relationships, litigation cost/benefit, coverage expectations, nontraditional loss exposures, and consumer service demands, described as follows:

- *Changes in products*. Insurers are constantly introducing new and more complex policy forms, policy endorsements, and policy exclusions. Consequently, producers must be more knowledgeable than ever before about insurance matters. Training on interpreting these new policies and forms, traditionally provided by the insurer, is often lacking.

- *Customer relationships*. Increasingly, like attorneys or accountants, producers are recognized as professionals. This professional status benefits the producer's image but also imposes a high standard of care on the producer and increases the likelihood of E&O claims. Additionally, emphasis on long-term relationships with customers means that producers are expected to know more about their customers' personal and business affairs and to provide adequate coverage in light of this increased knowledge.

- *Company relationships*. In the past, insurers rarely filed E&O claims against a contracted producer. Insurers supported their producers and generally did not take an adversarial position against them. However, this situation is rapidly changing. Insurers fight questionable claims more vigorously than in the past and, if called on to pay, can and do file suit against their producers.

- *Litigation cost/benefit*. Insurance agencies and brokerages have become popular targets in the search for a "deep pocket" to pay for uncovered losses. Insurers are likely to fight E&O claims because they have extensive corporate assets at risk in a legal dispute and have the economic resources available to support lengthy court battles. Agencies and brokerages are more concerned with their reputation and ability to serve customers in the future. Therefore, they do not undertake the level of legal resistance that insurers do and may be more inclined to settle than to engage in a protracted legal dispute. Consequently, people pursue E&O claims against producers to pay for losses that are not covered by the insurer even if the producer did not commit an error or omission.

- *Coverage expectations*. In the past, customers looked to insurance to cover potentially catastrophic losses. Increasingly, they seek compensation for losses considered insurable, even if insurance is typically available only in the surplus lines market or a government insurance pool. In an E&O lawsuit, a court may impose the doctrine of reasonable expectations, considering what a reasonable person would assume is covered by the insurance policy. In such cases, a court may require a the insurer to pay a claim under the policy even though the policy was not designed to cover that claim on the premise that a reasonable person would assume that the policy covered the claim. This result can be vastly different from what the insurance professional intended when arranging a customer's insurance. Consequently, more claims are being covered by the insured's own policy than by the producer's E&O policy.

- *Nontraditional loss exposures.* The ways in which the producer's customers can be exposed to loss are increasing and changing. Nontraditional loss exposures include environmental liability and pollution, computers and the Internet, e-commerce and intellectual property, the Americans with Disabilities Act, employment practices liability, telecommuting, home-based businesses, and terrorism. Product development to address these nontraditional loss exposures has been slow at best, leaving producers with additional E&O claims when the customer's needs are not met or when coverage is unavailable in the marketplace.

- *Consumer service demand.* Consumers' demands are also constantly increasing. Many want service to be better, faster, and less expensive than ever before. Responding to these demands may put an agency at an increased risk for an E&O claim because speed is often attained at the expense of accuracy.

Common Internal Causes

Most E&O claims are the result of a producer error, not an omission. If insurance professionals address the internal causes of errors and omissions, the majority of E&O claims may be reduced or eliminated. Common internal causes of errors and omissions include the following:

- *Inadequate training.* Agency principals cite many reasons that their personnel are not adequately trained. The most common are lack of time, lack of resources, and lack of motivation. Despite these constraints, agency principals must adequately train personnel to avoid E&O claims. Training, particularly related to the constantly changing areas of coverages and technology, should be built into each employee's development plan.

- *Lack of uniform policies and procedures.* Policies and procedures help ensure that tasks are performed as required. Most agencies, however, do not have uniform, circulated policies or procedures. Without them, agency personnel must rely on their judgment in many circumstances. Consequently, individuals develop separate systems of operation. Some systems may overlook tasks or allow them to be incorrectly performed, resulting in E&O claims.

- *Lack of consistency.* Even if policies and procedures are established, agency personnel often do not adhere to them. Treating one customer differently from another, for example, can be problematic in an E&O claim. Policies and procedures must be applied consistently to minimize the chances of an error or omission.

- *Time constraints.* Agencies and brokerages are confronted with increasing pressure to accomplish work in less time with fewer people. Haste leads to mistakes. To alleviate this pressure, agency staff must learn to use the tools available to work efficiently and to eliminate costly mistakes that lead to E&O claims. For example, an agency that uses all the functions and capabilities of its agency management system (AMS) and that requires its staff to consistently apply the agency's AMS policies and procedures should see an increase in speed and efficiency and a decrease in mistakes.

Sources of an Insurance Agent's Legal Responsibilities

E&O claims are based on producers' legal duties to the parties they serve in the insurance business. A producer primarily serves two parties—the customer and the insurer. Agency law dictates that when the producer acts as the insurer's representative or legal agent, that agent owes many duties to the insurer (principal). The producer also owes duties to customers. In addition, a growing and somewhat troublesome area of law involves duties owed to others who are customers of neither the producer nor the insurer.

The producer's legal responsibilities to the insurer derive from the common-law doctrine of negligence and the written contract between the agency and the insurer. The producer's legal responsibilities to another individual may derive from common-law theories of negligence and an implied contract to procure insurance that benefits that individual.

Under common law, negligence is defined as the failure to exercise the degree of care that a reasonably prudent person in a similar situation would exercise to avoid harming others. The prudent person against whom one is judged is generally a peer. The criteria against which actions are judged, therefore, are subject to change over time.

The doctrine of negligence implies that producers should act reasonably in both their professional and customer relationships, as follows:

- *Professional or salesperson.* One implication of the definition of negligence is that the higher the level of experience, education, or skills required, the higher the standard of care required. Therefore, insurance producers who present themselves as professionals through written or oral representations and appearances raise the standard of care against which their actions are judged. For example, a producer who offers more-complex products and services, such as commercial package policies and risk management services, is held to a higher standard of professional care than a salesperson offering magazines at a corner newsstand.
- *Customer relationships.* An established "course of dealing" or a "special relationship" with an insured can also affect the degree of the producer's legal responsibility to the insured. For example, if a producer consistently renews insurance policies for an insured over a period of years, the producer has established a "course of dealing" and may then be held liable

for failure to renew. A producer who counsels the insured on needed coverages, thereby creating a "special relationship" with the insured as an insurance consultant, can be held liable for failing to recommend a needed coverage the insured does not have at the time of a loss.

- *General duty to act reasonably*. A producer has a general duty to act as a reasonably prudent producer would act in the same or similar circumstances, for example, when advising a client or recommending coverages. This general duty to act reasonably has been less frequently applied over the years as courts place more responsibility on plaintiffs (insureds).

Management Tip

Agency procedures should be established to address the most common types of E&O claims. Priority should be given to implementing systems that reduce the possibilities of inadequate coverage, misinterpretation of policy provisions, and policy processing delays.

Agency's Common-Law Duties

Courts evaluate the negligence standard of care, actions that a "reasonable or prudent person" would or would not take, based on the facts or circumstances of a specific case. The standard of care against which an insurance agency is judged depends on the agency's policies and procedures at the time of the loss. A producer's duty to an insured, therefore, is constantly evolving.

Under common law, for a producer (or an individual) to be legally liable for negligence, the harmed party (the plaintiff) must prove all of the following elements of negligence:

- The agent's legal duty for the standard of care owed to the plaintiff
- The agent' failure to conform to the standard of care required in the situation, creating an unreasonable risk of harm
- A causal connection between the agent's negligent act and the plaintiff's harm (proximate cause)
- The plaintiff's actual loss or damage

Without proof of each of these elements, a person cannot successfully sue for negligence.

Agency's Common-Law Duties Owed to Customers

Under common law, an insurance agency has a duty to use the standard of care necessary to protect the customer's interest. If failure to use this standard results in bodily injury or property damage to the customer, the agency can be held liable for the injury or damage. The agency is also responsible for the negligent or fraudulent acts of its employees and producers.

Exhibit 4-3 summarizes the duties agencies owe to their customers and the common types of errors that can occur when agencies fail to adhere to the necessary standard of care in performing these duties.

EXHIBIT 4-3

Agency's Duties to Customers—Common Types of Errors

- Misrepresenting insurance coverage. A producer owes a duty not to misrepresent the existence or the extent of coverage provided by a policy.

- Failing to procure requested insurance. A producer who undertakes to procure insurance owes a duty to use reasonable diligence in attempting to place the insurance requested by the customer.

- Failing to notify the customer of inability to procure insurance. A producer owes a duty to inform the customer promptly if unable to place the requested insurance.

- Procuring inadequate coverage. A producer who agrees to provide insurance to a customer owes a duty to use reasonable care to obtain adequate insurance to meet the customer's needs.

- Failing to maintain requested insurance. A producer owes a duty to inform the customer when a renewal policy contains coverage changes.

- Failing to inform the customer of renewal. A producer owes a duty to inform the customer of premiums due for a renewal when the producer receives information about the policy expiration that is intended for the customer.

- Failing to investigate an insurer's financial condition. A producer owes a duty to place coverage with a solvent insurer, reasonably monitor an insurer's financial condition, disclose solvency information to the customer, and protect the customer when the risk of insolvency becomes too great.

- Failing to explain policy terms or coverage limitations. A producer who has a "special relationship" with the customer may owe a duty to explain policy terms or coverage limitations.

Agency's Common-Law Duties Owed to Its Insurer

A producer may be liable to an insurer for negligence or a breach of contract that causes harm to the insurer. In particular, the producer owes the insurer the duties of loyalty, fairness, honesty, and good faith. The producer must also keep the insurer informed about material matters that relate to the insurance or to the agency. An agency may also be liable for the negligent or fraudulent acts of agency employees or solicitors.

The agency/insurer contract creates a "special relationship" between the agency and insurer, thereby increasing the necessary standard of care. Additionally, an agency has a fiduciary relationship with an insurer that requires an extraordinary standard of care.

Exhibit 4-4 summarizes the duties agencies owe to their insurers and the common types of errors that can occur when agencies fail to adhere to the necessary standard of care in performing these duties.

EXHIBIT 4-4

Agency's Duties to Insurers—Common Types of Errors

- Making mistakes. A producer owes a duty to use reasonable diligence and care in conducting business with its insurers. An insurer may be held liable for a producer's error in processing an insured's request for coverage, but the insurer may then have a right to seek indemnification from the producer.

- Failing to follow instructions. A producer owes a duty to comply with an insurer's instructions promptly and fully and may be liable for any loss the insurer incurs as a result of the producer's failure to do so.

- Failing to disclose information. A producer has a fiduciary duty to the insurer to disclose any material information about the policies the insurer writes for the producer. Material information is any information that, if known by the insurer, would have affected the insurer's decision.

- Delaying the forwarding of information. A producer owes a duty to use reasonable diligence in forwarding information that has been requested by the insurer or that is material to the insurance.

- Exceeding express or implied authority. A producer owes a duty to understand and comply with binding authorities granted by the insurer and comply with all other terms of the agency/insurer agreement.

E&O Alert!

Does a producer have a duty to explain policy terms and coverages to customers? Does a producer have a duty to offer higher limits or additional coverages? Generally, the courts have answered "no" to both of these questions. As is the case with some E&O loss exposures, however, a producer can be sued for failing to explain or offer coverages or if customers dispute the coverage explanation provided even if there is no legal duty to do so or if no previous court decisions support the lawsuit. This possibility is why loss prevention measures against E&O claims are so important.

Customer relationships can affect the success or failure of a claim against the agency. An established "special relationship" with an insured can affect the degree of the producer's legal responsibility to the insured. For example, if a producer counsels the insured on policy terms or needed coverages, then a judge or jury would say that the producer has established a "special relationship" with the customer. The producer would be held liable for failing to explain a coverage or exclusion or for failing to mention a coverage that the insured does not have at the time of the loss. Without this special relationship, however, the courts have fairly consistently refused to hold the producer liable for an insured's failure to read and understand the policy or for not providing coverage for every conceivable loss.

Agency's Common-Law Duties to Others

A producer may be liable for errors or omissions that cause harm to persons with whom the producer has no customer relationship, such as lienholders, additional insureds, and certificate holders. Exhibit 4-5 summarizes the duties agencies owe to others and the common types of errors that can occur when agencies fail to adhere to the necessary standard of care in performing these duties.

EXHIBIT 4-5

Agency's Duties to Others—Common Types of Errors

- Failing to notify others of policy cancellation. A producer may owe a duty to notify lienholders and certificate holders when a policy is canceled.

- Failing to follow instructions. A producer owes a duty to comply with an insurer's instructions promptly and fully and may be liable for any loss the insurer incurs in relation to parties other than the insured as a result of the failure to do so.

- Failing to advise when coverage cannot be placed. A producer may owe a duty to advise a lienholder when coverage requested by the lienholder is not placed promptly.

Controlling E&O Loss Exposures

Although sound loss control can lower the probability of an E&O loss, the possibility of a claim cannot be eliminated. Therefore, *every producer faces the chance of an E&O loss.* A loss may result from careless behavior, from an unfortunate mistake, from a lack of knowledge, or simply from failure to ask the right question.

E&O loss control measures can be divided into two categories. Some measures aim to prevent losses from occurring (loss prevention). Other measures enable producers to defend themselves if an E&O claim occurs, thereby reducing the cost of the loss (loss reduction).

Measures to Prevent E&O Losses

Preventing E&O losses is one of the least costly ways of controlling the E&O loss exposure. The following measures may help producers prevent E&O claims:

- Using the risk management process with customers
- Knowing coverage availability and insurer quality
- Honoring binding authority
- Developing procedures to prevent E&O claims
- Handling claims with tact and diligence

Using the risk management process with customers can help producers prevent E&O claims that result when the producer fails to analyze a customer's needs and therefore fails to provide the necessary coverages or limits. This type of claim can occur if a producer agrees to duplicate previous coverage, to renew as is, or to provide the coverage the customer requests without first ascertaining the customer's actual needs. Such claims are much less likely to occur when a producer tries to identify all the customer's loss exposures and determine the best way to treat each one.

For some loss exposures, the risk management process may lead producers to suggest using retention rather than insurance. However, even when retention is in the customer's best interests, claim problems can arise. If a loss occurs for a retained loss exposure, the customer may state that the producer failed to provide insurance or that the producer failed to recommend the appropriate insurance. Recommendations to use retention should be carefully communicated to the customer. The decision to retain a loss exposure should be the result of a conscious decision by the customer and should be documented so the producer can prove that the customer was aware of the retained loss exposure.

When using the risk management process, producers should recognize the limits of their own expertise. The typical producer is not an accountant, engineer, or attorney. Producers should be frank with their customers about their limitations and, if possible, recommend another source of information that could provide knowledge in a specialized area. For example, producers should refer legal questions to the customer's attorney and tax questions to the customer's accountant.

Knowing coverage availability and insurer quality is another measure producers use to prevent E&O losses. E&O claims often arise because a producer tells a customer that a certain type of coverage is not available. After an uninsured loss occurs, customers may learn that their loss could have been covered by insurance. Before advising a customer that coverage is not available, a producer should determine whether coverage could be obtained from another source. Also, if coverage later becomes available, the producer should notify the customer.

Conversely, a producer may assure a customer that coverage can be placed, only to find that no underwriter will accept the loss exposure. Producers should not indicate that they can place coverage until they are certain that one or more insurers are willing to offer coverage.

Producers should know the quality of insurers they represent. If an insurer becomes insolvent or provides unsatisfactory service, affected insureds may file E&O claims against the producer who selected the insurer. Also, producers must remain updated on coverage changes by taking courses, reading periodicals, attending seminars, and continuously studying the changes in the insurance marketplace.

Producers can also help prevent E&O losses by honoring their binding authority. Producers are not usually granted unlimited binding authority in their agency contracts. Every producer who binds coverage must be aware of all restrictions on binding authority. If an unauthorized binder is issued, the practical effect may be that the agency has inadvertently become an insurer. Even if the insurer pays for a loss, it is likely to seek recovery from the producer who exceeded binding authority. All agency personnel should be informed of the scope of the agency's binding authority, which is contained in each insurer's agency agreement. Agency agreements should be updated to reflect any changes, and these changes should be distributed to employees.

Developing procedures to prevent E&O claims is an important measure producers use as part of their E&O loss prevention efforts. Failure to act and failure to act promptly are examples of major causes of E&O claims that sound agency procedures can minimize. Sound procedures apply not only to initial work flow but also to follow-up actions if procedures are not performed in a timely manner. Developing procedures to identify activities that are not performed (omissions) can be difficult but is an essential element in providing good service.

Procedures are needed in two areas that often cause E&O claims: processing renewals and processing policies and endorsements. Renewals should always be reviewed before the renewal date so that necessary changes or cancellations can be made before renewal. When the agency receives new policies and endorsements, staff should proofread them against the application or request to ensure that the coverage issued is the same as the coverage requested. Any changes should be investigated, documented, and explained to the insured. Equal care must be taken regarding accuracy of applications and endorsements that are electronically entered and issued at the agency via the Internet or direct agency interface.

Handling claims with tact and diligence is another way to prevent E&O losses. Insurance exists as a mechanism for paying claims; despite this fundamental purpose, claims are often mishandled. Those who handle claims must realize that each claimant has just experienced a personally traumatic event, and obtaining the necessary facts about the loss from the customer may be difficult under the stressful circumstances. Consequently, tact, courtesy, and patience in taking claim information and in handling claim settlements are important in helping prevent E&O claims.

Once the agency is aware of a claim, the customer should be advised of what steps he or she must take. For example, a customer who has suffered property loss should be reminded of the responsibility to protect property and to do nothing that may increase the loss, and the responsibility to comply with any other policy conditions relating to the loss. If the customer fails to comply with these policy provisions, the insurer can delay or deny claim payment.

E&O Alert!

Remember that a state's unfair claims practices act may require a producer to act on claims within a prescribed time frame. Agency personnel should know the act's provisions, and agency procedure manuals should reflect response time standards, at least in accordance with state law. Some states require that agency personnel receive specific training on the act annually or biennially.

The insurer should also be notified promptly of every claim reported to the agency. An agency standard for reporting claims to the insurer should be established, and all agency personnel must adhere to it.

Measures to Help Defend Against E&O Claims

Despite all the measures they may take to avoid or control their E&O loss exposures, producers may still find themselves involved in E&O claims. As discussed previously, some plaintiffs and even juries are in search of defendants with "deep pockets," and professionals are held to a higher degree of care in complex matters of understanding such as insurance.

E&O insurers encourage their customers to use certain measures to establish a primary line of defense against E&O lawsuits. Therefore, producers use the following measures to help establish a defense against lawsuits that could occur:

- Adopt a code of personal and business ethics.
- Develop and use standardized office forms, policies, and procedures.
- Purchase agents and brokers professional liability insurance to protect against E&O claims.
- Document, document, document! Put everything in writing, and log every transaction on the agency management system, including telephone conversations with insureds that require some action so that the e-file can be used as evidence if a claim ever depends on the producer's word against that of the customer bringing suit.
- Commit to a continuing professional education program for agency personnel.
- Use due diligence in obtaining information about insurer financial stability, claim procedures, and reputation.

Management Tip

Many people used to believe that agency automation would eliminate paper files and, therefore, be detrimental to agencies faced with E&O claims. But, depending on whether and how the information is processed, courts have tended to view computer records as more reliable than manual records. Because efficient use of an agency's management system automatically provides documentation of all transactions, technology may improve an agency's ability to defend against E&O claims.

Agents and Brokers Professional Liability Insurance

The preceding discussions about producer E&O loss exposures highlight the need to purchase professional liability insurance. Such policies are classified by the insurance industry as a type of professional liability coverage. They are designed specifically for agents and brokers but are commonly called agents and brokers errors and omissions, or E&O, liability insurance. In terms of its potential severity, the E&O loss exposure is too substantial for most agencies to retain. Some agencies purchase coverage on a mass-marketed basis, as members in an insurance trade association. Others obtain coverage on an individual basis.

Coverage Features

The specific provisions of agents and brokers professional liability insurance policies vary by insurer. This section discusses common coverage features and policy variations and suggests ways to analyze coverage to ensure that it provides the needed protection. Three sample E&O policies are included in Appendix B for reference and to illustrate how the wording of those policies varies among insurers.

Coverage features of typical E&O policies include the following:

- Insuring agreement
- Exclusions
- Limits and deductibles

Generally, E&O policies cover claims first made during the policy period that arise out of wrongful acts, errors, or omissions of the insured agent or broker. Most policies also include vicarious liability stemming from negligent acts, errors, or omissions of others for whom the insured is legally liable (such as licensed solicitors and employees). Insureds also receive defense protection and other supplementary coverages comparable to those found in most general liability policies. However, some E&O policies cover defense costs within the limit of liability, while others pay defense costs in addition to the policy limit.

All E&O policies feature an insuring agreement containing the insurer's obligations. The Policy Toolbox that follows includes the insuring agreements of three agents and brokers professional liability policies. These insuring agreements illustrate how policy wording varies and serve as a reminder of why producers must analyze E&O policies to ensure that their loss exposures are covered.

Some insurers include a provision that reserves the right to settle claims they deem expedient. Others include provisions that prevent any settlements without their insureds' consent. These provisions are significant because paying an E&O claim may damage an agency's reputation. By rejecting a settlement, the agency professes its innocence by agreeing to have the matter settled in court. In some policies, refusal to settle makes the insured liable for any judgment above the amount of the proposed settlement. Producers should know the nature of the settlement provisions of their E&O policies.

All E&O policies cover claims made against the producer during the policy period for acts or omissions that occurred during that period. However, as noted in the Policy Toolbox, policies differ in how or whether they cover a claim made during the policy period for an event that occurred before policy inception. Likewise, policies vary in whether they provide coverage for claims made in the future because of an event that occurred during the policy period. All agents and brokers professional liability forms are on a claims-made basis—that is, they apply only to claims made during the policy period. Policy variations are discussed in the next section.

Exclusions are also found in E&O policies. Some E&O policies contain comparatively few exclusions, and many apply to loss exposures best covered by other types of insurance. The exclusions common to these policies apply to claims arising from dishonest, fraudulent, criminal, or malicious acts; libel, slander, and other intentional torts; bodily injury and property damage liability; and failure to pay or collect premiums for policies the agent writes.

Another feature common to E&O policies is a section devoted to limits and deductibles. Available limits of liability generally start at $100,000 per claim with a $300,000 annual aggregate and go upward from that limit. Excess limits are available in primary or excess forms with limits higher than $10 million.

These high limits are commonly purchased by large agencies. Many producers opt for high limits when purchasing E&O insurance, despite the cost.

Policy Toolbox

Sample insuring agreements of insurance agents and brokers professional liability insurance policies that illustrate wording variations among insurers.

American International Specialty Lines Insurance Company

Errors and Omissions

To pay on behalf of the insured all sums which the Insured shall become legally obligated to pay as damages resulting from any claim or claims first made against the insured and reported in writing to the Company during the Policy Period for any Wrongful Act of the Insured or of any other person for whose actions the Insured is legally responsible, but only if such Wrongful Act occurs during or prior to the Policy Period and solely in rendering or failing to render professional services for others for a fee in the Insured's capacity as an Insurance Agent, Insurance Broker, Insurance Consultant or Notary Public.

Evanston Insurance Company

The Coverage

Professional Liability and Claims Made Clause: To pay on behalf of the Insured all sums in excess of the deductible amount stated in the Declarations which the Insured shall become legally obligated to pay as Damages as a result of CLAIMS FIRST MADE AGAINST THE INSURED DURING THE POLICY PERIOD by reason of an act, error, or omission which happened:

(a) during the Policy Period; or

(b) prior to the Policy Period provided that on the effective date of this policy the Insured has no knowledge of such act, error, or omission and there is no prior policy or policies which provide insurance for such liability or Claim resulting from such act, error, or omission whether or not the available limits of liability of such prior policy or policies are sufficient to pay any liability or Claim or whether or not the deductible provisions and amount of such prior policy or policies are different from this policy;

PROVIDED ALWAYS THAT such act, error, or omission arises out of professional services rendered or that should have been rendered by the Insured, or by any person for whose acts, errors, omissions the Insured is legally responsible, in the conduct of the Insured's profession as an insurance agent, insurance broker, general insurance agent, managing general insurance agent, managing general underwriter, surplus line broker, excess line broker and life insurance agent, including the following related activities connected therewith: notarizing, premium financing, servicing of insurance business of others, consulting, advising, engineering, appraising, claims adjusting and public relations activities.

Westport Insurance Corporation

Section I

A. INSURANCE OPERATIONS COVERAGE

   We will pay on behalf of the insured "loss" for which the insured is legally liable caused by a "wrongful act" committed by an insured arising out of "professional services" rendered to others.

E&O Alert!

Producers' E&O loss exposures, like other professional liability loss exposures, pose severity rather than frequency problems. Therefore, a frequently asked question is "How high a limit of E&O insurance should be purchased?" Although there is no correct answer to this question, one industry practice suggests that E&O limits should equal the largest limits of any property or liability policy written by the agency. However, most E&O losses result from coverage not placed by the producer. Therefore, the maximum limit available for purchase is more appropriate. Some E&O policy limits apply to defense costs as well as loss payments, meaning that cases that are expensive to defend may erode the limits of liability and leave a lower amount available to pay judgments or settlements. When considering E&O limits, producers should consider all these factors. Carrying a higher aggregate limit than the per-claim limit is also advisable because a single large claim in one year can wipe out a single per-claim/ aggregate limit and leave the agency uninsured for additional claims during the same year until other coverage can be purchased.

E&O policies usually contain a deductible of a least $1,000, and the trend is toward increasing deductibles to encourage producers to engage in loss control. Also, substantial premium credits may be granted for increased deductibles. Many agencies use partial retention by selecting high deductibles. Producers should also determine whether the deductible applies only to loss payments or to both loss payments and claim expenses, such as defense costs.

Variations Among E&O Policies

E&O policies are not all alike. An agency should carefully review an E&O policy before purchasing it.[12] Appendix B provides examples of policies used by three agents' and brokers' professional liability insurers. When reviewing the E&O policy, the agency should pay particular attention to the variations in the following provisions commonly found in E&O policies:

- Persons insured
- Organizations insured
- Coverage for prior acts
- Discovery period
- Other insurance
- Consulting activities
- Other activities
- Service on local boards and insurance committees
- Fraudulent acts of employees
- Personal injury liability

- Claim definition
- Exclusions
- Consent to settle
- Policy territory

Persons insured. Not all policies include producers who are independent contractors as insureds. Most policies cover agencies for the vicarious liability arising from the acts of independent contractors or others, but some do not. Producers should determine whether coverage applies to former employees and independent contracts. Agencies that are not traditional partnerships or corporations, such as limited liability companies (LLCs), may need special endorsements to cover their members and managers, which are equivalent to a corporation's stockholders and officers.

Organizations insured. Over the past several years, many agencies have acquired or merged with other agencies. Coverage provided by the E&O policy may not include so-called "predecessor firms." However, underwriters are often willing to include coverage for such firms when given the opportunity to evaluate the loss exposures. When an agency acquires or forms another agency entity during the policy period, some policies provide automatic coverage for the new entity, usually for a limited time after the acquisition.

Coverage for prior acts. E&O policies are written on a claims-made basis. All policies provide coverage for claims made during the policy period arising from an event that occurred during the policy period. For claims made during the policy period arising from prior events, coverage generally applies if the loss occurred after a retroactive date, as long as the producer did not know of a possible claim or could not have reasonably expected a claim. However, some policies exclude prior acts or charge separately to extend such coverage to prior years.

Discovery period. A variety of approaches are available to deal with claims filed after an E&O policy expires. Some policies provide coverage for a thirty- or sixty-day automatic discovery period. With the payment of an additional premium, the discovery period can sometimes be extended if the insurer cancels the policy, if the agency goes out of business as a result of the death or retirement of the agency principal, or if the agency is sold to another party. This extended discovery period provision should be examined carefully as the agency principal approaches retirement or if the agency is in a position to be acquired.

Other insurance. Policies also vary in how they respond when more than one policy may apply to a loss. Because coverage is not necessarily limited to events or claims occurring during the policy period, the chance that more than one policy provides coverage for a single claim often exists. When changing from one insurer to another, producers should be certain that continuous coverage exists for all potential claims.

Consulting activities. Agents and brokers professional liability policies generally cover loss exposures incurred only while the agent or broker (producer) is acting as an insurance agent or broker. The policies do not include liability arising out of consulting activities, such as preparing an insurance survey or performing a financial planning risk management audit for a fee.

Other activities. Activities other than consulting may create E&O loss exposures for which coverage might be questionable. Acting as a notary public, engaging in real estate operations, operating a premium finance company, performing accounting services (even helping a few customers with their tax returns), and providing legal advice are clearly outside the scope of the producer's normal insurance activities. With the trend toward the unbundling of services, incidental activities involving loss control services and appraisal work may also lead to questions about E&O coverage. Also, some agencies sell noninsurance products, such as prepaid legal services contracts, funeral contracts, mutual funds, variable annuities, and extended auto warranty contracts. The typical E&O policy covering operations as an insurance producer does not extend to these activities unless the insurer offers an endorsement to provide the coverage.

Service on local boards and insurance committees. If producers serve on committees responsible for handling the insurance of a public body, government organization, or private entity, they should pay special attention to the professional liability loss exposure. When the agency is not also providing the insurance products, E&O policies might exclude coverage because these activities do not arise from the named insured's business. The E&O policy can often be endorsed to provide such coverage.

Fraudulent acts of employees. Liability caused by dishonest, fraudulent, criminal, or malicious acts of the insured is usually excluded. However, some policies also exclude fraudulent or dishonest acts by the insured's employees, which can leave agency principals with a significant gap in coverage. The latter coverage is generally available, sometimes for additional premium.

Personal injury liability. The standard commercial general liability (CGL) policy covers specific types of personal injury loss exposures, including libel, slander, and invasion of privacy. However, most CGL policies written for insurance producers include some type of professional liability exclusion that eliminates coverage for these loss exposures relating to rendering services as an insurance producer. Some E&O policies fill this gap by specifically providing coverage within the insuring agreement or its definition of "wrongful acts."

Claim definition. Most E&O policies permit the insured to report potential claims to the insurer during the policy period when the agency becomes aware of an occurrence that could cause a claim against the agency in the future. Some policies, however, respond only to an actual claim, usually defined as a written notice of a demand for money or services. When the insurer permits the agency to report occurrences, the agency can be assured that any resulting future claim will be covered by the policy that was in force when the occurrence was reported. If the insurer does not permit incident reporting and the actual claim is made during a future policy period, the claim may not be covered, especially if the agency has changed insurers in the meantime.

Exclusions. The number and nature of exclusions vary significantly by E&O policy. Exclusions that producers should review carefully when considering policies offered by E&O insurers include the following:

- Punitive and multiplied (double, treble) damages
- Claims brought by one insured against another, especially when the agency permits employees to place their personal coverage within the agency
- Contractual liability
- Insolvency of an insurer or other risk-bearing entity
- Bodily injury or property damage with no exception for such claims arising from professional services rendered by an insured
- Pollution or other environmental loss exposures, such as mold, with no exception for such claims arising from professional services rendered by an insured

Consent to settle. Settlement disagreements occur with all kinds of liability insurance policies. With professional liability policies, an out-of-court settlement may seem unacceptable because it appears as though the professional is admitting to an error, and the settlement may damage that professional's reputation. Many professional liability policies formerly contained a provision to the effect that the insurer could not settle without the insured's consent. However, some policies now permit the insurer to settle any claim without the insured's consent. If the insured's consent is required, the policy generally includes a provision that limits the insurer's liability to the amount for which the claim could have been settled, should the insured want to contest the claim.

Any decision by an agency to contest a claim that the insurer wants to settle should be made with extreme care. For example, suppose a former customer files a lawsuit against an agency claiming $50,000 in damages because one of the insured's locations was omitted from the schedule of coverage and fire damaged a building at that location. Assume the producer is convinced that the policy was issued in accordance with the insured's instructions and suggests that the insured should have read the policy and discovered that this building was not covered. Although the producer is sure this defense is sound, the plaintiff is equally sure the claim is valid. Because of the plaintiff's superior credibility in the eyes of most juries, the insurer has some doubts about whether the agency could win the case and offers the plaintiff a $25,000 settlement. Also having some doubts concerning going to trial, the plaintiff is willing to settle for $25,000. Unless covered by an E&O policy that states that the agency must consent to any settlement, the agency can refuse to settle. Litigation could then proceed. Consider the following three possible outcomes of the litigation:

1. If the agency wins, the only expenses it will incur are those for the amount expended for time lost at trial, time away from the office, and other activities engaged in during the course of pursuing a defense. The agency's reputation is preserved, assuming that (and this is important) the people who were aware of the claim are also made aware of the final judgment.

2. If the plaintiff obtains a judgment for $50,000 against the agency, the insurer pays $25,000, and the agency pays $25,000. The agency may also incur additional defense costs and deductibles, depending on the specific terms of the E&O policy. The agency will not have preserved goodwill, and may have lost additional goodwill as a result of publicity accompanying the trial.

3. If the agency agrees to settle for $25,000, the insurer pays $25,000, minus the deductible the agency pays. Reputation may be damaged, but it will be mitigated by the fact that the claim is quickly settled without the publicity accompanying a trial. The public should recognize that an out-of-court settlement for less than the amount claimed is not the same as a judgment against the agency. Although some people may still view the agency as guilty because of a settlement, many settlements are made because that amount is less than the cost of defense. The public may realize this as well.

Policy territory. Many policies cover liability only in the U.S. and Canada. Coverage without territorial limitations is more desirable, particularly for agencies insuring international loss exposures or writing ocean marine coverage on import or export cargo insurance.

After purchasing an E&O policy, the agency should remain aware of coverage that is in force and any policy conditions that may restrain the agency's activities. Just as conscientious producers review their customers' policy provisions, they should also thoroughly analyze their own policies.

It should be noted that E&O policies are not designed to preserve an agency's goodwill. They are not intended to be an indirect form of property-casualty insurance for the agency's customers, providing them with coverage regardless of whether the agency has sold insurance that specifically addresses all of their loss exposures.

E&O policies do protect an agency against claims that are enforceable by law. These policies provide liability protection in the strictest sense of the term, and they protect an agency against financial loss from an E&O claim, despite careful attempts to control the loss exposure.

Management Tip

E&O insurers require not only new business applicants but also insureds at renewal to complete detailed applications. A properly completed application can make a big difference in whether the insurer offers a policy and, if so, at what premium and on what terms and conditions. When applying for new coverage, agencies should submit loss runs from prior E&O carriers for at least five years and the résumés of key personnel. Whether applying for new or renewal coverage, agencies should provide a narrative on each claim or occurrence reported in the last five years, including a summary of the allegations, claim status or disposition, and brief comments on what new procedures the agency has implemented to prevent similar claims in the future. Agencies applying for first-time coverage should include résumés of key agency personnel along with a business plan describing the agency's formation and long-term business strategy. The application should be submitted well in advance of the anticipated effective date to give the underwriter time to carefully review the submission and avoid a last-minute quote that could prove relatively expensive.

REVIEW

Key Words and Phrases

Define or describe each of the words and phrases found in this assignment.

Countersignature laws (p. 4.12)

Unfair trade practices (p. 4.13)

Review Questions

1. Explain how each of the following federal regulations affect producers: (pp. 4.7–4.10)

    a. Fair Credit Reporting Act

    b. Gramm-Leach-Bliley Act

    c. Electronic Signatures in Global and National Commerce Act (ESIGN)

REVIEW

d.   USA Patriot Act

e.   Sarbanes-Oxley Act

f.   CAN-SPAM Act

g.   Telemarketing and Consumer Fraud and Abuse Prevention Act
     and the Do Not Call Implementation Act

h.   Telephone Consumer Protection Act

2. Explain how each of the following areas of state regulation affects producers: (pp. 4.11–4.16)

   a. Licensing laws

   b. Unfair trade practices acts

   c. Unfair claims settlement practices acts

   d. Handling of premiums

   e. Dealing with suitable insurers

REVIEW

3. What is an error or omission? (p. 4.17)

4. What are seven common external causes of errors and omissions claims? (pp. 4.18–4.19)

5. What are four common internal causes of errors and omissions claims? (pp. 4.19–4.20)

6. To whom might a producer be liable for an errors and omissions (E&O) claim? (p. 4.20)

7. Describe the common-law duties an insurance agency owes to customers, insurers, and others. (pp. 4.21–4.24)

8. What measures can an agency use to prevent E&O losses?
   (p. 4.24)

9. "Document, document, document!" Explain the relevance of this
   advice to a producer's E&O coverage. (p. 4.27)

10. Describe the coverages shown in the insuring agreement that
    are generally available to producers through agents and brokers
    professional liability insurance. (pp. 4.28–4.29)

11. Describe areas in which E&O insurance policies can vary.
    (pp. 4.31–4.35)

12. What types of consent to settle provisions are found in E&O poli-
    cies? (pp. 4.34–4.35)

Application Questions

1. During the last three weeks, the following events occurred at the Joyce Insurance Agency. Describe what effect, if any, they may have on the agency's E&O loss exposure.

   a. Jim Joyce, the agency's owner, received his CPCU designation.

   b. A new loss control expert was added to the agency's staff.

   c. The agency has contemplated the purchase of a local real estate firm.

2. Applying the risk management process is often proposed as a method for preventing E&O claims in an agency environment. Why is this process a useful loss prevention tool?

3. Measures for controlling E&O loss exposures fall into two distinct categories—those used to prevent losses and those used to defend against claims.

   a. Describe the measures that could be used to prevent E&O claims in your agency.

   b. Describe the measures that could be used to establish a defense against E&O claims.

REVIEW

Answers to Assignment 4 Questions

NOTE: These answers are provided to give students a basic understanding of acceptable types of responses. They often are not the only valid answers and are not intended to provide an exhaustive response to the questions.

Review Questions

1. Federal laws affect producers in the following ways:

    a. Fair Credit Reporting Act—Producers may be responsible for providing appropriate notice to applicants that consumer reports may be obtained in the application process.

    b. Gramm-Leach-Bliley Act—Producers must establish policies about the collection and disclosure of customers' nonpublic personal financial information.

    c. Electronic Signatures in Global and National Commerce Act (ESIGN)—Ensures the validity and legal effects of insurance contracts and other documents entered into electronically.

    d. USA Patriot Act—Sets reporting and compliance requirements for life insurers. Property-casualty and health operations of insurers, insurance agents, and brokers are exempt.

    e. Sarbanes-Oxley Act—Tightens internal accounting controls and holds company executives, including insurers who fall under the law's requirements, responsible for financial misdeeds.

    f. CAN-SPAM Act—Affects the use of e-mail messages sent by solicitors, including producers; exempts messages to customers that facilitate, complete, or confirm a commercial transaction.

    g. Telemarketing and Consumer Fraud and Abuse Prevention Act and the Do Not Call Implementation Act—The primary federal law governing telemarketing practices; includes provisions applicable to telemarketers under national do-not-call regulations. Can affect how producers solicit new business accounts.

    h. Telephone Consumer Protection Act—The "Junk Fax Law" makes it illegal to send an unsolicited ad to a telephone facsimile machine or computer or other device and requires that all fax messages carry the sender's identity and phone number. This law can influence how producers contact customers and solicit new business.

2. Producers are affected by the following areas of state regulation:

    a. Licensing laws—Producers must be licensed in each state in which they transact business and must pass an insurance department-sponsored examination that is administered either by the department or by an independent testing service.

    b. Unfair trade practices acts—Producers must carefully examine the state provisions regarding methods of competition and advertising or risk cease and desist orders, loss of license, or heavy fines.

    c. Unfair claims settlement practices acts—Producers must carefully examine the state provisions regarding time frames for communicating with claimants and policyholders or face regulatory penalties or possible errors and omissions claims.

REVIEW

d. Handling of premiums—Typically, producers collect premiums on the insurer's behalf and act as the insurer's fiduciary. Premiums must be kept in a separate trust account and must not be commingled with other personal or business funds. Failure to comply can subject the producer to penalties, fines, loss of license, or imprisonment.

e. Dealing with suitable insurers—Producers should use due diligence before recommending an insurer to a customer. If a producer places business with an unauthorized insurer, that insurer's insolvency could result in an E&O claim against the producer.

3. An error is the failure to perform correctly. An omission is the failure to perform at all.

4. The following are seven common external causes of errors and omissions claims:

   (1) Changes in products—Producers must stay updated on new policy forms, endorsements, and policy exclusions.

   (2) Customer relationships—Customers expect a high standard of care from the producer.

   (3) Company relationships—Insurers are more likely to file suit against their producers than they have been in the past.

   (4) Litigation cost/benefit—Insurance agencies are viewed as a "deep pockets" recovery resource in litigation because of the existence of E&O coverage; therefore, insurers are more inclined to fight E&O claims.

   (5) Coverage expectations—Customers increasingly expect losses to be covered under their insurance policies, and courts are increasingly inclined to agree.

   (6) Nontraditional loss exposures—Producers are exposed to E&O loss when the market is slow to offer products to cover these loss exposures.

   (7) Consumer service demand—Consumer demand for speedy, inexpensive service may expose producers to E&O loss.

5. Four common internal causes of errors and omissions claims are as follows:

   (1) Inadequate training—Time and resource constraints and lack of motivation contribute to inadequate training.

   (2) Lack of uniform policies and procedures—Policies and procedures often are not uniform and circulated; therefore, tasks are not performed as required.

   (3) Lack of consistency—Agency policies and procedures are not followed.

   (4) Time constraints—Pressures to perform tasks in less time with fewer people leads to mistakes.

6. A producer may be liable to the following parties:
   • Customers (insureds)
   • Insurers
   • Other individuals, such as leinholders, additional insured, and certificate holders

7. An insurance agency owes the following common-law duties:
   • Customers—to use the standard of care necessary to protect the customer
   • Insurers—loyalty, fairness, honesty; to act in good faith; and to keep them informed of material matters that relate to the insurance or the relationship

- Others—The agency may be liable for errors or omissions that cause harm to persons with whom the agency has no customer relationship, such as lienholders, additional insureds, and certificate holders.

8. An agency can use the following measures to prevent E&O losses:
   - Use the risk management process with customers
   - Know coverage availability and insurer quality
   - Honor binding authority
   - Develop procedures to prevent E&O claims
   - Handle claims with tact and diligence

9. Documenting conversations and communications between agency personnel and a customer or an underwriter establishes credibility to defend against E&O claims. The outcome of a claim often depends on the producer's word against that of the customer bringing suit.

10. Coverages that are generally available to producers through agents and brokers professional liability insurance include the following:
    - Claims made during the policy period that result from wrongful acts, errors, or omissions of the insured agent or broker
    - Vicarious liability stemming from negligent acts, errors, or omissions of others for whom the insured is legally liable
    - Defense protection and other supplementary coverages

11. Areas in which agents' E&O insurance policies can vary include the following:
    - Persons insured—The E&O policy may not include producers who are independent contractors and former employees. Nontraditional partnerships or corporations may need special endorsements to cover their members and managers.
    - Organizations insured—The E&O policy may not include predecessor firms. Underwriters can extend this coverage after evaluating the loss exposures.
    - Coverage for prior acts—E&O policies are written on a claims-made basis. Coverage for prior acts generally applies if the loss occurred after a retroactive date, as long as the agent did not know of a possible claim or could not have reasonably expected a claim. Some policies exclude prior acts or charge separately to extend coverage to prior years.
    - Discovery period—E&O policies vary in the way they provide coverage for a discovery period. With payment of an additional premium, the discovery period might be extended if the insurer cancels the policy or if the agency goes out of business due to death, retirement, or sale.
    - Other insurance—E&O policies vary in the way they respond when more than one policy may apply to a loss. When changing from one insurer to another, agents should be certain that continuous coverage exists for all potential claims.

- Consulting activities—E&O policies generally cover only the exposures incurred while the agent or broker is acting as a producer and do not include liability resulting from consulting activities, such as preparation of an insurance survey or risk management audit.

- Other activities—Activities other than consulting may create E&O loss exposures for which coverage is questionable.

- Service on local boards and insurance committees—When the producer serves on a committee responsible for handling insurance but the agency is not also providing the insurance products, E&O policies might exclude coverage because these activities do not stem from the named insured's business. The E&O policy can be endorsed to provide coverage.

- Fraudulent acts of employees—E&O policies exclude liability caused by fraudulent acts of the insured and sometimes exclude fraudulent acts by employees of the insured (endorsed for additional premium).

- Personal injury liability—Some E&O policies fill the gap resulting from CGL exclusions for professional liability loss by providing coverage within the insuring agreement or the definition of "wrongful acts."

- Claim definition—Most E&O policies permit the insured to report potential claims to the insurer during the policy period, while others respond only to written notice of a demand for money or services.

- Exclusions—The number and nature of exclusions varies significantly by E&O policy.

- Consent to settle—Some E&O policies permit the insurer to settle any claim without the insured's consent or limit the insurer's liability to the amount for which the claim could have been settled, if the insured contests the claim.

- Policy territory—Many E&O policies cover liability only in the U.S. and Canada. Some agencies might consider coverage without territorial limitations.

12. The following are types of consent to settle provisions found in E&O policies:

- The insurer may settle any claim without the insured's consent.

- The insurer may not settle a claim without the insured's consent.

- If consent of the insured is required, a provision limits the insurer's liability to the amount for which the claim could have been settled, if the insured contests the claim.

Application Questions

1. a. Jim's CPCU designation may increase the firm's loss exposure to E&O claims because, in the event of an E&O suit against Jim and the firm, a court and jury may hold Jim to a higher standard of professional conduct than someone without a professional designation.

   b. The loss control expert could introduce new E&O loss exposures and potential claims based on the quality of loss control services he or she provides. The agency must check its E&O policy to see how broad its coverage is. Services other than the selling of insurance policies may not be covered under the E&O policy. The agency should check with its E&O insurer to determine whether it needs a policy endorsement to broaden the coverage provided.

REVIEW

c. An entirely new business with its own unique E&O loss exposures is being contemplated. The new loss exposures would probably not be covered by the existing policy and would require new E&O coverage. Additionally, if the purchase is made, the Anderson Agency should determine whether their E&O underwriter will allow coverage for "predecessor firms" under their current E&O policy after a thorough underwriting review.

2. The risk management process is an excellent prevention tool in an agency environment because it stresses identifying and addressing all exposures. E&O claims arise because of improper identification or treatment of loss exposures. Risk management can prevent losses with continual follow-up and review of all account activities. Insurers typically offer E&O insurance to agencies with the understanding that those agencies are practicing good E&O risk management.

3. a. To prevent E&O claims, a producer can use the risk management approach with customers. Additionally, knowing insurance coverages and insurers helps a producer ensure that all options available have been checked for coverage placement with a quality insurer and that the policies in effect provide all the coverage that is necessary. Thoroughly understanding and honoring the binding authority granted by various insurers prevents stepping beyond such authority. If a producer exceeds binding authority, coverage can be jeopardized, leading to a possible E&O claim. Developing procedures to prevent E&O claims ensures that all customers are treated consistently. Finally, claims must be handled with tact and diligence. The customers must be informed of the duties they must perform, and the producer must make sure that all paperwork is properly completed.

b. One measure the agency can use to defend against E&O claims is to adopt a code of personal and business ethics. Another measure is to develop and use standard office forms, policies, and procedures. Treating customers inconsistently can be one of the most significant causes of errors and thus E&O claims. The agency should also purchase agents and brokers errors and omissions insurance to provide claim protection. This coverage is the "insurance agent's insurance" and can be the difference between a producer staying in business and having financial difficulties—even if the producer is found not liable for the E&O suit. Document, document, document! The agency should put everything in writing and log every transaction, including telephone conversations with insureds that require action. The agency should commit to a continuing education program and use due diligence in researching insurer financial stability, claim procedures, and reputation.

ETHICS AND THE PRODUCER

The potential penalties for violating a regulation or being held liable for an error or omission can be strong motivators for encouraging producers to obey the law. But obeying the law or avoiding lawsuits does not necessarily mean that someone is acting ethically. Ethical behavior is based on the principles of being honest, acting with integrity, and treating people fairly. Consequently, ethical behavior strives to do more than avoid what is wrong.

Nature of Ethics

Honest businesspeople follow personal codes of behavior to ensure fair and honorable dealings in their business practices. **Ethics** is the study of what constitutes good and bad behavior, dealing with moral duty and obligation.

Ethical behavior is not motivated by legal restrictions or the threat of sanctions. Rather, ethical behavior is motivated by self-respect and integrity as well as altruism. Often, what is ethical is defined in relation to what is unethical. However, the many gray areas between ethical and unethical acts can make it difficult to define what is ethical.

As businesspeople, insurance producers make many decisions using their discretion. As the level of discretion in decision making increases, the likelihood of encountering ethical dilemmas also increases. This is so because many choices are not clearly right or wrong. For example, producers often derive their income from commissions, and they earn commission income only when they make a sale. The commission is normally some percentage of the premium so that, in general, the more insurance producers sell, the larger their commission income. This arrangement can create several ethical dilemmas, particularly because producers have responsibilities to both insureds and insurers. A producer who analyzes a customer's needs from a risk management perspective often recommends noninsurance techniques for financing certain types of losses. However, advising a potential customer not to buy an insurance policy may conflict with the producer's sales goals. Although producers can sometimes charge a consulting fee, many states prohibit this practice or require special licensing. Also, there are practical limits on the amount of sales time a producer can invest in giving free, if helpful, advice. Yet providing inadequate or incorrect advice violates the ethical principle of acting with integrity.

The fact that selling a large premium policy yields a higher commission can tempt producers to sell more insurance than needed, to sell higher-priced coverage when equivalent coverage is available at a lower price, or to recommend the policy with the highest commission percentage. It is unethical for a producer to purport to meet a customer's needs by recommending a particular coverage solely because it benefits the producer. But is it always ethical for a producer representing several insurers to sell the least expensive coverage or the one with the lowest commission? Not necessarily, because there are qualitative differences between insurers and their coverages and services as well as the financial and underwriting stability they offer.

Ethics
The study of what constitutes good and bad behavior, dealing with moral duty and obligation.

Under what circumstances should a producer recommend that a customer purchase coverage from a competitor? Does the producer have an ethical duty to refer a customer to another producer who can better serve the customer? The opportunity to place business with more than one insurer increases the potential for conflict of interest. Insurers use various incentives to encourage certain mixes or volumes of business. (Such practices also affect exclusive agents.) Insurers offering many types of insurance prefer a spread of business among the types of insurance products, and they offer contingent commissions, preferred agency contracts, or other valuable incentives for producing a certain volume of business. Incentives strengthen the insurer's relationship with the insurance agency—a strong relationship has many benefits, including mutual volume growth and profitability and an understanding of each others' marketing preferences. But should a producer select an insurer to achieve a certain level of premium volume in order to earn the incentive, even if the producer would otherwise recommend another insurer? Conversely, should a producer ignore insurer premium volume goals and select insurers solely on the basis of low price or other similar criteria?

Ethical Decision Making

Although discussing ethics in general is easy, making specific ethical decisions is more difficult. In a sense, the law defines and requires minimum acceptable behavior. Insurance department regulations prescribe what producers can and cannot do. Court decisions on professional liability claims define some minimum standards of behavior below which a producer is held liable. But what nonlegal guidelines can producers use to deal with the many ethical dilemmas that confront them on a daily basis? Kenneth Blanchard and Norman Vincent Peale suggest answering the following three questions as an "ethics check" when considering a course of action.[13]

1. *Is it legal?* Will I be violating civil law or company policy?

2. *Is it balanced?* Is it fair to all concerned in the short term as well as the long term? Does it promote win-win relationships?

3. *How will it make me feel about myself?* Will it make me proud? Would I feel good if my decision were published in the newspaper? Would I feel good if my family knew about it?

Situation-based approach
An approach to ethical decision making that is based on the best possible outcome, given the circumstances.

Rule-based approach
An approach to ethical decision making that is based on rules that apply regardless of the circumstances.

This method of ethical decision making is practical and informal. A more formal way to make ethical decisions involves three approaches that are commonly used in the field of ethics: the situation-based approach, the rule-based approach, and the people-based approach. Using a **situation-based approach**, producers decide what the best possible outcome would be, given the circumstances. Using the **rule-based approach**, producers follow rules that apply to the situation, regardless of the circumstances. Using a **people-based approach**, producers consider how they would want to be treated in the same situation. No single approach is best for every situation, even within a given profession. Also, these approaches have their weaknesses: the decision maker must decide what rules to follow, consider when and under what circumstances the rules were made, and consider whether those rules still apply. Exhibit 4-6 illustrates approaches to ethical decision making regarding issues that may involve producers.

People-based approach
An approach to ethical decision making that is based on how the decision maker would want to be treated in the same situation.

EXHIBIT 4-6

Illustration of Approaches to Ethical Decision Making

Following a series of hurricanes in an area, an insurer's claim department staff, working with several local agents—some of whom had draft authority—was faced with an ethical dilemma. Should they pay the insureds who lost their homes $5,000 to help them pay for temporary housing and living expenses before thoroughly investigating their claims, or should they withhold payments until the claims have been investigated thoroughly and coverage has been confirmed? When the department staff and agency principals discussed the dilemma, they used three approaches, as follows:

- *Situation-based approach*: They should write the checks. The small amount of funds that may be paid fraudulently would be dwarfed by the legitimate needs of insureds with valid claims. In the long run, the goodwill that the insurer and agencies would reap from providing immediate relief would more than compensate for any financial loss related to fraud.

- *Rule-based approach*: They could ask their producers from that area, in particular, those without draft authority, to vouch for their insureds before making the payments; they could ask producers or insureds for enough information on the amount of coverage, home location, and years insured to generate reasonable credibility, or they could arrange to pay nearby hotels and restaurants directly for temporary housing and meals.

- *People-based approach*: They should make the payment. The insurer staff and agencies would consider how they would want to be treated. If they lost everything they owned, quick payment is exactly what they would want.

Producers have an ethical and legal obligation to keep certain information confidential. They have access to a significant amount of personal information about insureds, claimants, and other third parties, much of which is private and some of which could harm others if it were to become public. Such confidential information includes the following:

- Medical records
- Department of motor vehicle (DMV) records
- Financial reports (Dun and Bradstreet reports)
- Underwriting data (such as an insured's employment history or limits of liability)
- Insurance scores

Conflict of interest
A situation in which a decision maker's personal interests incline him or her to make decisions that may adversely affect customers or employers.

Producers must also avoid conflicts of interest. They should make decisions based on the best interests of their customers and the insurer. Any time a decision maker's personal interests incline him or her to make decisions that may adversely affect customers or employers, a **conflict of interest** arises.

Guidelines for ethical decision-making are also provided by various professional organizations that have developed codes of ethics.

Codes of Ethics

Code of ethics
The minimum standards of expected behavior for those to whom the code applies.

Many insurance and noninsurance organizations have adopted written codes of ethics. Codes of ethics define ethical behavior in a formal, structured way, prescribing a level of behavior higher than that required by law. However, even a rigorous code of ethics does not guarantee ethical behavior. A **code of ethics** establishes minimum standards of expected behavior for those to whom the code applies.

Management Tip

Many agencies include ethical behavior as a component of their mission or vision statements. Employees, customers, insurers, and competitors can see that the agency values ethical behavior, and this enhances the agency's image in the public's eyes. Ethical management should be as much a part of an organization's culture as is an adherence to quality standards.

Many codes do not include penalties for not adhering to standards. Other codes reserve the right to penalize or discharge any individual who engages in unethical behavior. The implication is that any individual employed by or associated with the organization promulgating the code is, by definition, ethical. One such organization is the American Institute for Chartered Property Casualty Underwriters. All current CPCU candidates become bound by the rules of the CPCU Code of Professional Ethics when they matriculate with the American Institute. Any candidate who violates a rule may have the CPCU designation deferred, denied, or revoked. The rules are also enforceable and binding on every CPCU whose designation was conferred after 1976 and also on many CPCUs designated before 1976 who have voluntarily elected to be bound by the code. A detailed disciplinary procedure ensures that all rights are preserved and a fair hearing is granted. Sanctions less severe than revoking the designation are imposed for minor code violations.

The ethics code of the American Institute sets high minimum standards of ethical behavior, and enforcement of the code adds credibility and stature to the CPCU professional designation. Excerpts from the Canons and Rules of the *Code of Professional Ethics of the American Institute for Chartered Property Casualty Underwriters* are reproduced in Appendix C of this assignment. Other organizations publish codes of ethics to which members can voluntarily subscribe, including the Independent Insurances Agents and Brokers of America (IIABA) and the National Association of Insurance Women (NAIW). The NAIW's code of ethics is reproduced in Exhibit 4-7.

EXHIBIT 4-7

Code of Ethics

National Association of Insurance Women—Code of Ethics

The National Association of Insurance Women (International), both collectively and as individual members, aspires to, actively promotes, and pledges adherence to the following ethical principles:

Professionalism:

- Through competence in the performance of duties,

- Through continued education and training in insurance and its related disciplines, and

- Through cooperation and good relations with colleagues and associates, both within and without the insurance industry.

Service:

- Through conduct in accordance with the highest standards of business performance in a positive and enthusiastic manner,

- Through encouragement of others in the insurance field to achieve maximum levels of competence, and

- Through communication with clients and with the general public to achieve broader understanding of the role of insurance in our society.

Integrity:

- Through strict honesty and moral courage in all transactions,

- Through diligence in representing the interest of clients and of the general public, and

- Through adherence to the spirit of competition.

Reprinted with permission of the National Association of Insurance Women.

What these codes and the codes of most other professions have in common is a spirit of putting the interests of others before those of the professional. When this spirit is compromised, the result is often ethically questionable.

Ethical behavior is central to professionalism, discussed next.

PROFESSIONALISM

This section examines professionalism in relation to insurance producers. The people whom society traditionally recognize as professionals, such as physicians, attorneys, and the certified public accountants, are held to higher standards of conduct in their professions than are practitioners in other fields. The definition of what constitutes a profession is debatable. However, in addition to specialized knowledge, the following are typically identified as characteristics of a profession:

1. Commitment to high ethical standards
2. Prevailing attitude of altruism
3. Recognition of the importance of mandatory educational preparation and training
4. Recognition of the importance of mandatory continuing education
5. Membership in a formal association or society
6. Independence of action
7. Public recognition as a profession

Commitment to High Ethical Standards

Professionalism requires a person to develop and adhering to personal standards of ethical behavior. Individuals can continuously compare their personal standards against an ideal. This comparison is what guides ethical decision making, thereby promoting professional conduct.

The decision to commit to high ethical standards is personal and cannot be forced upon someone by a written code. However, the existence of a written code can serve as the ideal and can provide a set of benchmarks to which an individual's personal ethical behavior can be compared.

Attitude of Altruism

Altruism
Unselfish concern for the welfare of others or selflessness; in ethics, the principle that the general welfare of society should take precedence over one's own interests.

Professionals are expected to have an attitude of altruism. This attitude may be the most important characteristic of professionalism. **Altruism** may be defined as unselfish concern for the welfare of others, or selflessness. In ethics, altruism is the principle that the general welfare of society should take precedence over one's own interests. The goal of altruism is embodied in Canon 1 of the CPCU Code—"CPCUs should endeavor at all times to place the public interest above their own."

To illustrate, an insurance agent demonstrates an attitude of altruism when she opens the agency for business to take care of customers the morning after a tornado strikes their area, even though her own home has been severely damaged. An attitude of altruism is also demonstrated when scores of claim representatives from various insurers descend upon a damaged area, working long hours under difficult conditions to help residents repair their homes and lives.

Mandatory Educational Preparation and Training, and Mandatory Continuing Education

Almost every definition of a professional recognizes the importance of having specialized knowledge. Extensive study is required for members of the "learned professions," such as law and medicine. Specialized knowledge is also required for producers to be licensed to practice in their chosen specialties. The level of competence required to pass state licensing exams is a starting point. To provide quality service, maintain customer trust, and make sound decisions, producers must constantly expand their knowledge.

To accomplish this, producers must participate in education and training programs; read industry publications; and attend seminars sponsored by insurers, producer organizations, insurance education providers, the CPCU Society, and others. The goal of continuing professional development is stated in Canon 2 of the CPCU Code—"CPCUs should seek continually to maintain and improve their professional knowledge, skills, and competence." Many CPCUs accomplish this by participating in the AICPCU's Continuing Professional Development (CPD) program, which encourages them to reach and maintain CPD qualifier status by writing articles, attending or teaching classes, or engaging in other industry-related activities.

Membership in a Formal Association or Society

Another characteristic required of professionals is membership in a formal association or society. Such organizations typically provide opportunities to serve the public. For example, they promote professionalism by providing a forum to discuss important issues, by conducting research, and by educating members.

Many insurance associations and societies exist. Several national organizations, such as the IIABA and the National Association of Professional Insurance Agents (PIA), have state and local associations whose members work together toward common goals and have shared interests. Other organizations, such as the Society of Financial Service Professionals and the CPCU Society, consist of members who have obtained one or more professional insurance designations and who have an interest in, among other things, maintaining and strengthening the professionalism of the insurance industry. The NAIW also provides education, fellowship, and networking opportunities for its members.

Independence of Action

Professionalism is also characterized by independence of action. A producer needs independence to make and implement decisions. Just as a lawyer or a surgeon has the independence to take action in a courtroom or an operating theater to resolve professional dilemmas, a producer requires independence to make a decision and to take action.

Producers have this independence to varying degrees. For example, compared to an exclusive agent, an independent agent or broker deals with more insurers and, therefore, has more independence and a greater opportunity to place business with the insurer for which the business is best suited. Also, ownership of expirations gives an independent agent the freedom to remove business from an insurer that is not performing in the customer's best interests and place it elsewhere or even to discontinue representing an insurer.

Even a producer employed by a large exclusive agency is generally permitted to act independently within certain guidelines. However, the question inevitably arises, "Can a producer who derives an income only by selling insurance truly act in the customers' best interests when acting independently?"

Most discussions about insurance commissions and ethical behavior conclude that a producer can perform ethically even if remunerated on a commission basis—but the system makes it difficult. In the past, few insurance organizations have supported basing compensation on net premiums produced (the policy premium prior to any loading of the agent's or broker's commissions) with a separate specified fee for the producer's services. Lack of support was due to the difficulties in quantifying the value of producer services and related uncertainties in budgeting for the agency's income. However, more producers are now moving toward specified fee compensation. Although such compensation is still a controversial topic and subject to regulations in certain states, producers may want to consider this alternative to commissions to increase their independence of action.

Public Recognition as a Profession

Medicine, law, and certified public accounting are generally recognized as professions. Deserving members of these professions receive an extra degree of respect in recognition of their high standing in society. Other occupational groups aspire to the stature of these professions and to the recognition they receive. Because they provide products and services vital to the wellbeing of individuals, businesses, and the economy, insurance producers tend to believe that their occupation should also receive the recognition given to other professions.

There are many reasons that insurance production can be regarded as a profession. Among them are the vital benefits producers provide as part of selling their products and services. These benefits include restoring businesses to pre-loss conditions and providing loss prevention and reduction advice. Additional reasons relate to a professional's duty and ethics. Independent insurance consultant and author Ken Brownlee suggests (in *Winning by the Rules: Ethics and Professionalism*) that "While insurance is not a true profession in the same sense as medicine, law, and other recognized professions, it is a professional vocation. The individuals within the field can be—perhaps *should* be—professionals. What that translates to is a matter of both legal and ethical duty. The legal duty owed by any professional is much higher than for a nonprofessional. Even the slightest breach of duty exposes a professional to an allegation of malpractice. If we in the vast arena of insurance intend to be professionals, then we must gear our ethics to perform above the normal standard."[14]

Although many people involved in insurance would support the idea that the insurance producer is a professional, the general public may not agree. Consideration of the characteristics of professionalism as they relate to producers may provide some common ground.

PRODUCER AS A PROFESSIONAL

One does not become a professional merely by engaging in a certain occupation; by joining any particular group, association, or organization; or by earning a designation. Likewise, one does not become a professional by assenting to a code of ethics. These activities promote professionalism. However, the true test of whether producers are professionals is how they conduct themselves in their daily business dealings.

Insurance producers who aspire to be professionals should do the following:

- Dedicate themselves to the insurance and risk management industry and demonstrate support for industry insurers, producers, and related participants
- Offer quality insurance programs and represent quality insurers
- Place the customer's interests above their own self-interests

For example, a producer aspiring to be a professional would not make disparaging comments about another agent or insurer or withhold information from an insurer that may affect the customer's premium. Rather, a producer aspiring to be a professional would participate in industry professional groups and societies and engage in continuing education as either a student or instructor.

Inherent in these requirements are the important personal characteristics of altruism and ethical behavior. Those who are altruistic and ethical in all their business dealings will gain professional recognition, and such recognition can contribute to prosperity and self-satisfaction. Self-satisfaction can be considered inner prosperity. It can be more rewarding than monetary prosperity.

Insurance professionals are in an enviable position in many respects. They may know all the ultimate rewards of caring for others, and they have the satisfaction of knowing that they serve vital needs. The services insurance producers provide hold them to a high standard of professional care equal to the standards for attorneys, physicians, and certified public accountants, for example. While insurance alone cannot save a life, it can pay for the medical treatment that will. It can replace the income of a disabled wage earner, send a son or daughter to medical or law school, and pay for quality medical and legal care. It can protect the owners of homes and automobiles from lawsuits. It can replace a dwelling destroyed by windstorm so that the inhabitants will have a decent place to live. It can protect individuals and businesses from financial ruin.

The insurance producer who engages in ethical, professional business practices will demonstrate a commitment to learning and service that will benefit his or her customers and demonstrate a high standard of care that other professionals can follow.

Key Words and Phrases

Define or describe each of the words and phrases found in this assignment.

Ethics (p. 4.49)

Situation-based approach (p. 4.50)

Rule-based approach (p. 4.50)

People-based approach (p. 4.51)

Conflict of interest (p. 4.52)

Code of ethics (p. 4.52)

Altruism (p. 4.54)

Review Questions

13. Explain why a producer using risk management techniques might encounter difficult ethical questions. (p. 4.49)

14. Producers have access to a great deal of personal information about insureds, claimants, and other parties which they have an ethical and legal obligation to keep confidential. Describe these types of confidential information. (pp. 4.51–4.52)

15. What are seven characteristics of a profession? (p. 4.54)

16. What behaviors are expected of insurance producers who aspire to professionalism? (p. 4.57)

Application Questions

4. Illustrate how each of the seven characteristics of a profession applies to an insurance producer.

5. Because of a change in underwriting eligibility, one of your customers, Jack's Garden Center, has been renewed on a commercial package policy instead of the businessowners policy that was used last year.

    a.   What responsibilities do you have to the customer when delivering the renewal?

    b.   Could this change of policies lead to an E&O claim? How?

Answers to Assignment 4 Questions

NOTE: These answers are provided to give students a basic understanding of acceptable types of responses. They often are not the only valid answers and are not intended to provide an exhaustive response to the questions.

Review Questions

13. Difficult ethical questions may arise when a producer determines that a noninsurance technique—for which the producer earns no commission—may be the best risk management solution for an insured. There are practical limits on the amount of sales time a producer can divert to giving free advice, but providing improper advice is not ethical. Additionally, producers who charge fees for risk management consulting services must ensure they adhere to state regulations and sound ethical principals.

14. Types of information producers have an ethical and legal obligation to keep confidential include the following:
    - Medical records
    - Department of motor vehicle (DMV) records
    - Financial reports (Dun and Bradstreet reports)
    - Underwriting data (such as an insured's employment history or limits of liability)
    - Insurance scores

15. The seven characteristics of a profession are as follows:
    (1) Commitment to high ethical standards
    (2) Prevailing attitude of altruism
    (3) Mandatory educational preparation and training
    (4) Mandatory continuing education
    (5) A formal association or society
    (6) Independence of action
    (7) Public recognition as a profession

16. Insurance producers who aspire to professionalism should do the following:
    - Dedicate themselves to the insurance and risk management industry and demonstrate support for industry insurers, producers, and related participants
    - Offer quality insurance programs and represent quality insurers
    - Place the customer's interests above their own self-interests

Application Questions

4. The seven characteristics of a profession apply to an insurance producer in the following ways:
    (1) A commitment to high ethical standards—A producer can encounter challenging ethical situations, such as determining the commission on which his or her compensation is based or determining an optimal insurance program for the customer.

(2) A prevailing attitude of altruism—A professional in a service field must put the interests of others first. For example, a producer should always consider the needs of the customer above his or her own personal or business needs, even if the consequence is that the producer receives less compensation or has to refer the customer to another producer.

(3) Mandatory educational preparation and training—A producer must be thoroughly competent in the technical aspects of the profession. Producers should receive a level of education and training that prepares them to deal professionally with their customers and to make reliable coverage and product recommendations.

(4) Mandatory continuing education—A producer must maintain a level of professional excellence by participating in continuing education throughout his or her career. Producers should engage in continuing education and training, particularly in the area of new product offerings.

(5) Membership in a formal association or society—A producer should work toward becoming a member of a formal association or society, such as by attaining the CPCU designation for membership in the CPCU Society, or by attaining membership in the Risk and Insurance Management Society, Inc. (RIMS).

(6) Independence of action—The insurance marketing system should allow a producer to act independently in making and implementing decisions.

(7) Public recognition as a profession—Producers are increasingly regarded as professionals in part because of the products and services vital to the well-being of others that they provide.

5. a. The producer must explain to the owner of Jack's Garden Center why the renewal is on a commercial package policy instead of the businessowners policy that was used last year. The producer should point out that the unendorsed CPP lacks some of the favorable features of the BOP (no coinsurance and loss of income coverage) and should carefully explain any other coverage differences between the CPP and the BOP that may apply specifically to Jack's Garden Center and could otherwise give rise to an E&O loss exposure. In thoroughly explaining the underwriting decision that went into the change in policy form, the producer must ensure that the customer understands the reasons for the decision, particularly if it resulted in a significant premium increase (the producer will want to assure Jack's Garden Center that the form change was not made for the purpose of any monetary benefit).

   b. If the new coverage is not thoroughly explained to the customer and a loss occurs that would have been covered by the BOP but is not covered by the CPP, the agent is definitely a target for an E&O claim. To prevent an E&O claim, the producer may wish to have the owner of Jack's Garden Center sign the renewal proposal, indicating his understanding of the renewal's revised terms.

SUMMARY

Insurance producers, like other practitioners in the insurance business, are subject primarily to state regulation. The U.S. Congress recognized its right to regulate the insurance business but deferred that right to the states as long as they perform well; therefore, few federal regulations apply. Federal regulations affecting agents originate from the Securities and Exchange Commission; the Federal Emergency Management Agency; the Department of Transportation; the Federal Trade Commission, which enforces the Fair Credit Reporting Act; the Gramm-Leach-Bliley Act; the Electronic Signatures in Global and National Commerce Act (ESIGN); the USA Patriot Act; the Sarbanes-Oxley Act; The CAN-SPAM Act; the Telemarketing and Consumer Fraud and Abuse Act and Do Not Call Implementation Act, and the Telephone Consumer Protection Act. Principal areas of state regulation affecting producers include licensing, unfair trade practices, the handling of premiums, and choice of insurers.

Common law also influences the way agents and agencies behave in their business dealings. Producers and agencies are subject to loss from their errors and omissions in many activities. Insurance producers are ideal targets for E&O claims brought by insureds, insurers, and others. The insurance business is technically complex, and the producer is subject to laws and regulations that are sometimes obscure. E&O coverage itself may be responsible for many E&O claims against producers—the producer is sometimes the sole party remaining with a convenient source of recovery for an aggrieved claimant. Being a technical expert, following all the laws and rules, and implementing and enforcing procedures may not keep an agency out of the courthouse, but it will make it easier for the agency's E&O insurer to defend the lawsuit.

Producer E&O claims are the result of many causes, both internal and external. Interplay can exist among the internal and external causes. Examples of common external causes include changes in products and customer relationships, litigation cost/benefit, customer coverage expectations, nontraditional loss exposures, and customer service demands. Examples of common internal causes include inadequate training, lack of uniform policies and procedures, lack of consistency, and time constraints.

An insurance agency has legal responsibilities to customers, insurers, and others. E&O losses typically result from either the failure of the producer or agency to do something the courts or regulators have determined should be done or from doing something the courts or regulators have determined should not be done. Common errors affecting customers include misrepresenting insurance coverage, failing to procure required insurance, failing to notify a customer of inability to procure proper insurance, failing to inform a customer of renewal, failing to investigate an insurer's financial condition, and failing to explain policy terms or coverage limitations. Common errors affecting insurers include failing to follow instructions, failing to disclose information, delaying the forwarding of information, and exceeding express or implied authority. Common errors based on duties owed to others include failing to notify others of policy cancellation, failing to follow instructions, and failing to advise when coverage cannot be placed.

E&O loss exposures are controllable. Producers and agencies can adopt policies and procedures to prevent E&O claims, or assist in the defense of an E&O claim. When E&O insurance is purchased, producers must examine the coverage provided as seriously as they would examine coverages for customers because there are no standardized E&O forms.

Various professional organizations have promulgated ethical standards of behavior, and some organizations make ethical decisions using one of three approaches: the situation-based approach, the rule-based approach, and the people-based approach. Other organizations have published codes of ethics, which are higher standards of behavior than those required by law.

One result of ethical conduct is being recognized as an insurance professional. Common attributes of a profession or professional include a commitment to high ethical standards, an attitude of altruism, educational preparation, continuing education, membership in a formal association or society, independence of action, and public recognition.

ASSIGNMENT NOTES

1. 15 U.S.C. § 1011–1015.
2. 15 U.S.C. § 1011 et seq.
3. 15 U.S.C. § 1681.
4. 15 U.S.C. § 6801–6809 et seq.
5. 15 U.S.C. § 7001.
6. Public Law 107-56 [H.R. 3162].
7. 18 U.S.C. § 1514A.
8. U.S. S877 (2003).
9. 15 U.S.C. §§ 1601–1608.
10. 15 U.S.C. §§ 1601–1608 (1994), as amended by H.R. 395.
11. 47 U.S.C. § 227.
12. Discussion contained in this section draws on materials contained in *Professional Liability Insurance* (Dallas, Tex.: International Risk Management Institute, 1997), vol. 2, p. XE. 1–25.
13. Kenneth Blanchard and Norman Vincent Peale, *The Power of Ethical Management* (New York: Ballantine Books, 1996), pp. 7–17.
14. Ken Brownlee, *Winning by the Rules: Ethics and Success in the Insurance Profession* (Erlanger, Ken.: The National Underwriter Company, 2001), p. 178.

Appendix A

Unfair Trade Practices Act—Excerpts

UNFAIR TRADE PRACTICES ACT—EXCERPTS

UNFAIR TRADE PRACTICES ACT

Section 1.   Purpose

The purpose of this Act is to regulate trade practices in the business of insurance in accordance with the intent of Congress as expressed in the Act of Congress of March 9, 1945 (Public Law 15, 79th Congress) and the Gramm-Leach-Bliley Act (Public Law 106-102, 106th Congress), by defining, or providing for the determination of, all such practices in this state that constitute unfair methods of competition or unfair or deceptive acts or practices and by prohibiting the trade practices so defined or determined. Nothing herein shall be construed to create or imply a private cause of action for a violation of this Act.

Section 3.   Unfair Trade Practices Prohibited

It is an unfair trade practice for any insurer to commit any practice defined in Section 4 of this Act if:

A. It is committed flagrantly and in conscious disregard of this Act or of any rules promulgated hereunder; or

B. It has been committed with such frequency to indicate a general business practice to engage in that type of conduct.

Section 4.   Unfair Trade Practices Defined

Any of the following practices, if committed in violation of Section 3, are hereby defined as unfair trade practices in the business of insurance:

A. Misrepresentations and False Advertising of Insurance Policies. Making, issuing, circulating, or causing to be made, issued or circulated, any estimate, illustration, circular or statement, sales presentation, omission or comparison that:

(1) Misrepresents the benefits, advantages, conditions or terms of any policy; or

(2) Misrepresents the dividends or share of the surplus to be received on any policy; or

(3) Makes a false or misleading statement as to the dividends or share of surplus previously paid on any policy; or

(4) Is misleading or is a misrepresentation as to the financial condition of any insurer, or as to the legal reserve system upon which any life insurer operates; or

(5) Uses any name or title of any policy or class of policies misrepresenting the true nature thereof; or

(6) Is a misrepresentation, including any intentional misquote of premium rate, for the purpose of inducing or tending to induce the purchase, lapse, forfeiture, exchange, conversion or surrender of any policy; or

(7) Is a misrepresentation for the purpose of effecting a pledge or assignment of or effecting a loan against any policy; or

(8) Misrepresents any policy as being shares of stock.

B. False Information and Advertising Generally. Making, publishing, disseminating, circulating or placing before the public, or causing, directly or indirectly to be made, published, disseminated, circulated, or placed before the public, in a newspaper, magazine or other publication, or in the form of a notice, circular, pamphlet, letter or poster, or over any radio or television station, or in any other way, an advertisement, announcement or statement containing any assertion, representation or statement with respect to the business of insurance or with respect to any insurer in the conduct of its insurance business, which is untrue, deceptive or misleading.

C. Defamation. Making, publishing, disseminating, or circulating, directly or indirectly, or aiding, abetting or encouraging the making, publishing, disseminating or circulating of any oral or written statement or any pamphlet, circular, article or literature which is false, or maliciously critical of or derogatory to the financial condition of any insurer, and which is calculated to injure such insurer.

D. Boycott, Coercion and Intimidation. Entering into any agreement to commit, or by any concerted action committing any act of boycott, coercion or intimidation resulting in or tending to result in unreasonable restraint of, or monopoly in, the business of insurance.

E. False Statements and Entries.

(1) Knowingly filing with any supervisory or other public official, or knowingly making, publishing, disseminating, circulating or delivering to any person, or placing before the public, or knowingly causing directly or indirectly, to be made, published, disseminated, circulated, delivered to any person, or placed before the public, any false material statement of fact as to the financial condition of an insurer.

(2) Knowingly making any false entry of a material fact in any book, report or statement of any insurer or knowingly omitting to make a true entry of any material fact pertaining to the business of such insurer in any book, report or statement of such insurer, or knowingly making any false material statement to any insurance department official.

F. Stock Operations and Advisory Board Contracts. Issuing or delivering or permitting agents, officers or employees to issue or deliver, agency company stock or other capital stock, or benefit certificates or shares in any common law corporation, or securities or any special or advisory board contracts or other contracts of any kind promising returns and profits as an inducement to purchase insurance.

G. Unfair Discrimination.

(1) Making or permitting any unfair discrimination between individuals of the same class and equal expectation of life in the rates charged for any life insurance policy or annuity or in the dividends or other benefits payable thereon, or in any other of the terms and conditions of such policy.

(2) Making or permitting any unfair discrimination between individuals of the same class and of essentially the same hazard in the amount of premium, policy fees or rates charged for any accident or health insurance policy or in the benefits payable thereunder, or in any of the terms or conditions of such policy, or in any other manner.

Drafting Note: In the event that unfair discrimination in connection with accident and health coverage is treated in other statutes, this paragraph should be omitted.

(3) Making or permitting any unfair discrimination between individuals or risks of the same class and of essentially the same hazard by refusing to insure, refusing to renew, canceling or limiting the amount of insurance coverage on a property or casualty risk solely because of the geographic location of the risk, unless such action is the result of the application of sound underwriting and actuarial principles related to actual or reasonably anticipated loss experience.

(4) Making or permitting any unfair discrimination between individuals or risks of the same class and of essentially the same hazards by refusing to insure, refusing to renew, canceling or limiting the amount of insurance coverage on the residential property risk, or the personal property contained therein, solely because of the age of the residential property.

(5) Refusing to insure, refusing to continue to insure, or limiting the amount of coverage available to an individual because of the sex, marital status, race, religion or national origin of the individual; however, nothing in this subsection shall prohibit an insurer from taking marital status into account for the purpose of defining persons eligible for dependent benefits. Nothing in this section shall prohibit or limit the operation of fraternal benefit societies.

(6) To terminate, or to modify coverage or to refuse to issue or refuse to renew any property or casualty policy solely because the applicant or insured or any employee of either is mentally or physically impaired; provided that this subsection shall not apply to accident and health insurance sold by a casualty insurer and, provided further, that this subsection shall not be interpreted to modify any other provision of law relating to the termination, modification, issuance or renewal of any insurance policy or contract.

(7) Refusing to insure solely because another insurer has refused to write a policy, or has cancelled or has refused to renew an existing policy in which that person was the named insured. Nothing herein contained shall prevent the termination of an excess insurance policy

on account of the failure of the insured to maintain any required underlying insurance.

(8) Violation of the state's rescission laws at [insert reference to appropriate code section].

Drafting Note: A state may wish to include this section if it has existing state laws covering rescission and to insert a reference to a particular code section.

Source: NAIC Unfair Trade Practices Act, 2001 edition. Copyright National Association of Insurance Commissioners. Reprinted with permission. Further reprint or distribution strictly prohibited.

Appendix B

Sample E&O Insurance Policies

AMERICAN INTERNATIONAL SPECIALTY LINES INSURANCE COMPANY

(a capital stock company, herein called the Company)

NOTICE: THIS IS A CLAIMS MADE FORM, EXCEPT TO SUCH EXTENT AS MAY OTHERWISE BE PROVIDED HEREIN, THE COVERAGE OF THIS POLICY IS LIMITED GENERALLY TO LIABILITY FOR ONLY THOSE CLAIMS THAT ARE FIRST MADE AGAINST THE INSURED AND REPORTED IN WRITING TO THE COMPANY WHILE THE POLICY IS IN FORCE. PLEASE REVIEW THIS POLICY CAREFULLY AND DISCUSS THE COVERAGE THEREUNDER WITH YOUR INSURANCE AGENT OR BROKER.

INSURANCE AGENTS AND BROKERS PROFESSIONAL LIABILITY POLICY

In consideration of the payment of the premium, and in reliance upon the statements in the application and Declarations attached hereto and made a part hereof, and subject to the limits of liability stated in Item 3 of the Declarations and the terms and conditions contained herein, the Company hereby agrees as follows:

INSURING AGREEMENTS

1. ERRORS AND OMISSIONS

   To pay on behalf of the Insured all sums which the Insured shall become legally obligated to pay as damages resulting from any claim or claims first made against the Insured and reported in writing to the Company during the Policy Period for any Wrongful Act of the Insured or of any other person for whose actions the Insured is legally responsible, but only if such Wrongful Act occurs during or prior to the Policy Period and solely in rendering or failing to render professional services for others for a fee in the Insured's capacity as an Insurance Agent, Insurance Broker, Insurance Consultant or Notary Public.

2. DEFENSE COSTS, CHARGES & EXPENSES (INCLUDED IN THE LIMITS OF LIABILITY)

   With respect to any such Wrongful Act for which insurance is afforded by this policy under Insuring Agreement 1 above, the Company shall, as part of and subject to the limits of liability:

   a) have the right and duty to defend any suit brought against the Insured seeking damages on account of a Wrongful Act, even if such suit is groundless, false or fraudulent, but the Insured shall not admit liability for or settle any claim or suit or incur any cost, charge or expense without the written consent of the Company, and the Company shall have the right to make such investigation and conduct negotiations and, with the written consent of the Insured, enter into such settlement of any claim or suit as the Company deems expedient.

If the Insured refuses to consent to any settlement recommended by the Company and acceptable to the claimant, the Company's duty to defend the Insured shall then cease and the Insured shall thereafter at his own expense negotiate or defend such claim or suit independently of the Company and the Company's liability shall not exceed the amount of damages for which the claim or suit could have been settled if such recommendation was consented to, plus defense costs, charges and expenses incurred by the Company, and defense costs, charges and expenses incurred by the Insured with the Company's written consent, up to the date of such refusal.

The Company shall not be obligated to pay any claim or judgment or to defend or continue to defend any suit after the applicable limit of the Company's liability has been exhausted by payments of judgments and/or settlements and/or other items included within the limits of liability.

b)   pay all expenses incurred by the Company in any suit defended by the Company and brought against the Insured alleging a Wrongful Act, all costs taxed against the Insured in any such suit, and all interest on the entire amount of any judgment therein which accrues after entry of the judgment and before the Company has paid, tendered or deposited in court that part of the judgment which does not exceed the limit of the Company's liability thereon.

c)   Pay premiums on appeal bonds required in any suit defended by the Company and brought against the Insured alleging a Wrongful Act, and/or premiums on bonds to release attachments for an amount not in excess of the applicable limit of liability of this policy, but without any obligation to apply for or furnish any such bonds.

d)   Pay all reasonable expenses, other than loss of earnings, incurred by the Insured at the Company's request.

DEFINITIONS

1.   **Insured** means the individual, partnership, corporation or other entity named in Item 1 of the Declarations and shall include any partner, director, officer or employee thereof solely while acting within the scope of his duties as such.

2.   **Policy Period** means the period from the inception date of this policy shown in Item 2 of the Declarations to the earlier of the expiration shown in Item 2 of the Declarations or the effective date of cancellation of this policy.

3.   **Wrongful Act** means any actual or alleged:

a)   negligent act, error or omission; or,

b)   false arrest, detention, or imprisonment; or,

49606 (1/90)

c)   the publication or utterance of a libel or slander or of other defamatory or disparaging material, or a publication or utterance in violation of an individual's right of privacy; or,

d)   wrongful entry or eviction, or other invasion of the right of private occupancy.

EXCLUSIONS

This policy does not apply:

a)   to any claim alleging fraud, dishonesty, criminal or malicious acts or omissions; however, if such allegations are subsequently disproven by a final adjudication favorable to the Insured, then the Company shall reimburse the Insured for all reasonable defense costs, charges and expenses which would have been collectible under this policy;

b)   to any claim alleging discrimination;

c)   to any claim for or alleging bodily injury to, or sickness, disease or death of any person, or damage to or destruction of any property, including the loss of use thereof;

d)   to any claim seeking non-pecuniary relief;

e)   to any claim based upon, arising out of, due to or involving directly or indirectly, the insolvency, receivership, bankruptcy, liquidation or financial inability to pay, of any insurance company in which the Insured has placed or obtained any insurance or bond;

f)   to any claim brought about or contributed to by any commingling of funds or accounts, nor to any claim for sums received by any Insured or credited to any Insured's account nor to any claim for fees, premiums, taxes, commissions or brokerage monies;

g)   to any Wrongful Act committed prior to the beginning of the Policy Period, if on or before the inception date of this policy any Insured knew or could have reasonably foreseen that such Wrongful Act did or could lead to a claim or suit;

h)   to any claim arising out of the activities of any Insured in regard to any "employee pension benefit plan" and/or "employee welfare benefit plan", as those terms are defined in the Employee Retirement Income Security Act of 1974, as amended, sponsored by any Insured or any firm which any Insured owns or controls, or in regard to any such plan in which any Insured is a participant or a named fiduciary as that term is used under the Employee Retirement Income Security Act of 1974 as amended;

49606 (1/90)

i)   to any claim arising out of or connected with the performance or failure to perform services for any person or entity:

   (1)   which is owned by or controlled by any Insured; or

   (2)   which owns or controls any Insured; or,

   (3)   which is affiliated with any Insured through any common ownership or control; or,

   (4)   in which any Insured is a director, officer, partner or principal stockholder;

(j)   to any claim arising directly or indirectly out of any actual or alleged discharge, dispersal, release, escape, or use of asbestos, toxic substances or pollutants, including but not limited to any failure to effect and maintain insurance or bond with respect thereto;

k)   to any claim brought by one Insured under this policy against another Insured;

l)   to fines, penalties, or punitive, exemplary or multiplied damages; however, only where permitted by law, this policy shall cover, subject to all the terms, conditions and exclusions contained herein, up to $5,000 punitive, exemplary or multiplied damages, as part of and not in addition to the limits of the Company's liability otherwise afforded by this policy;

m)   to any Wrongful Act committed with knowledge that it was a Wrongful Act;

n)   to any claim arising out of notarized certification or acknowledgement of a signature without the physical appearance at the time of said notarization before such notary public as Insured hereunder of the person who is or claims to be the person signing.

SPECIAL PROVISIONS

1.   LIMITS OF LIABILITY

The limit of liability stated in the Declarations as applicable to "Each Wrongful Act or series of continuous, repeated or interrelated Wrongful Acts" is the limit of the Company's liability for all amounts payable hereunder in settlement or satisfaction of claims, judgments or awards and defense costs, charges and expenses arising out of the same Wrongful Act or series of continuous, repeated or interrelated Wrongful Acts, without regard to the number of Insureds, claims, demands, suits or proceedings or claimants. If additional claims are subsequently made which arise out of the same Wrongful Act or series of continuous, repeated or interrelated Wrongful Acts as claims already made and reported to the Company, all such claims, whenever made, shall be considered first made within the Policy Period or the extended reporting period in which the earliest claim arising out of such Wrongful Act was first made and reported to the Company, and all such claims shall be subject to one such limit of liability.

49606 (1/90)

The limit of liability stated in the Declarations as "Aggregate" is, subject to the above provisions respecting "Each Wrongful Act or series of continuous, repeated or interrelated Wrongful Acts", the limit of the Company's liability for all amounts payable hereunder in settlement or satisfaction of claims, judgments or awards and defense costs, charges and expenses arising out of claims first made and reported to the Company during the Policy Period or during the extended reporting period. The aggregate limit of liability for the extended reporting period shall be part of, and not in addition to, the aggregate limit of liability for the Policy Period.

The inclusion herein of more than one Insured shall not operate to increase the limits of the Company's liability.

Defense costs, charges and expenses, as well as amounts paid in settlement or satisfaction of claims, judgments or awards are subject to the applicable limits of liability. All defense costs, charges and expenses shall first be subtracted from the limit of liability with the remainder, if any, being the amount available to pay damages.

2.   DEDUCTIBLE

The Company shall only be liable for those amounts payable hereunder in settlement or satisfaction of claims, judgments or awards, defense costs, charges and expenses which are in excess of the deductible stated in Item 4 of the Declarations. This deductible shall apply to each Wrongful Act and shall be borne by the Insured and remain uninsured. For purposes of the deductible, claims arising out of the same Wrongful Act or out of a series of continuous, repeated or interrelated Wrongful Acts shall be considered as arising out of one Wrongful Act, and only one deductible amount shall apply thereto.

3.   LOSS PROVISIONS

The Insured shall, as a condition precedent to the availability of the rights provided under this policy, give written notice to the Company as soon as practicable during the Policy Period, or during the extended reporting period (if applicable), of any claim made against the Insured. Notice given by or on behalf of the Insured to any authorized representative of the Company, with particulars sufficient to identify the Insured, shall be deemed notice to the Company.

4.   SPECIAL REPORTING CLAUSE

If during the Policy Period or during the extended reporting period (if the right is exercised by the Insured in accordance with Provision 5), the Insured shall become aware of any occurrence which may reasonably be expected to give rise to a claim against the Insured for a Wrongful Act which first occurs during or prior to the Policy Period, and provided the Insured gives written notice to the Company during the Policy Period or the extended reporting period (if applicable) of the nature of the occurrence and specifics of the possible Wrongful Act, any claim which is subsequently made against the Insured arising out of such Wrongful Act shall be treated as a claim made during the Policy Period.

-5-

5.   EXTENDED REPORTING PERIOD

If the Company or the Insured shall cancel or refuse to renew this policy, the Insured shall have the right, upon payment of an additional premium of 50% of the total annual premium, to a period of twelve (12) months following the effective date of such cancellation or non-renewal (herein referred to as the extended reporting period) in which to give written notice to the Company of claims first made against the Insured during said twelve (12) month period for any Wrongful Act committed during or prior to the Policy Period and otherwise covered by this policy.

The rights contained in this clause shall terminate, however, unless written notice of such election together with the additional premium due is received by the Company within thirty (30) days of the effective date of cancellation or non-renewal. This clause and the rights contained herein shall not apply to any cancellation resulting from non-payment of premium.

GENERAL CONDITIONS

1.   This policy only applies to Wrongful Acts committed in, and suits brought against the Insured in, the United States of America, its territories or possessions, or Canada.

2.   All notices of claims, applications, demands or requests provided for in this policy shall be in writing and addressed to Michael Mitrovic, Esq., Attorney at Law, P.O. Box 2603, Jersey City, N.J. 07303.

3.   The Insured shall cooperate with the Company and, upon the Company's request, assist in making settlements, in the conduct of suits or proceedings, and in enforcing any right of contribution or indemnity against any person or organization who may be liable to the Insured. The Insured shall attend hearings, trials and depositions and shall assist in securing and giving evidence and obtaining the attendance of witnesses. The Insured shall not, except at his own cost, voluntarily make any payment, assume any obligation or incur any expense.

4.   No action shall lie against the Company unless, as a condition precedent thereto, there shall have been full compliance with all the terms of this policy, nor until the amount of the Insured's obligation to pay shall have been finally determined either by judgment against the Insured after actual trial or by written agreement of the Insured, the claimant and the Company. Any person or organization or the legal representative thereof who has secured such judgment or written agreement shall thereafter be entitled to recover under this policy to the extent of the insurance afforded by this policy. No person or organization shall have any right under this policy to join the Company as a party to any action against the Insured to determine the Insured's liability nor shall the Company be impleaded by the Insured or his legal representative.

5.   In the event of any payment under this policy, the Company shall be subrogated to all the Insured's rights of recovery therefor, and the Insured shall execute and deliver

49606 (1/90)

instruments and papers and do whatever else is necessary to secure such rights. The Insured shall do nothing to prejudice such rights. Any amount recovered in excess of the Company's total payment shall be restored to the Insured, less the cost to the Company of recovery.

6.   Such insurance as is provided under this policy shall apply only as excess over any other valid and collectible insurance.

7.   This policy may be cancelled by the Insured by surrender of this policy to the Company or by giving written notice to the Company stating when thereafter such cancellation shall be effective. This policy may also be cancelled by the Company by mailing to the Insured by registered, certified, or other first class mail, at the Insured's address shown in Item 1 of the Declarations, written notice stating when, not less than thirty (30) days thereafter, the cancellation shall be effective. The mailing of such notice as aforesaid shall be sufficient proof of notice and this policy shall terminate at the date and hour specified in such notice. If this policy shall be cancelled by the Insured, the Company shall retain the customary short rate proportion of the premium hereon. If this policy shall be cancelled by the Company, the Company shall retain the pro rata proportion of the premium hereon. Payment or tender of any unearned premium by the Company shall not be condition of cancellation, but such payment shall be made as soon as practicable.

8.   Assignment of interest under this policy shall not bind the Company until its consent is endorsed hereon; however, subject otherwise to the terms hereof, this policy shall cover the estate, heirs, legal representative, or assigns of the Insured in the event of the Insured's death, bankruptcy, insolvency or being adjudged incompetent.

9.   Bankruptcy or insolvency of the Insured or the Insured's estate shall not relieve the Company of any obligation hereunder.

10.   Notice to any agent or knowledge possessed by any agent or by any other person shall not effect a waiver or a change in any part of this policy or estop the Company from asserting any right under the terms of this policy; nor shall the terms of this policy be waived or changed, except by endorsement issued to form a part of this policy and signed by an authorized representative of the Company.

11.   The Insured first named in Item 1 of the Declarations shall be the sole agent of all Insureds hereunder for the purpose of effecting or accepting any amendments to or cancellation of this policy, for the payment of premium and the receipt of any return premiums that may become due under this policy, and the exercising or declining to exercise any right to an extended reporting period.

12.   Service of Suit

It is agreed that in the event of failure of the Company to pay any amount claimed to be due hereunder, the Company, at the request of the Insured, will submit to the jurisdiction of a court of competent jurisdiction within the United States. Nothing in this condition constitutes or should be understood to constitute a waiver of the Company's rights to commence an action in any court of competent jurisdiction in the United States to remove an action to a United States District Court or to seek a transfer of a case to another court as permitted by the laws of the United States or of any state in the United States.

It is further agreed that service of process in such suit may be made upon Counsel, Legal Department, American International Specialty Lines Insurance Company, c/o American International Surplus Lines Agency, Inc., Harborside Financial Center, 401 Plaza 3, Jersey City, NJ 07311, or his or her representative, and that in any suit instituted against the Company upon this contract, the Company will abide by the final decision of such court or of any appellate court in the event of any appeal.

Further, pursuant to any statute of any state, territory, or district of the United States which makes provision therefor, the Company hereby designates the Superintendent, Commissioner, or Director of Insurance, other officer specified for that purpose in the statute, or his or her successor or successors in office as its true and lawful attorney upon whom may be served any lawful process in any action, suit, or proceeding instituted by or on behalf of the Insured or any beneficiary hereunder arising out of this contract of insurance, and hereby designates the above named Counsel as the person to whom the said officer is authorized to mail such process or a true copy thereof.

IN WITNESS WHEREOF, the Company has caused this policy to be signed by its president and secretary and signed on the declarations page by a duly authorized representative of the Company.

SECRETARY

PRESIDENT

SHAND MORAHAN & COMPANY, INC.

INSURANCE AGENTS AND BROKERS
PROFESSIONAL LIABILITY INSURANCE POLICY

Underwriting Manager:

Shand Morahan & Company, Inc.

Shand Morahan Plaza

Evanston, Illinois 60201

INSURER: **EVANSTON INSURANCE COMPANY**
(A stock insurance company, herein called the Company, which except
in Illinois is a non-admitted insurer, writing pursuant to the surplus lines
laws and not under the jurisdiction of the Insurance Commissioner.)

Shand Morahan Plaza
Evanston, Illinois 60201
(847)866-2800

In consideration of the payment of the premium, the undertaking of the Named Insured to pay the deductible as described herein and in the amounts stated in the Declarations, in reliance upon the statements in the application attached hereto and made a part hereof, and subject to the limits of liability shown in the Declarations, and subject to all the terms of this insurance, the Company agrees with the Named Insured as follows:

The Insured

1.   **The Insured:** The unqualified word "Insured", whenever used in this policy, means:

(a)   the Named Insured herein defined as the individual, partnership, or corporation named in Item 1 of the Declarations;

(b)   any partner, officer, director, stockholder or employee of the Named Insured solely while acting within the scope of his duties as such;

(c)   any former partner, officer, director or employee of the Named Insured solely while acting within the scope of his duties as such;

(d)   the heirs, executors, administrators, assigns and legal representatives of each Insured above in the event of death, incapacity or bankruptcy.

2.   **Limited Additional Insureds:** Solicitors or office brokers specifically named under Item 7 of the Declarations are Insureds hereunder, but only with respect to any act, error or omission happening during the period of their affiliation with the Named Insured and then only as respects insurance handled or placed through the Named Insured.

The Coverage

1.   **Professional Liability and Claims Made Clause:** To pay on behalf of the Insured all sums in excess of the deductible amount stated in the Declarations which the Insured shall become legally obligated to pay as Damages as a result of CLAIMS FIRST MADE AGAINST THE INSURED DURING THE POLICY PERIOD by reason of an act, error or omission which happened:

(a)   during the Policy Period; or

(b)   prior to the Policy Period provided that on the effective date of this policy the Insured has no knowledge of such act, error or omission and there is no prior policy or policies which provide insurance for such liability or Claim resulting from such act, error or omission whether or not the available limits of liability of such prior policy or policies are sufficient to pay any liability or

Claim or whether or not the deductible provisions and amount of such prior policy or policies are different from this policy;

PROVIDED ALWAYS THAT such act, error or omission arises out of professional services rendered or that should have been rendered by the Insured, or by any person for whose acts, errors or omissions the Insured is legally responsible, in the conduct of the Insured's profession as an insurance agent, insurance broker, general insurance agent, managing general insurance agent, managing general underwriter, surplus line broker, excess line broker and life insurance agent, including the following related activities connected therewith: notarizing, premium financing, servicing of insurance business of others, consulting, advising, engineering, appraising, claims adjusting and public relations activities.

It is a condition precedent to coverage under this policy that all Claims be reported in compliance with the section CLAIMS 1, Notice of Claim or Suit.

Claim, whenever used in this policy, means a demand received by the Insured for money or services, including the service of suit or institution of arbitration proceeding against the Insured.

Claim Expenses, whenever used in this policy, means: (a) fees charged by any lawyer designated by the Company; (b) all other fees, costs and expenses resulting from the investigation, adjustment, defense and appeal of a Claim, if incurred by the Company; and (c) fees charged by any lawyer designated by the Insured with the written consent of the Company. However, Claim Expenses does not include salary charges of regular employees or of the officials of the Company.

Damages, whenever used in this policy, means the monetary portion of any judgment, award or settlement and does not include: (a) punitive or exemplary damages, any damages which are a multiple of compensatory damages, or fines or penalties or sanctions; or (b) the restitution of consideration paid to the Insured for services or goods; or (c) judgments or awards deemed uninsurable by law.

Policy Period, whenever used in this policy, means the period from the inception date of this policy to the policy expiration date as set forth in the Declarations or its earlier termination date, if any.

2. Defense, Settlement: With respect to any Claim covered herein and subject to the applicable limits of liability:
(a) The Company shall investigate and defend any such Claim made against the Insured, even if any of the allegations of any such Claim are groundless, false or fraudulent, but the Company shall not be obligated to pay any Damages or to defend or to continue to defend or to pay Claim Expenses for any Claim after the available limits of the Company's liability have been tendered to the Insured or into the court or exhausted by payment of Damages and/or Claim Expenses;
(b) The Insured shall cooperate with the Company in the defense, investigation and settlement of any Claim all without cost to the Company. The Insured will assist the Company in effecting any rights of indemnity, contribution or apportionment available to the Insured or the Company. Upon the Company's request, the Insured shall: (1) submit to examination and interview by a representative of the Company, under oath if required; (2) attend hearings, depositions and trials; (3) assist in effecting settlement, securing and giving evidence, obtaining the attendance of witnesses in the conduct of suits; (4) give a written statement or statements to the Company's representatives and meet with such representatives for the purpose of determining coverage and investigating and/or defending any Claim.

(c) The Insured shall not, with respect to any Claim covered under this policy, except at the Insured's personal cost, make any payment, admit liability, settle Claims, assume any obligation, agree to arbitration or any similar means of resolution of any dispute, waive any rights or incur Claim Expenses without prior written Company approval. Any costs and expenses incurred by the Insured prior to the Insured giving written notice of the Claim to the Company shall be borne by the Insured and will not constitute satisfaction of the deductible either in whole or in part.

(d) The Company shall not settle any Claim without the consent of the Named Insured. If, however, the Named Insured shall refuse to consent to any settlement recommended by the Company and shall elect to contest the Claim or continue any legal proceedings in connection with such Claim, then the Company shall not be obligated to pay Claim Expenses incurred subsequent to such refusal. Furthermore, the Company's liability for such Claim shall not exceed the amount for which the Claim could have been so settled and Claim Expenses incurred up to the date of such refusal. Such amounts are subject to the provisions of the section LIMITS OF LIABILITY.

3. **Discovery Clause:** If during the Policy Period the Insured first becomes aware of any specific act, error or omission in professional services for which coverage is provided under THE COVERAGE 1, and if the Insured shall during the Policy Period give written notice to the Company of:

(a) the specific act, error or omission; and

(b) the injury or damage which has or may result from such act, error or omission; and

(c) the circumstances by which the Insured first became aware of such act, error or omission;

then any Claim subsequently made against the Insured arising out of such act, error or omission shall be deemed for the purposes of this insurance to have been made on the date on which such written notice is received by the Company.

The Insured shall cooperate fully with the Company as provided in THE COVERAGE 2, and any investigation conducted by the Company or its representatives shall be subject to the terms set forth in this policy as applicable to a Claim.

The Exclusions

This Policy Does Not Apply:

(a) to any Claim made against an Insured who intentionally commits, permits, or directs the commission of, or acquiesces in the commission of any dishonest, fraudulent, criminal, malicious or knowingly wrongful act or omission. Furthermore, this policy shall not apply to any Claim made against a partner, officer, director, or stockholder of the Named Insured for any dishonest, fraudulent, criminal, malicious or knowingly wrongful act or omission committed by, at the direction of, or with the knowledge or acquiescence of another partner, officer, director or stockholder of the Named Insured;

(b) to any Claim arising out of notarized certification or acknowledgement of a signature without the physical appearance at the time of said notarization before such notary public as insured hereunder of the person who is or claims to be the person signing said instrument;

(c) to any Claim based upon, arising out of, due to or involving directly or indirectly the insolvency, receivership, bankruptcy, liquidation or financial inability to pay, of any insurance company, reinsurer, risk retention group or captive (or any other self-insurance plan or trust by whatsoever name) in which the Insured has placed or obtained coverage for a client or an account;

(d)   to any Claim for or based upon libel, slander, invasion of privacy or discrimination;

(e)   to any Claim based upon or arising out of the commingling of monies or accounts, or to any Claim for loss monies received by the Insured or credited to the Insured's account or to any Claim for fees, premiums, taxes, commissions or brokerage monies;

(f)   to any Claim made by or against any business enterprise not named in the Declarations, which is or was wholly or partially owned, operated, or managed by the Insured; or to any Claim made against the Insured solely because the Insured is or was a partner, officer, director, or stockholder in, or under common ownership, operation, or management with any such firm;

(g)   to any Claim arising out of the Insured's activities as a fiduciary under the Employee Retirement Income Security Act of 1974 and its amendments or any regulation or order issued pursuant thereto;

(h)   to any Claim based upon, arising from, or in any way involving management or ownership of any insurance company by the Insured;

(i)   to any Claim based upon, arising from, or in any way involving the sale of mutual funds or variable annuities;

(j)   to liability assumed by the Insured under any contract or agreement, unless such liability would have attached to the Insured even in the absence of such contract or agreement;

(k)   to any Claim based upon, arising from, or in any way involving pollution and which results in:

    (1)   personal injury or bodily injury, including, but not limited to, sickness, disease, occupational disease, disability, shock, death, mental or emotional anguish, or mental or emotional injury; and/or

    (2)   physical injury, destruction or damage, loss of use, diminution in value, contamination, loss of rental revenue or income as to any tangible personal or real property, including but not limited to, any building, structure, fixture, site or location; and/or

    (3)   expenditures to correct or clean up any actual or potential health threat arising from the presence of pollution in any form in or on any tangible personal or real property, including any costs and expenses of:

        i.   inspecting any such property for pollution;
        ii.   investigating for and/or preparing of any remedial action plan;
        iii.   remediating and/or cleaning up and/or nullifying any pollution;
        iv.   monitoring the level of pollution;
        v.   monitoring the health of any person;

except that if a Claim shall have been brought against the Insured alleging an act, error or omission arising out of those services specified under The Coverage 1., then the Company will afford a defense for such Claim or suit without liability, however, for Damages arising from the items referenced in (1) and/or (2) and/or (3), of this exclusion.

Pollution, whenever used in this exclusion, includes any pollutant in any form including, but not limited to, smoke, vapors, soot, fumes, acids, alkalis, chemicals, liquids, gases, thermal pollutants, waste materials, seepage and all other irritants or contaminants of any kind, nature or quantity.

Territory

The insurance afforded applies worldwide, provided that the Claim is made or suit is brought within the United States of America, its territories and possessions or Canada.

Limits of Liability

1.   Limit of Liability--Professional Liability--Each Claim: The liability of the Company for the combined total of Damages and Claim Expenses for each Claim FIRST MADE AGAINST THE INSURED DURING THE POLICY PERIOD shall not exceed the amount stated in the Declarations for "each Claim".

2.   Limit of Liability--Professional Liability--Policy Aggregate: Subject to 1. Limit of Liability--Each Claim, the liability of the Company for the combined total of Damages and Claim Expenses shall not exceed the amount stated in the Declarations as "aggregate" as a result of all Claims FIRST MADE AGAINST THE INSURED DURING THE POLICY PERIOD.

3.   Deductible: The deductible amount stated in the Declarations shall be paid by the Named Insured and shall be applicable to the combined total of Damages and Claim Expenses for each Claim.

Such amounts shall, upon written demand by the Company, be paid by the Named Insured within ten days. The total payments requested from the Named Insured in respect of each Claim shall not exceed the deductible amount stated in the Declarations.

The determination of the Company as to the reasonableness of the Claim Expenses shall be conclusive on the Named Insured.

4.   Multiple Insureds, Claims and Claimants: The inclusion herein of more than one Insured or the making of Claims or the bringing of suits by more than one person or organization shall not operate to increase the Company's limit of liability. Two or more Claims arising out of a single act, error or omission or a series of related acts, errors or omissions shall be treated as a single Claim. All such Claims, whenever made, shall be considered first made within the Policy Period, in which the earliest Claim arising out of such acts, errors or omissions was first made, and all such Claims shall be subject to the same limit of liability and deductible.

5.   Payment of Claim Expenses: Subject to the Named Insured's obligation to pay the deductible as set forth in LIMITS OF LIABILITY 3, the Company shall pay all Claim Expenses, up to the applicable limit of liability.

Claims

1.   **Notice of Claim or Suit:** As a condition precedent to the right to the protection afforded by this insurance, the Insured shall, as soon as practicable, give to the Company written notice directed to **Shand Morahan & Company, Inc., Shand Morahan Plaza, Evanston, Illinois 60201,** of any Claim made against the Insured.

In the event suit is brought against the Insured, the Insured shall IMMEDIATELY forward to the Company through SHAND MORAHAN & COMPANY, INC., every demand, notice, summons or other process received by the Insured or by the Insured's representative.

2.   **Subrogation:** In the event of any payment under this policy, the Company shall be subrogated to all the Insured's rights of recovery therefor against any person or organization and all amounts recoverable, and the Insured shall execute and deliver instruments and papers and do whatever else is necessary to secure such rights. The Insured shall do nothing after the claim to prejudice such rights. Any recovery shall be used to pay: first, subrogation expenses; second, payments in excess of the deductible by the Insured; third, payments by an excess insurer; fourth, payments made by a primary insurer; and, last, reimbursement of the Insured's deductible.

The Company shall not exercise any such rights, against any individual or entity identified in THE INSURED. Notwithstanding the foregoing, however, the Company reserves the right to exercise any rights of subrogation against an Insured in respect of any Claim brought about or contributed to by the dishonest, fraudulent, criminal or malicious act or omission of such Insured.

3.   **Action Against the Company:** No action shall lie against the Company unless, as a condition precedent thereto, the Insured shall have fully complied with all the terms of this policy, nor until the amount of the Insured's obligation to pay shall have been fully and finally determined either by judgment against the Insured after actual trial or by written agreement of the Insured, the claimant and the Company.

Nothing contained in this policy shall give any person or organization any right to join the Company, as a co-defendant in any action against the Insured to determine the Insured's liability. Bankruptcy or insolvency of the Insured or of the Insured's estate shall not relieve the Company of any of its obligations hereunder.

4.   **False or Fraudulent Claims:** If any individual or entity identified in THE INSURED shall commit fraud in presenting or maintaining any Claim as regards amount or otherwise, this insurance shall become void as to such Insured from the date such fraudulent Claim is presented or maintained.

Other Conditions

1.   **Applications:** By acceptance of this policy, the Insured agrees that the statements in the application are the Insured's representations, that they shall be deemed material and that this policy is issued in reliance upon the truth of such representations and that this policy embodies all agreements existing between the Insured and the Company, or any of its agents, relating to this insurance.

2.   **Other Insurance:** Subject to the limitation of coverage as set forth in THE COVERAGE 1 for prior insurance, this insurance shall be in excess of the amount of the applicable deductible of this policy and any other valid and collectible insurance available to the Insured whether such other insurance is stated to be primary, contributory, excess, contingent or otherwise, unless such other insurance is written only as a specific excess insurance over the limits of liability provided in this policy.

3.   **Changes:** Notice to any agent or knowledge possessed by any agent or other person acting on behalf of the Company shall not affect a waiver or a change in any part of this policy or estop the Company from asserting any right under the terms of the policy, nor shall the terms of this policy be waived or changed, except by endorsement issued to form a part of this policy.

4. Assignment: Assignment of interest under this policy shall not bind the Company unless its consent is endorsed hereon.

5. Cancellations: This policy may be cancelled by the Named Insured by surrender thereof to the Company or to Shand Morahan & Company, Inc., Shand Morahan Plaza, Evanston, Illinois 60201 or by mailing to the aforementioned written notice stating when thereafter such cancellation shall be effective. If cancelled by the Insured, the Company shall retain the customary short rate proportion of the premium.

This policy may be cancelled by the Company or by Shand Morahan & Company, Inc., by mailing to the Named Insured at the address stated in the Declarations, written notice stating when, not less than thirty (30) days thereafter, such cancellation shall be effective. However, if the Company cancels the policy because the Insured has failed to pay a premium or deductible when due, this policy may be cancelled by the Company by mailing a written notice of cancellation to the Insured stating when, not less than ten (10) days thereafter, such cancellation shall be effective. The mailing of notice as aforementioned shall be sufficient notice and the effective date of cancellation stated in the notice shall become the end of the Policy Period. Delivery of such written notice to the Named Insured by the Company, or Shand Morahan & Company, Inc., shall be equivalent to mailing. If cancelled by the Company or Shand Morahan & Company, Inc., earned premium shall be computed pro rata. Premium adjustment may be made at the time cancellation is effected or as soon as practicable thereafter.

6. Audit: The Company may examine and audit the Insured's books and records at any time during the Policy Period and within three years after the final termination of this policy, as far as they relate to the subject matter of this policy.

7. Service of Suit: Except with respect to policies issued for Named Insureds domiciled in Illinois, it is agreed that in the event of the failure of the Company to pay any amount claimed to be due hereunder, the Company at the request of the Named Insured will submit to the jurisdiction of any court of competent jurisdiction within the United States and will comply with all requirements necessary to give such court jurisdiction, and all matters arising hereunder shall be determined in accordance with the law and practice of such court. Nothing contained in this clause constitutes nor should be understood to constitute a waiver of the Company's right to commence an action in any court of competent jurisdiction in the United States, to remove an action to a United States District Court or to seek a transfer of a case to another court, as permitted by the laws of the United States or of any State in the United States. In any suit instituted against it upon this contract, the Company will abide by the final decision of the court or of any appellate court in the event of an appeal.

Lord, Bissell & Brook, whose address is 115 S. LaSalle, Chicago, IL 60603, is authorized and directed to accept service of process on behalf of the Company in any such suit and/or upon the request of the Insured, Lord, Bissell & Brook will enter a general appearance upon the Company's behalf in the event such suit shall be instituted.

Further, pursuant to any statute of any state, territory or district of the United States which makes provision therefor, the Company hereon hereby designates the Superintendent, Commissioner or Director of Insurance or other officer specified for that purpose in the statute, or his successor(s) in office, as their true and lawful attorney, upon whom may be served any lawful process in any action, suit or proceeding instituted by or on behalf of the Named Insured or any beneficiary hereunder arising out of this contract of insurance, and hereby designates the above named as the person to whom the said officer is authorized to mail such process or a true copy thereof.

Definitions - Reference

Certain words are specifically defined for the policy and the definitions are to be found in the sections set forth below:

Claim, Claim Expenses, Damages, Policy Period **See The Coverage**
Pollution **See The Exclusions**

IN WITNESS WHEREOF, the Company has caused this policy to be signed by its President and Secretary, but this policy shall not be valid unless countersigned on the Declarations page by a duly authorized representative of the Company.

Secretary   President

EIC 3081 2/96

Westport Insurance Corporation

Administrative Office:
5200 Metcalf
Overland Park, Kansas 66201

Domiciliary Office
237 East High Street
Jefferson City, Missouri 65102

**THIS IS A CLAIMS MADE POLICY
PLEASE READ CAREFULLY**

DECLARATIONS

Policy Number: ABC-00000
Renewal of Policy: PAL206419

A.   Named Insured: J.W. Smith & Associates

B.   Address: 1234 Walter Blvd.
                            Anytown, PA 00000

PRO

C.   Policy Period: From: 12:01 A.M. January 1, 200X   To: 12:01 A.M. January 1, 200Y
                            Local time at the address stated herein

D.   Policy Aggregate Limit of Liability for all "coverage units": **$1,000,000**

E.1.   Coverage – **CLAIMS EXPENSES ARE IN ADDITION TO THE LIMIT OF LIABILITY FOR THE COVERAGES UNITS LISTED IN THIS SECTION E.1.:**

"Coverage Unit"	"Coverage Unit" Per Claim Limit of Liability	"Coverage Unit" Aggregate Limit of Liability	Deductible Each Claim	Deductible Aggregate Each "Policy Period"	"Retroactive Date"
Insurance Industry Professional Liability	$ 500,000	$ 1,000,000	$ 2,500	$ 7,500	Full Prior Acts
N/A	N/A	N/A	N/A	N/A	N/A

Experience Credit Applied

E.2.   Coverage – **CLAIMS EXPENSES ARE INCLUDED WITHIN THE LIMIT OF LIABILITY FOR THE COVERAGES UNITS LISTED IN THIS SECTION E.2.:**

"Coverage Unit"	"Coverage Unit" Per Claim Limit of Liability	"Coverage Unit" Aggregate Limit of Liability	Deductible Each Claim	Deductible Aggregate Each "Policy Period"	"Retroactive Date"
N/A	N/A	N/A	N/A	N/A	N/A

F.   Total Premium: $ 4,793.00

Date: May 02, 2006

Declarations W-1001 (06/99)

Page 1 of 2
Insured Copy

Westport Insurance Corporation

GENERAL TERMS & CONDITIONS

Throughout this "policy" the words "you" and "your" refer to the "named insured" shown in the Declarations. The words "we," "us," and "our" refer to the company providing the insurance. The word "insured" means any person or organization qualifying as such in each "coverage unit." Other words and phrases that appear in quotation marks have special meaning. Refer to DEFINITIONS.

These terms and conditions shall constitute the GENERAL TERMS & CONDITIONS of the "policy" and shall apply to all "coverage units" issued by us as part of the "policy." Such terms and conditions may be specifically amended in a "coverage unit" solely for that "coverage unit."

In consideration of the payment of the premium and in reliance upon the statements in the application and supplements, and subject to the Declarations and all terms of the "policy," we agree with you as follows:

I.   **REPORTING AND NOTICE**

INSURED'S DUTIES in the event of "claim" or any "potential claim":

A.   The insured shall not, without our written consent, do any of the following:

1.   Admit liability;

2.   Participate in any settlement discussions nor enter into any settlement; or

3.   Incur any costs or expense.

B.   The insured shall:

1.   provide written notice of any "claim" to us or the producing agent shown on the Declarations Page as soon as practical. Any "potential claims" must be reported to us in writing during the "policy period" or Extended Reporting Period. If, during the "policy period," you, or any owner, officer or partner of the "named insured" first become aware of a "potential claim" and give written notice of such "potential claim" to us during the "policy period," any "claims" subsequently made against an insured arising from the "potential claim" shall be considered to have been made during the "policy period" that you, or any owner, officer or partner of the "named insured" first became aware of such "potential claim";

2.   provide copies of all documents we request;

3.   cooperate with us and the attorney we retain to defend you, and, upon our request, attend hearings and trials and assist in effecting settlements, securing and giving evidence, obtaining the attendance of witnesses, and in the conduct of "suits";

4.   include within any notice of "claim" or "potential claim" a description of the "claim" or "potential claim," the alleged "wrongful act(s)," including the date(s) it was committed, a summary of the facts upon which the "claim" or "potential claim" is based, the alleged or potential damage or "loss" that may result from the "wrongful act," the names of actual or potential claimants, the names of insured(s) and employee(s) against whom the "claim" was or may be made, and the date and circumstances by which you, or any owner, officer or partner of the "named insured" first became aware of the "claim," or "potential claim."

Notice to us under the "policy" shall be given to:

> Westport Insurance Corporation
> 5200 Metcalf
> Overland Park, KS 66201
> Attention: Westport Claims Department
> Telephone Number: 1-800-241-3470
> Facsimile Number: 1-800-388-0931

All notices under the "policy" shall be in writing, shall comply with the time requirements as stated in the "coverage units," and shall be given by confirmed facsimile, prepaid express courier, certified U.S. Mail, return receipt requested.

Except as provided in the Termination of Coverage Section of these GENERAL TERMS & CONDITIONS, any notice shall be effective on the date of our receipt at the above address.

II.   EXCLUSIONS

In addition to the Exclusions contained in each "coverage unit," the following exclusions apply to all "coverage units."

This "policy" shall not apply to any "claim" based upon, arising out of, attributable to, or directly or indirectly resulting from:

A.   BODILY INJURY, PROPERTY DAMAGE. "Claims" for:

1.   bodily injury, sickness, disease, or death of any person; or

2.   injury to or destruction of any property, including the loss of use of the property.

B.   CONTRACTUAL LIABILITY. Any liability assumed by the insured under contract, unless the insured would have been legally liable in the absence of such contract.

C.   ERISA, COBRA. "Claims" arising out of any duties or activities assumed under contract by an insured as a plan administrator or fiduciary under the Employee Retirement Income Security Act of 1974 (ERISA), the Pension Benefits Act or the Consolidated Omnibus Budget Reconciliation Act of 1986 (COBRA) including any amendments, regulations, or enabling statutes pursuant thereto, or any other similar federal, state, or provincial statute or regulation.

D.   FUNDS. Conversion, misappropriation, or improper commingling of client funds or funds held for the benefit of a client.

E.   INSURED VS. INSURED. "Claims" or disputes:

1.   between insureds under this "policy." However, this exclusion does not apply if the "wrongful act" arises out of "professional services" by an insured rendered to such other insured as a client, provided the insured rendering such "professional services" does not have an equity interest in the property to be insured; or

2.   by an enterprise which one or more insureds have a total of ten percent (10%) or more equity interest, or operate, control, or manage; or

3.   by an enterprise which either has a ten percent (10%) or more equity interest in an insured or, operates, controls, or manages an insured.

F.   INTENTIONAL ACTS. Any "claim" for Intentional acts, including but not limited to acts of dishonesty, fraud, criminal conduct, malice, or assault and battery.

G.   PERSONAL PROFIT. Any insured having gained, in fact, any personal profit or advantage to which he or she was not legally entitled.

H.   PRIOR CLAIMS. Any act, error, omission, circumstance, or "personal injury" occurring prior to the effective date of this "policy," or any Employers Reinsurance Corporation or Westport Insurance Corporation "policy" this "policy" replaces, if you or any owner, officer or partner of the "named insured" at the effective date knew of a "claim" or a "potential claim."

III.   DEFINITIONS

In addition to the Definitions contained in each "coverage unit," the following Definitions shall apply to all "coverage units":

A.   CLAIM. "Claim" or "claims" means:

1.   that an insured has received a summons, a subpoena, or any other notice of legal process;

2.   that an insured has received notice of any "suit";

3.   that an insured has received notice of a written demand, or a written demand for money or services; or

4.   that an insured has received a request to provide a recorded statement.

B.   CLAIM EXPENSE. "Claim expense" or "claim expenses" means:

1.   all expense incurred in the defense of any "claim" or "potential claim" first made against an insured seeking damages for a "wrongful act" even if a "claim" or "potential claim" is groundless, false, fraudulent, or for an amount less than your Deductible;

2.   fees charged by any lawyer, designated by us, or required by law to defend the interests of any insured; and

3.   if authorized by us, all other fees, costs, and expenses resulting from the investigation, adjustment, defense, or appeal of any "claim," or "potential claim" including but not limited to:

a.   all costs taxed against any insured in any "suit";

b.   all prejudgment and post judgment accrued interest on that portion of any judgment which does not exceed the applicable Limit of Liability. If we tender or pay a "loss" on any judgment up to our Limits of Liability, we have no further obligation to pay any additional interest;

  c. all premiums on bonds to release attachments and appeal bonds, limited to that portion of a bond which does not exceed the "policy" Limit of Liability. We will obtain the bond on behalf of the insured. You shall reimburse us for the additional cost of the bond we obtain for any exposure in excess of our Limit of Liability;

  d. all reasonable expenses incurred by an insured at our request while assisting us in the investigation and defense of any "claim" or "potential claim," or

  e. Reimbursement for loss of earnings or temporary staff due to an insured attending depositions or trials at our request. Such reimbursement is subject to $100 per insured per day and a maximum of $1,000 per "policy period."

"Claims expenses," except as provided in B.3.e., shall not include salaries, loss of earnings, or expenses of regular employees, our officials, or you.

C. COVERAGE UNIT. "Coverage unit" means the terms, conditions, definitions, and exclusions as stated in each attachment hereto for each of the coverages selected by the insureds and listed in the Declarations including endorsements thereto. Each "coverage unit" is a separate and distinct coverage.

D. INSURED. Insured is defined in each "coverage unit." Refer to the Who Is An Insured section of each "coverage unit."

E. LOSS. "Loss" is defined in each "coverage unit."

F. NAMED INSURED. "Named Insured" means the person or entity listed in the Declarations.

G. POLICY. "Policy" means the combination of:

  1. all "coverage units" issued by us to you and listed in the Declarations; and

  2. these GENERAL TERMS & CONDITIONS.

H. POLICY PERIOD. "Policy period" means the period stated in the Declarations, unless terminated earlier pursuant to the Termination Of Coverage Section of these GENERAL TERMS & CONDITIONS.

I. POTENTIAL CLAIM. "Potential claim" means that you, or any owner, officer or partner of the "named insured" has become aware of a proceeding, event, or development which has resulted in or could in the future result in the institution of a "claim" against the insured.

J. RETROACTIVE DATE. "Retroactive date" means the date, as specified in the Declarations or in any endorsement attached hereto, on or after which any "wrongful act," as defined in each of the attached "coverage units," must have occurred in order for "claims" arising therefrom to be covered under this "policy." "Claims" arising from any "wrongful act," as defined in each of the attached "coverage units," occurring prior to this date are not covered by this "policy."

K. SUIT. "Suit" means a civil proceeding alleging "loss" against an insured for a "wrongful act." "Suit" includes arbitration or other alternative dispute resolution proceedings to which the insured must submit, or does submit with our consent, and in which "loss" is requested.

L.   WRONGFUL ACT. "Wrongful act" is defined in each "coverage unit."

IV.   LIMITS OF LIABILITY

A.   All Limits of Liability shall apply in excess of the Deductible. All amounts paid in satisfaction of "claims" are subject to the applicable Limit of Liability. All "claim expenses" shall be in addition to the applicable Per Claim Limit of Liability.

B.   Our liability for the combined total of all "loss," as defined in each of the attached "coverage units," shall not exceed the amount stated in the Declarations as Per Claim Limit of Liability for that "coverage unit."

C.   There shall be no stacking of "coverage unit" limits. If more than one "coverage unit" covers a "claim," our liability for the combined total of all "loss" for the "claim" shall not exceed the highest single Per Claim Limit of Liability as stated in the Declarations for the "coverage unit(s)" which cover the "claim."

D.   Our liability for the combined total of all "loss" for all "claims" covered by a "coverage unit" shall not exceed the amount stated in the Declarations as Aggregate Limit of Liability for that "coverage unit."

E.   Our liability under the "policy" for the combined total of all "loss" for all "claims" covered by any and all "coverage unit(s)" shall not exceed the amount stated in the Declarations as Policy Aggregate Limit of Liability.

V.   DEDUCTIBLE

You shall be responsible for the Deductible indicated on the Declarations shown as "each claim." The Deductible applies to "loss" and not "claim expenses." The total Deductible you shall be responsible to pay during the "policy period" will not exceed the aggregate each "policy period" amount shown on the Declarations.

VI.   SUBROGATION

If we pay any "loss" or "claim expense," we have subrogation rights of the insured against any person or organization. The insured(s) shall execute all papers we require and shall do everything that may be necessary to preserve, secure, and pursue our rights, including the execution of such documents as may be necessary to enable us to bring "suit" in the name of the insured(s). All insureds shall cooperate with us and do nothing to jeopardize, prejudice, or terminate such rights. We shall not exercise any subrogation rights against any insured(s), unless the "claim" arises from any dishonest, fraudulent, or malicious act, error, or omission of such insured.

VII.   REIMBURSEMENT TO COMPANY

If we have paid any amounts as "loss" in satisfaction of any "claims" in excess of the applicable Limit of Liability, or have paid "loss" within the amount of the applicable Deductible, you shall be liable to us for any and all such amounts and, shall pay such amounts to us within 30 days of our demand.

VIII.   CHANGES

No change or modification of this "policy" shall be effective except when made by a written endorsement to this "policy" which is signed by our authorized representative.

IX.   NO ASSIGNMENT

Neither this "policy" nor any insured's interest in this "policy" may be assigned without our written consent.

X.   TERMINATION OF COVERAGE

The "policy" shall terminate at the earliest of the following:

A.   if the "policy" is terminated for failure to pay a premium when due, the effective date of cancellation stated in a written notice of cancellation from us to you, provided such notice is received by you at least ten (10) days prior to the effective date of cancellation. The mailing of such notice shall be sufficient notice and the effective date of cancellation stated in the notice shall become the end of the "policy period." Any earned premium shall be computed pro rata;

B.   if the "policy" is terminated by us for any reason other than non-payment of premium, the effective date of cancellation stated in our written notice of cancellation, provided you receive such notice at least thirty (30) days prior to the effective date of cancellation. The mailing of such notice shall be sufficient notice and the effective date of cancellation stated in the notice shall become the end of the "policy period." Any earned premium shall be computed pro rata;

C.   upon your surrender of the "policy" to us or upon our receipt of your written notice of termination stating when thereafter such cancellation shall be effective. Any earned premium shall be computed in accordance with the customary short rate table and procedure; or

D.   upon expiration of the "policy period" as set forth in the Declarations.

XI.   EXTENDED REPORTING PERIOD:

A.   EXTENDED REPORTING PERIOD TERMS. The following provisions are applicable to all Extended Reporting Periods:

1.   The Extended Reporting Periods cover "claims" arising out of "wrongful acts" that occurred prior to cancellation or expiration of the "policy" and on or after any "retroactive date" applicable to the expired or terminated "policy."

2.   If you have obtained a replacement "policy," the Extended Reporting Period will apply only in the event the replacement "policy" limits have been exhausted for a "claim" that qualifies for coverage under this section.

3.   The Limit of Liability during the final "policy period" immediately preceding the cancellation or non-renewal of the "policy" shall apply to "claims" reported during the final "policy period" together with "claims" reported during the Extended Reporting Period.

4.   If any Extended Reporting Period option is exercised, it cannot be terminated by us or you.

B. AUTOMATIC EXTENDED REPORTING PERIOD. If we or you choose to cancel or not renew this "policy," this "policy" will apply to "claims" first made against you and reported in writing to us during the sixty (60) days immediately following the date of cancellation or expiration.

C. OPTIONAL EXTENDED REPORTING PERIODS. Subject to the above identified terms and conditions, payment of all outstanding premiums or Deductibles due, and your electing within sixty (60) days from the date of cancellation or non-renewal of the "policy," the following Extended Reporting Periods are available:

1. If we or you choose to cancel or not renew the "policy," you have the right to extend the time for reporting "claims" made against any insured under the "policy" per the following schedule. The additional premium for the Extended Reporting Period shall be:

Extended Reporting Period	Additional Premium
12 months	50% of the last annual premium of this "policy"
36 months	100% of the last annual premium of this "policy"

You must send us written notice of your intent to purchase the option along with the annual expiring premium stated on the Declarations page within sixty (60) days of the cancellation or non-renewal of the "policy."

2. In addition to the above, we will issue an Extended Reporting Period Endorsement for an unlimited period at no additional premium following the cancellation or non-renewal of this "policy" provided that:

a. you are the sole owner and the sole producer; and

b. retire from the profession of insurance and your retirement is for reasons other than a suspension, revocation, or surrender of your license; and

c. you have reached the age of 65 and have been insured by us for 10 consecutive years prior to the "policy" termination or cancellation.

3. In addition to the above, if you are the sole owner and sole producer, we will issue a 10 year Extended Reporting Period endorsement at no additional premium provided:

a. cancellation or termination of the "policy" is due to your death or you are totally and permanently disabled during the "policy period"; and

b. in the event of disability, you are continuously totally and permanently disabled from your profession for a minimum of six (6) months after issuance of this "policy"; and

c. any death or total and permanent disability does not arise from a self-inflicted injury, suicide, alcohol, or drug abuse; and

d. satisfactory written evidence of death or total and permanent disability is provided by you or your legal representative within sixty (60) days of death or total and permanent disability.

4.   In addition to the above, if this "policy" is canceled by you, due to your merger, consolidation, or sale to another entity, or death or retirement of the owner, you shall also have the right to purchase an Extended Reporting Period provided:

a.   such merger, consolidation, or sale is not due to suspension, revocation, or surrender of an insured's license; and

b.   you send us written notice of your intent to purchase the option along with the annual expiring premium within sixty (60) days of the cancellation or non-renewal of the "policy."

Schedule:

Extended Reporting Period for Sale, Merger, Death, or Retirement	Premium (the percent of the last annual premium)
3 years	100%
4 years	120%
5 years	140%
6 years	155%
7 years	170%
8 years	185%
9 years	195%
10 years	200%

XII. MULTIPLE INSUREDS, CLAIMS, AND CLAIMANTS

The inclusion of more than one insured in any "claim" or the making of "claims" by more than one person or organization shall not increase the Limits of Liability or the Deductible. Two or more "claims" arising out of a single "wrongful act," as defined in each of the attached "coverage units," or a series of related or continuing "wrongful acts," shall be a single "claim." All such "claims," whenever made, shall be considered first made on the date on which the earliest "claim" was first made arising out of such "wrongful act," as defined in the applicable "coverage unit," and all such "claims" are subject to one Per Claim Limit of Liability and Deductible.

XIII. OTHER INSURANCE

Except as provided in the Exclusions in this "policy," if there is other insurance applicable to a "claim" covered by this "policy," this "policy" shall be deemed excess insurance over and above the applicable Limits of Liability of all such other insurance unless such other insurance is specifically written as excess insurance over the Limits of Liability provided in the "policy."

XIV. ACTION AGAINST US

No action shall lie against us unless, as a condition precedent thereto, all insureds shall have fully complied with all the GENERAL TERMS & CONDITIONS of this "policy" and the terms and conditions of all attached "coverage units," and not until the amount of all insureds' obligations to pay has been finally determined either by judgment against all insureds after actual trial or by written agreement of you, the claimant, and us.

Nothing contained in the "policy" shall give any person or organization any right to join us as a co-defendant in any action against any insured to determine any insured's liability.

XV. APPLICABLE LAWS

Any terms of the "policy" which are in conflict with any laws and regulations governing the "policy" are hereby amended to conform to such laws and regulations.

XVI. TERRITORY

This "policy" applies to "wrongful act(s)" that occur anywhere in the world, but the insured's responsibility to pay "loss" must be determined in a "suit" on the merits or in a settlement to which we have agreed.

XVII. WAIVER

Our failure to insist on strict compliance with any of the terms, provisions, or conditions to coverage of these GENERAL TERMS & CONDITIONS or the attached "coverage units" or the failure to exercise any right or privilege shall not operate or be construed as a waiver thereof or of any subsequent breach thereof or a waiver of any other terms, provisions, conditions, privileges, or rights.

XVIII. ENTIRE AGREEMENT

By acceptance of this "policy," all insureds reaffirm as of the effective date of this "policy" that (a) the statements in the Declarations and your most recent application(s) and all information communicated by the insureds to us are true and accurate and are all insureds' agreements and representations, (b) this "policy" is issued in reliance upon the truth and accuracy of such representations which are material to our issuance of this "policy" and (c) this "policy" embodies all agreements between all insureds and us or any of our agents relating to this insurance.

IN WITNESS WHEREOF, we have caused the signatures of our executive officers to be affixed hereto, and have caused this "policy" to be countersigned by our authorized representative.

WESTPORT INSURANCE CORPORATION

President   Secretary

Westport Insurance Corporation

INSURANCE INDUSTRY PROFESSIONAL LIABILITY COVERAGE UNIT
THIS IS A CLAIMS MADE POLICY. PLEASE READ CAREFULLY.

I. INSURING AGREEMENTS

A. INSURANCE OPERATIONS COVERAGE.

We will pay on behalf of the insured "loss" for which the insured is legally liable caused by a "wrongful act" committed by an insured arising out of "professional services" rendered to others.

B. ADDITIONAL COVERAGES.

We will pay on behalf of the insured "loss" caused by "wrongful acts" committed by an insured in connection with your insurance operations arising from the following:

1. Responding to a complaint or defending an investigation brought by any state regulatory agency, insurance department, or other government agency arising from your insurance operation. You must:

    a. provide prompt written notice to us and obtain our written consent before responding; and

    b. agree to the use of legal counsel that we choose or approve.

    This coverage does not apply to salaries of your personnel, loss of income, fines, penalties, return of fees or commissions, or reimbursement of premiums. The most we will pay under this additional coverage is $25,000 per "policy period" for all "loss" and "claim expenses." This coverage is part of, and not in addition to, the Limit of Liability shown in the Declarations.

2. Services rendered in teaching a formal insurance course, but we will only cover "claims" first made against the insured by a student or former student for a "wrongful act" of the insured causing such student to incur legal liability.

3. Services rendered as a notary public.

4. Services rendered as an insurance consultant.

5. Premium financing services provided by you to your clients for insurance products placed through your agency.

6. Loss control, risk management, or anti-fraud services rendered in connection with insurance placed through your agency.

7. Advertising activities for your insurance operations.

8. Services as a licensed registered representative rendered in connection with the sale and servicing of variable life and variable annuity products.

9. An insured's testimony as an expert witness in connection with insurance related litigation.

C. CLAIMS TO WHICH THIS INSURANCE APPLIES. Insuring Agreement, Part A and B apply to "potential claims" and "claims" first made against an insured during the "policy period" arising out of a "wrongful act" taking place on or after the "retroactive date" shown in the Declarations and within the coverage territory.

D. CATASTROPHE EXTRA EXPENSE. We will pay up to $10,000 per catastrophe subject to a per "policy period" aggregate limit of $25,000 for the actual extra expenses incurred by you as a result of a catastrophe during the "policy period" beginning on the date of a catastrophe and for thirty (30) days thereafter. The extra expense incurred must be incurred by you only to assist in the insurance claims processing needs of your customer(s) who have been affected by the catastrophe. The catastrophe must be a declared catastrophe by the Property Claims Services. A $500 Deductible for each "claim" shall apply to each "claim" made under this paragraph. Limits provided by this paragraph are part of and not in addition to the limits provided by this "policy."

E. SUBPOENA. If, during the "policy period," you receive a subpoena for documents or testimony relating to your business services and the subpoena is not related to a "claim" under this "policy," we will, at your request and upon receipt of a copy of the subpoena, retain legal counsel to advise you regarding the document production or to represent you during testimony. We will pay the expenses incurred in providing advice regarding the production of documents, review of the documents prior to production, your preparation for testifying, and representation during testimony. The maximum amount payable, regardless of the number of subpoenas reported or the number of insureds subject to all subpoenas shall be $5,000 per "policy period." The Deductible shall not apply to this provision, however any payments made by us under this provision will be included within the applicable Limit of Liability and not in addition thereto. Any notification you give us of such subpoena shall be deemed to be notification of a "potential claim" under this "policy." If this "potential claim" ultimately results in a "claim" any expenses we have paid will be included in "claim expense."

II. WHO IS AN INSURED

A. INDIVIDUAL. If you are an individual, you and your spouse are insureds, but only with respect to the conduct of a business of which you are the sole owner.

B. PARTNERSHIP. If you are a partnership, you, your partners and their spouses, and former partners and their spouses are insureds, but only with respect to the conduct of your business.

C. LIMITED LIABILITY COMPANY. If you are a limited liability company, you are an insured. Your members and former members are also insureds, but only with respect to the conduct of your business. Your managers and former managers are insureds, but only with respect to their duties as your managers.

D. OTHER ORGANIZATIONS. If you are an organization other than a partnership or limited liability company, you are an insured. Your officers, directors, and former officers and directors, are insureds, but only with respect to their duties as your officers or directors. Your stockholders are also insureds, but only with respect to "loss" for which the Insuring Agreement, Part A or B would apply.

E.   OTHER INSUREDS. Each of the following is also an insured:

1.   Your employees and former employees but only for acts within the scope of their employment by you and while performing duties related to the conduct of your insurance operations.

2.   Any independent contractor while acting within the scope of their duties as your subproducer.

3.   The heirs, executors, administrators, or legal representatives of an insured in the event of death, incapacity, or bankruptcy of the insured, but only to the extent that such insured would otherwise be covered by this "policy."

F.   NEWLY ACQUIRED. Any organization you newly acquire or form, and over which you maintain ownership or majority interest will qualify as an additional insured if there is no other similar insurance available to that organization. However:

1.   Coverage under this provision is afforded only until the 90th day after you acquire or form the organization or the end of the "policy period," whichever is earlier;

2.   Coverage does not apply to "wrongful acts" committed before you acquired or formed the organization unless agreed to by us and endorsed to this "policy"; and

3.   An additional premium may be charged from the date you acquired or formed the organization.

III.   DEFENSE, INVESTIGATION, AND SETTLEMENT OF CLAIMS

As respects such insurance as is afforded by this "coverage unit," we shall:

A.   have the right and duty to defend, investigate, and conduct any settlement negotiations arising from "claims" first made based upon alleged "wrongful acts" of an insured. We have the right to select the attorney to represent and defend the insured for any "claim" that is made against them.

B.   not settle any "claim" without your consent. If we recommend a settlement to you which is acceptable to the claimant, and you do not agree with us and would rather contest the matter, our ultimate liability will be limited to the total of:

1.   the amount for which the "claim" could have been settled at that time, plus

2.   the amount of "claim expense" that was incurred up to the time we made the recommendation.

We shall not be obligated to pay any "loss" or defend or continue to defend any "claim" after the Per Claim Limit of Liability or Aggregate Limit of Liability under this "coverage unit" has been exhausted by payment of "loss" or the deposit in a court having jurisdiction of sums exhausting the Per Claim Limit of Liability or Aggregate Limit of Liability.

IV.   EXCLUSIONS

In addition to those Exclusions contained in the GENERAL TERMS & CONDITIONS, this "coverage unit" shall not apply to any "claim" based upon, arising out of, attributable to, or directly or indirectly resulting from:

A.   BODILY INJURY, PROPERTY DAMAGE. As respects this "coverage unit," the BODILY INJURY, PROPERTY DAMAGE Exclusion in the GENERAL TERMS AND CONDITIONS is amended to the following:

BODILY INJURY, PROPERTY DAMAGE. This "coverage unit" shall not apply to any "claim" based upon, arising out of, attributable to, or directly or indirectly resulting from:

1.   BODILY INJURY, PROPERTY DAMAGE. "Claims" for:

a.   bodily injury, sickness, disease, or death of any person. This exclusion shall not apply to "claims" arising directly out of the act of placing insurance for others as a managing general insurance agent, general insurance agent, insurance agent or insurance broker; or

b.   injury to or destruction of any property, including the loss of use of the property.

B.   CONTRACTUAL LIABILITY. As respects this "coverage unit" the Contractual Liability Exclusion in the GENERAL TERMS AND CONDITIONS is deleted in its entirety.

C.   FUNDS. As respects this "coverage unit," the Funds Exclusion in the GENERAL TERMS AND CONDITIONS is amended to the following:

FUNDS. "Claims" for commissions, fees, taxes, reimbursement, or the failure to collect, pay, or return premiums or commingling of funds.

D.   INTENTIONAL ACTS. As respects this "coverage unit" the Intentional Acts Exclusion in the GENERAL TERMS AND CONDITIONS is amended to the following:

INTENTIONAL ACTS. Any "claim" for intentional acts, including but not limited to acts of dishonesty, fraud, criminal conduct, malice, or assault and battery. However, this exclusion does not apply to those insureds described in the section, Who Is An Insured, paragraphs A, B, C, D, or E of this "coverage unit" who do not personally participate in or ratify the acts identified above and who notify us once such act has been discovered.

E.   PRIOR CLAIMS. As respects this "coverage unit," the Prior Claims Exclusion in the GENERAL TERMS AND CONDITIONS is amended to the following:

PRIOR CLAIMS. Any act, error, omission, circumstance, or "personal injury" occurring prior to the effective date of this "policy," or any Employers Reinsurance Corporation or Westport Insurance Corporation "policy" this "policy" replaces, if you or any owner, officer or partner of the "named insured" at the effective date knew of a "claim."

F.   THIRD PARTY ADMINISTRATOR. "Claims" against an insured arising out of third party administrator activities, whether the insured performs such activities for a fee or no fee.

G.   VIATICALS. "Claims" arising from, based upon, or in connection with a viatical settlement.

V.   DEFINITIONS

In addition to the Definitions contained in the GENERAL TERMS AND CONDITIONS, as respects such insurance as is afforded by this "coverage unit," the following Definitions shall apply:

A.   LOSS.   "Loss" means amounts payable by an insured in settlement of "claims" or in satisfaction of judgments or awards including punitive and multiple damages where permitted by law, if covered by the Insuring Agreement. "Loss" does not include fines and penalties.

B.   PERSONAL INJURY.   "Personal Injury" means libel, slander, or invasion of privacy committed by the insured.

C.   PROFESSIONAL SERVICES.   "Professional Services" means activities as a managing general insurance agent, general insurance agent, insurance agent, or insurance broker.

D.   WRONGFUL ACTS.   "Wrongful act" or "wrongful acts" means any negligent act, error, omission, or "personal injury" of an insured or any person for whose acts the insured is legally liable in rendering services for others.

VI.   LIBERALIZATION

If, during the "policy period" we adopt revised provisions for this "policy" in order to afford, without additional premium, broader insurance to all insureds of the types of professionals covered by this "policy," such provision will apply to this "policy" effective the date the provision has been approved by the appropriate regulatory authority and such revision shall apply only to "claims" first made, or "potential claims" of which you first became aware, after the date of such approval.

IN WITNESS WHEREOF, the Corporation has caused the signatures of its executive officers to be affixed hereto, and has caused this "policy" to be countersigned by an authorized representative of the Corporation.

WESTPORT INSURANCE CORPORATION

President   Secretary

Westport Insurance Corporation

INSOLVENCY EXCLUSION

It is agreed that the Exclusions Section of the General Terms and Conditions is amended to include the following exclusion:

INSOLVENCY. The financial inability to pay, insolvency, receivership, bankruptcy or liquidation of any insurance company, any Individual Practice Association, Health Maintenance Organization, Preferred Provider Organization, Dental Service Plan, Risk Retention Group, Risk Provider Group, self-insured plan or any pool, syndicate, association, or other combination formed for the purpose of providing insurance or reinsurance, or any healthcare provider or any reinsurer with which the insured directly placed the subject risk; however, this exclusion does not apply if, at the time the insured placed the subject risk with any of the above-described entities, such entity or entities were rated by AM Best as B+ or higher, or alternatively, such entities were guaranteed by a governmental body or bodies and/or operated by a governmental body or bodies (including but not limited to assigned risk plans, Joint Underwriting Association's, fair plans), or the insured placed the coverage with a County Mutual reinsured by carriers rated B+ or higher.

All other terms and conditions of this policy shall remain unchanged.

This endorsement forms a part of the policy to which attached, effective on the inception date of the policy unless otherwise stated herein.

(The information below is required only when this endorsement is issued subsequent to the preparation of the policy.)

Endorsement Effective   **Policy No.**
Named Insured

                                       WESTPORT INSURANCE CORPORATION

Countersigned.

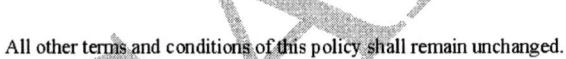

_____
Authorized Representative   President   Secretary

Endorsement Serial No. SP 1 938 0402

Appendix C

Code of Professional Ethics of
the American Institute for CPCU

CODE OF PROFESSIONAL ETHICS OF THE AMERICAN INSTITUTE FOR CPCU

CANON 1—ALTRUISM

CPCUs should endeavor at all times to place the public interest above their own.

Rules

R1.1 A CPCU has a duty to understand and abide by all Rules of conduct which are prescribed in the Code of Professional Ethics of the American Institute.

R1.2 A CPCU shall not advocate, sanction, participate in, cause to be accomplished, otherwise carry out through another, or condone any act which the CPCU is prohibited from performing by the Rules of this Code.

CANON 2—CONTINUING PROFESSIONAL COMPETENCE

CPCUs should seek continually to maintain and improve their professional knowledge, skills, and competence.

Rules

R2.1 A CPCU shall keep informed on those technical matters that are essential to the maintenance of the CPCU's professional competence in insurance, risk management, or related fields.

CANON 3—LEGAL CONDUCT

CPCUs should obey all laws and regulations, and should avoid any conduct or activity which would cause unjust harm to others.

Rules

R3.1 In the conduct of business or professional activities, a CPCU shall not engage in any act or omission of a dishonest, deceitful, or fraudulent nature.

R3.2 A CPCU shall not allow the pursuit of financial gain or other personal benefit to interfere with the exercise of sound professional judgment and skills.

R3.3 A CPCU shall not violate any law or regulation relating to professional activities or commit any felony.

CANON 4—DILIGENT PERFORMANCE

CPCUs should be diligent in the performance of their occupational duties and should continually strive to improve the functioning of the insurance mechanism.

Rules

R4.1 A CPCU shall competently and consistently discharge his or her occupational duties.

R4.2 A CPCU shall support efforts to effect such improvements in claims settlement, contract design, investment, marketing, pricing, reinsurance, safety engineering, underwriting, and other insurance operations as will both inure to the benefit of the public and improve the overall efficiency with which the insurance mechanism functions.

CANON 5—MAINTAINING AND RAISING PROFESSIONAL STANDARDS

CPCUs should assist in maintaining and raising professional standards in the insurance business.

Rules

R5.1 A CPCU shall support personnel policies and practices which will attract qualified individuals to the insurance business, provide them with ample and equal opportunities for advancement, and encourage them to aspire to the highest levels of professional competence and achievement.

R5.2 A CPCU shall encourage and assist qualified individuals who wish to pursue CPCU or other studies which will enhance their professional competence.

R5.3 A CPCU shall support the development, improvement, and enforcement of such laws, regulations, and codes as will foster competence and ethical conduct on the part of all insurance practitioners and inure to the benefit of the public.

R5.4 A CPCU shall not withhold information or assistance officially requested by appropriate regulatory authorities who are investigating or prosecuting any alleged violation of the laws or regulations governing the qualifications or conduct of the insurance business.

CANON 6—PROFESSIONAL RELATIONSHIPS

CPCUs should strive to establish and maintain dignified and honorable relationships with those whom they serve, with fellow insurance practitioners, and with members of other professions.

Rules

R6.1 A CPCU shall keep informed on the legal limitations imposed upon the scope of his or her professional activities.

R6.2 A CPCU shall not disclose to another person any confidential information entrusted to, or obtained by, the CPCU in the course of the CPCU's business or professional activities, unless a disclosure of such information is required by law or is made to a person who necessarily must have the information in order to discharge legitimate occupational or professional duties.

R6.3 In rendering or proposing to render professional services for others, a CPCU shall not knowingly misrepresent or conceal any limitations on the CPCU's ability to provide the quantity or quality of professional services required by the circumstances.

CANON 7—PUBLIC EDUCATION

CPCUs should assist in improving the public understanding of insurance and risk management.

Rules

R7.1 A CPCU shall support efforts to provide members of the public with objective information concerning their risk management and insurance needs and the products, services, and techniques which are available to meet their needs.

R7.2 A CPCU shall not misrepresent the benefits, costs, or limitations of any risk management technique or any product or service of an insurer.

CANON 8—INTEGRITY OF THE CPCU DESIGNATION

CPCUs should honor the integrity of the CPCU designation and respect the limitations placed on its use.

Rules

R8.1 A CPCU shall use the CPCU designation and the CPCU key only in accordance with the relevant Guidelines promulgated by the American Institute.

R8.2 A CPCU shall not attribute to the mere possession of the designation depth or scope of knowledge, skills, and professional capabilities greater than those demonstrated by successful completion of the CPCU program.

R8.3 A CPCU shall not make unfair comparisons between a person who holds the CPCU designation and one who does not.

R8.4 A CPCU shall not write, speak, or act in such a way as to lead another to reasonably believe the CPCU is officially representing the American Institute, unless the CPCU has been duly authorized to do so by the American Institute.

CANON 9—INTEGRITY OF THE CODE

CPCUs should assist in maintaining the integrity of the Code of Professional Ethics.

Rules

R9.1 A CPCU shall not initiate or support the CPCU candidacy of any individual known by the CPCU to engage in business practices which violate the ethical standards prescribed by this Code.

R9.2 A CPCU possessing unprivileged information concerning an alleged violation of this Code shall, upon request, reveal such information to the tribunal or other authority empowered by the American Institute to investigate or act upon the alleged violation.

R9.3 A CPCU shall report promptly to the American Institute any information concerning the use of the CPCU designation by an unauthorized person.

Index

Page numbers in boldface refer to definitions of Key Words and Phrases.